NOESIS ULTIMATE GUIDE

(With complete explanations of all answers)

(I.C.S.E)

BIOLOGY

(CLASS X)

Author

Er. SAJAL KUMAR GHOSH
M.I.E

NOESIS PUBLICATION
KAIGA, KARNATAKA

First Edition: FEB-2021

Popular books of the author are:

1) **A textbook of Objective Mechanical Engineering.**
2) **A complete Guide to Internal Combustion Engine*.**
3) **A Complete Guide to MCQ, Class 10 [CBSE/NCERT] Science.**
4) **A Complete Guide to MCQ, Class 10 [CBSE/NCERT] Social Science.**
5) **A Complete Guide to MCQ, Class 10 [CBSE/NCERT] Mathematics.**
6) **A Complete Guide to MCQ, Class 9   [CBSE/NCERT] Science.**
7) **A Complete Guide to MCQ, Class 9   [CBSE/NCERT] Social Science.**
8) **A Complete Guide to MCQ, Class 9   [CBSE/NCERT] Mathematics.**
9) **A Complete Guide to MCQ, Class 8   [CBSE/NCERT] Science.**

All books are available in Amazon. in,Flipkart.Com, Notionpress.com and with many other online booksellers.

***This book is in Press.**

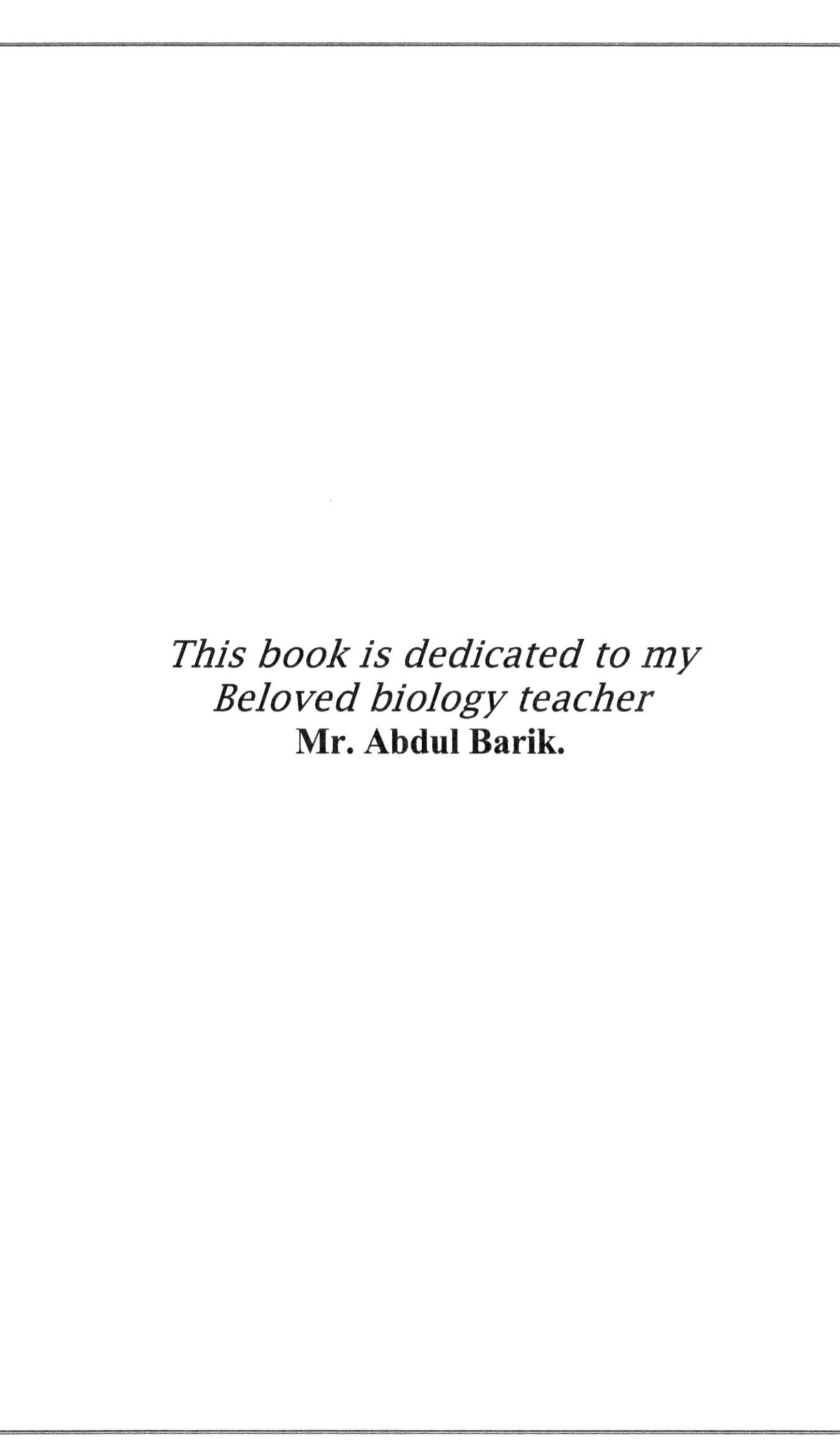

This book is dedicated to my
Beloved biology teacher
Mr. Abdul Barik.

PREFACE

Noesis Ultimate Guide For Biology [Class X] has been written in accordance with the latest syllabus of biology prescribed by the Council for the Indian school certificate examination, New Delhi. This book will help students to prepare for their examination in a simple & quick method. The present book will help you to self-understand the question style and subject in a better way.

Unique features of this book

- Book written in very simple, easy to understand student-friendly language.

- The conventional type questions are also answered on point basis.

- Too many questions have been generated to understand the types of questions could be asked by the council in the upcoming exam.

- All chapters of biology syllabus has been covered.

- All questions are made at par with the ICSE question standard.

- Every questions have answerd point to point basis.

- Previous years questions are also answered to understand the questioning style of the council.

- About 10 types of questions have been prepared for Section-I so that students could understand types of question in different format.

I hope this book will prove very useful to the students and teachers. Suggestions and constructive criticism for the further improvement of the book would be gratefully acknowledged and should incorporate in coming editions.

Er. Sajal Kumar Ghosh

About the Author

Full name of the author:
Er. SAJAL KUMAR GHOSH.

Current Affiliation: M.I.E, M-Tech.

E-mail ID:
skghosh100@gmail.com

Teaching/Professional Experience:

a) Private tutor since 1998 at PUC-2 level (22 Years' experience).
b) Scientific Staff in Nuclear power Plant and Commissioning expert in engineering safety systems. Professional Experience (e.g. Industry, Consultancy) He is working in a Nuclear Power Plant under Govt. PSU of Dept. of Atomic Energy since 2004. He was involved in commissioning of engineering safety features and ventilation systems of 220×2 MWe PHWR Nuclear power plants. Presently associated with Nuclear Power Program of India. He has vast 16 years of experience in commissioning of ventilation and engineering safety features systems in nuclear power plants and testing of related equipment at par with atomic energy regulatory norms.

Membership of Associations/Societies: Member of The Institution of Engineers (India), Kolkata.

Follow me on www.facebook.com/skghosh100

Follow me on https://twitter.com/skghosh100

WhatsApp me +91-9972707631. (For your education related queries only)

Watch my video lectures **You Tube**
www.youtube.com/noesisonlinetutor

Table of contents

Cell Division & Structure of Chromosome.

SECTION-I

Q:Type:[1] Name the followings:

1. Who discovered the cell?
2. Name smallest known cell in the world.
3. Name the largest cell in the world.
4. Name the smallest plant cell in the world.
5. Name the largest plant cell in the world.
6. Name the largest cell in our body.
7. Name largest cell organelles.
8. Organelle helps in the formation of RNA.
9. The cell organelle could trap the solar energy.
10. The cell organelle helps for intercellular digestion.
11. The cell organelle helps to secret.
12. The cytoplasmic organelles help in the manufacture of starch.
13. The cell organelle synthesis lipid.
14. The shortest phase of mitosis.
15. The type of cell division methods.
16. The method of cell division caused variation.
17. The type of cell division occurs in the cells of the reproductive organs.
18. Nitrogen bases paired by two hydrogen bonds in DNA.
19. Nitrogen bases paired by three hydrogen bonds in DNA.
20. The shortest phase of mitosis.
21. The chromosomes with satellites.
22. The substances formed chromatin.
23. The area where crossing over has taken place during prophase of meiotic I.
24. The membrane disappears during the late prophase.
25. The cell organelle synthesis protein.
26. The nitrogenous base does not contain RNA.
27. The nitrogenous base does not contain DNA.
28. The cell never divides.
29. The phases which combined called interphase.
30. The cell division method of prokaryotic cells.
31. Smallest anon-membranous cell membrane.
32. Smallest a membranous cell membrane.
33. The portion of the chromosome which lightly stain.
34. Inactive X chromosome of the human body.
35. The phase of Karyokinesis when the size of chromosomes normally measured.
36. Chromosomes which bear round, elongated and knob-like structure.

A:Type:[1] Answer :

1.	Robert Cook.		19.	Cytosine and Guanine
2.	Mycoplasma.		20.	Anaphase.
3.	Egg cell of Ostrich.		21.	Sat chromosomes.
4.	Wolffia cell.		22.	DNA & Protein.
5.	Cycas.		23.	Along equator.
6.	Ovum.		24.	Nuclear membrane.
7.	Nucleus.		25.	Ribosome.
8.	Nucleolus.		26.	Thymine.
9.	Plastids.		27.	Uracil.
10.	Lysosome.		28.	Nerve cell.
11.	Golgi apparatus.		29.	G1,S and G2 phases.
12.	Plastids.		30.	Binary cell division.
13.	Endoplasmic reticulum.		31.	Ribosome.
14.	Anaphase.		32.	Peroxisome.
15.	Mitosis, Meiosis and Binary fission.		33.	Euchromatin.
16.	Meiosis.		34.	Barr body.
17.	Meiosis.		35.	Metaphase.
18.	Adenine and Thymine.		36.	Sat-chromosome.

Q:Type:[2] Write the exact location:

1.	Cristae.		8.	Plastids.
2.	Centromere.		9.	Nucleolus.
3.	Uracil.		10.	Chiasmata.
4.	Thymine.		11.	Protein synthesis.
5.	Largest human cell.		12.	Sex region.
6.	Histone molecules.		13.	Kline filter syndrome.
7.	Meiosis cell division.		14.	Lamp brush chromosome.

A:Type:[2] Answer & Explanation:

1) *Cristae*: Inner membrane of Mitochondrion.

2) *Centro mere*: at the junction of chromatids.

3) *Uracil*:RNA (Note: DNA does not contain Uracil)

4) *Thymine*: DNA (Note: RNA does not contain Thymine)

5) *Largest human cell*: Fallopian tube [Ovum] of the female body.

6) *Histone molecules*: Nucleosome (Note: DNA strand winds around it)

7) *Meiosis cell division*: Reproductive cells.

8) *Plastids*: Plant cell

9) ***Nucleolus***: Within the Nucleus.

10) ***Chiasmata***: Located where crossing over takes place.

11) ***Protein synthesis***: Ribosome.

12) ***Sex region***: Y type chromosome of a sex cell.

13) ***Klinefelter syndrome***: Male having extra X chromosome i.e. XXY.

14) ***Lamp brush chromosome***: Amphibian Oocyte.

Q:Type:[3] Find Odd terms:

1. Uracil, thymine, adenine, DNA

2. Cytosine, adenine, thymine, RNA

3. Histone, thymine, adenine, Guanine.

4. Leptotene, Pachytene, Diplotene, Cytokinin

5. Spore, crossing over, mitosis, Chiasmata.

6. Watson &Crick, Walther Fleming, W.Waldeyer, Robert Hook.

7. Ribosome, Mitochondria, Golgi apparatus, ER.

8. G1 phase, M phase,G2 phase, S phase.

9. Plastid, dictyosomes, cell membrane, Lysosome.

10. Lysosome, Centriole, centrosome, Plastid.

A:Type:[3] Answer & Explanation:

1. **Uracil**, thymine, adenine, DNA

Explanation: Uracil does not present in DNA.

2. Cytosine, adenine, **thymine**, RNA

Explanation: thymine does not present in RNA.

3. **Histone**, thymine, adenine, Guanine.

Explanation: except Histone all are nitrogen bases of DNA.

4. Leptotene, Pachytene, Diplotene,**Cytokinin**

Explanation: Cytokinin is the hormone and others are stages of Prophase Iin Meiosis .

5. Spore, crossing over, **mitosis**, Chiasmata.

Explanation: Mitosis related to somatic cell and others arerelated to reproductive cell division.

6. Watson &Crick,Walther Fleming, W.Waldeyer, **Robert Hook.**

Explanation: Robert Hook related to the invention of cell and others are related to chromosome.

7. Ribosome, **Mitochondria,** Golgi apparatus, ER.

Explanation: Except mitochondria all others synthesis either protein or enzymes.

8.   G1 phase, **M phase,**G2 phase, S phase.

Explanation: except m phase, all others come under interphase.

9. Plastid, dictyosomes, cell membrane, **Lysosome.**

Explanation: all given organelles are present only in plant cell except Lysosome.

10. Lysosome, Centriole, centrosome, **Plastid.**

Explanation: plastid found only in plant cells.

Q:Type:[4] Match the Column:

Sl. No	Column A	Sl. No	Column B
1	Thymine	A	Cleavage in animal cell
2	Karyotype	B	Guanine
3	Histone	C	Bundle of microtubules
4	Dictyosomes	D	Satellites
5	Meta centric Chromosome.	E	Interphase
6	Body cell	F	DNA
7	S phase	G	Idiogram
8	Uracil	H	T shape chromosome
9	Selectively permeable cell organelle	I	Granules
10	Cytosine	J	RNA
11	amembranous cell organelle	K	Adenine
12	Sub metacentric Chromosome.	L	Autosomes

13	Smallest amembranous cell organelle	M	X-chromosome inactive
14	Puckering	N	V shape chromosome
15	Barr body chromosome	O	Ribosome
16	Aster	P	Cell membrane
17	Sat chromosome	Q	Plant Golgi apparatus

A:Type:[4] Answer & Explanation:

Sl. No	Column A	Sl. No	Column A
1.	Thymine	k	Adenine
Expl.	Adenine pairs with thymine.		
2.	Karyotype.	G	Idiogram.
Expl.	Diagrammatic representation of a Karyotype of a species is called an ideogram.		
3.	Histone	F	DNA
Expl.	DNA strands winds around a core of eight histone molecules.		
4.	Dictyosomes	Q	Plant Golgi apparatus
Expl.	Plant Golgi apparatus is called Dictyosomes.		
5.	Meta centric Chromosome.	N	V shape chromosome
Expl.	The shape of the metacentric is V shape.		
6.	Body cell	L	Autosomes.
Expl.	Body cell chromosomes are called autosomes.		
7.	S phase	E	Interphase.
Expl.	S phase is a part of interphase (Interphase = G1+S+G2).		
8.	Uracil	J	RNA
Expl.	Uracil nitrogen base is present in RNA but absent in DNA.		
9.	Selectively permeable cell organelle	P	Cell membrane
Expl.	The cell membrane is a selectively permeable cell organelle but cell walls are freely permeable.		
10.	Cytosine	B	Guanine
Expl.	Cytosine bonded with Guanine by 3 hydrogen bond.		
11.	Amembranous cell organelle	I	Granules
Expl.	Granules are amembranous cell organelle.		

Sl. No	Column A	Sl. No	Column A
12.	Sub metacentric Chromosome.	H	T shape chromosome.
Expl.	Sub metacentric Chromosome is a T-shape chromosome.		
13.	Smallest amembranous cell organelle	O	Ribosome
Expl.	The smallest amembranous cell organelle is Ribosome.		
14.	Puckering	A	Cleavage in animal cell
Expl.	The first sign of cleavage in animal cells is puckering.		
15.	Barr body chromosome	M	X-chromosome inactive
Expl.	An inactive X-chromosome is Barr body chromosome.		
16.	Aster	C	Bundle of microtubules
Expl.	A bundle of microtubules fibers radiating out from each cell pole during cell division is called aster.		
17.	Sat chromosome.	D	Satellites.
Expl.	Chromosomes with satellites are called sat chromosomes.		

Q:Type:[5] Write the special functional activities of the followings:

1	S-phase of cell division	2	Chromosome	3	Phosphate in DNA
4	Crossing over	5	G1 phase	6	Golgi apparatus
7	Lysosome	8	Centrosome	9	Vacuoles
10	Anaphase	11	Telophase II.	12	Diakinesis
13	Nucleosome	14	Idiogram	15	Organizer

A:Type:[5] Answer & Explanation:

1) **S-phase of cell division:** Replication of DNA, synthesis of Histone proteins and duplication of chromosome occurs.

2) **Chromosome:** carry genetic codes from one generation to another.

3) **Phosphate in DNA:** phosphate bonds connect sugar molecules in series in DNA.

4) **Crossing over:** creates a new combination of genes for variation.

5) **G1 phase:** synthesis RNA and proteins.

6) **Golgi apparatus:** synthesis and secretion of enzymes, the formation of the cell wall.

7) **Lysosome:** intercellular digestion is the main purpose.

8) **Centrosome:** Initiate and regulates cell division.

9) **Vacuoles:** store water and other substances including waste materials of cell.

10) **Anaphase:**Cleaves the cohesion rings holding together the sister chromatids which leading to the chromosome separation.

11) **Telophase II:** Meiosis end with this stage and here two groups of chromosomes once again get enclosed by a nuclear envelope.

12) **Diakinesis:**The final stage of meiotic prophase 1 is called Diakinesis and here chromosomes are fully condensed.

13) **Nucleosome:**it helps DNA to wind up and stand.

14) **Idiogram:**It helps to presume to represent the evolutionary relationship.

15) **Organizer:** formation of nucleolus from Nucleolar chromosome.

Q:Type:[6] True or False:

1) Duplicated chromosomes remain attached at a point called the centrosome.
2) Crossing over occurs during mitosis.
3) Cytokinesis refers to the division of the nucleus.
4) Karyokinesis is referred to as the division of the nucleolus.
5) The resting phase of mitosis is called interphase.
6) Uracil is one of the nitrogen base present in DNA.
7) Mitosis is the type of cell division occurring in the cells of the injured part of the body.
8) Meiosis produced gametes.
9) During mitosis 4 daughter cells are produced.
10) Crossing over occurs during prophase II.
11) The time required for mitosis is less than meiosis.
12) The kinetochore is a cube-shaped structure.
13) Sub-meta centric chromosomes are T-shaped.
14) Cytosine and Guanine are bonded by three hydrogen bonds.
15) Thymine is a pyrimidine based nitrogen base.
16) Meiosis II is called reduction division.
17) Amitosis cell division involves nuclear changes.
18) Replication of DNA takes place during the G2 phase.
19) Nucleolus produces ribosomes.
20) Aster rays formed during the Metaphase of mitosis.
21) Duplicated chromosomes remain attached at a point termed centrosome.

A:Type:[6] Answer & Explanation:

1) **[True]**Duplicated chromosomes remain attached at a point called the centrosome.
2) **[False]** Crossing over occurs during meiosis.
3) **[False]**Cytokinesis refers to the division of the cytoplasm.
4) **[False]**Karyokinesis is referred to as the division of the nucleus.
5) **[True]**The resting phase of mitosis is called interphase.
6) **[False]**Uracil is one of the nitrogen base present in RNA.
7) **[False]**Mitosis is the type of cell division occurring in the cells of all part of the body.
8) **[True]**Meiosis produced gametes.
9) **[False]**During meiosis 4 daughter cells are produced.
10) **[False]**Crossing over occurs during prophase I.
11) **[True]** Time required for mitosis is less than meiosis.
12) **[False]**Kinetochore is a disc-shaped structure.
13) **[False]**Sub-meta centric chromosomes are J/L-shaped.
14) **[True]** Cytosine and Guanine are bonded by three hydrogen bonds.
15) **[True]** Thymine is a pyrimidine based nitrogen base.
16) **[True]** Meiosis II is called reduction division.
17) **[True]** Amitosis cell division involves nuclear changes.
18) **[False]** Replication of DNA takes place during S-phase.
19) **[True]** Nucleolus produces ribosomes.
20) **[True]** Aster rays formed during Metaphase of mitosis.
21) **[False]** Duplicated chromosomes remain attached at a point termed centromere.

Q:Type:[7] Fill in the blanks:

1) Two arms of the chromosome joined at the Centre is called________.
2) Crossing over takes place during________ of meiosis.
3) Crossing over leads to _________.
4) G1,S& G2 phase all together is called _________.
5) Each homologous pair of chromosome contains ________ Chromatids.
6) Nuclear membrane gradually disappears during ______ of mitosis.
7) Protein synthesis takes place during cell cycle in ______&_____ phase.
8) _________ organelle of the cell also contains DNA other than nucleus.
9) __________ is the smallest amembranous cell organelle.
10) Kinetochore is _________shaped structure.
11) Chromatin consists of ______5 of Histones protein.
12) Histone wind up by DNA is called _________.
13) Thyamin does not found in ________ nucleic acid.
14) Chromosomes with _______ are called a sat chromosome.
15) Barr chromosome is inactive ______ chromosome.
16) Chromosomal end is known as _________.
17) Duplication of DNA occurs in the ______ phase of the cells cycle.

18) In Humans, meiosis takes place in _____ and ______.
19) Chiasmata formation takes place during______.
20) Fluid-filled spaces enclosed by membrane called _______.

A:Type:[7] Answer:

1.	Centromere.	**11.**	60%.
2.	Prophase I.	**12.**	Nucleosome.
3.	Variation.	**13.**	Ribo.
4.	Interphase.	**14.**	Satellite.
5.	Four.	**15.**	X
6.	Prophase.	**16.**	Centromere.
7.	G1 & G2	**17.**	S
8.	Mitochondria.	**18.**	Gonad, Ovary.
9.	Ribosome.	**19.**	Crossing over.
10.	Disc.	**20.**	Tonoplast.

Q:Type:[8] Write One difference of pair (on the given parameter).

1	RNA and DNA	*structure*
2	ER and Golgi apparatus	*function*
3	Golgi apparatus & Ribosome	*structure*
4	Liver cell & skin cell	*structure*
5	Mitosis & Meiosis	*function*
6	Nucleolar chromosome & Sat chromosome	*structure*
7	Meiosis I & Meiosis II	*function*
8	Cytokinesis during mitosis in Animal cell & Plant cell	*function*
9	Spindle formation of animal and plant cell	*source*
10	Adenine & Thymine	*Chemistry*
11	Heterochromatin & Euchromatin	*stain*
12	Crossing over & Spindle formation	*function*
13	Autosomes & Sex chromosome.	*Number.*

A:Type:[8] Answer& Explanation:

1) **[Structure]** RNA contains all the nitrogen bases except thymine but DNA contains all the nitrogen bases except Uracil.

2) **[Function]** ER main function in the cell is to produce a supportive framework but the main function of the Golgi apparatus is to synthesis and secrets enzymes, hormones etc.

3) **[Structure]** Golgi apparatus is membranous but ribosome is amembranous organelle.

4) **[Structure]** liver cell is plate-like shape but skin cells are cubic shape.

5) **[Function]** Mitosis helps to produce daughter somatic cells to grow, replacement, repair but Meiosis helps to reproduce by producing reproductive cells.

6) **[Structure]**the number of Nucleolar chromosome in a nucleus is only two but sat chromosomes may exist or may not exist in the nucleus.

7) **[Function]** Meiosis I is a heterotypic division whereas meiosis II is a homotypic division.

8) **[Function]** Cytokinesis in an animal cell is a centripetal type but in a plant cell, it is centrifugal type.

9) **[Source]** spindle formation of the animal cell takes place through asters but in a plant cell, it takes place through microtubules.

10) **[Chemistry]** Adenine is nitrogen-based purine but Thymine is a nitrogen-based pyrimidine.

11) **[Stain]** Heterochromatin is the dark staining part of a chromosome and remains condensed but Euchromatin is that part of a chromosome that stain lightly and partially condensed.

12) **[Function]** crossing over function is to get a new combination of genes to get variation.

13) **[Number]** Autosomes are 22 pairs of chromosomes responsible for various traits in the organism. Sex chromosomes are single pairs of chromosomes involved in reproduction and sex determination in an organism.

Q:Type:[9] Choose the correct answer(MCQ):

1. A phase which is the reverse of prophase is

a)metaphase**b)**anaphase **c)**telophase **d)** interphase.

2. the area where crossing over takes place is known as

a)aster**b)**Chiasmata**c)**Cristae**d)**centromere.

3.a diagrammatic representation of karyotype is called

a)PolyGram. b)ideogram c)phonogram. d)graffiti.

4.size of a chromosome normally measured during

a)metaphase. b)anaphase c)G1 phased) interphase.

5.synthesis of RNA takes place during

a)G1 phase. b)S phase. c)M phased)G2 phase.

6. Replication of DNA takes place during

a)G1 phase b)S phase c)M phase d) G2 phase.

7.Interphase is the sum of the following phases

a)G1,S,Mb)G1,S,G2c)S,M,G2d)G1,G2.

8.Double membrane sausage-like structure found in

a)mitochondrion. b)Golgi apparatus. c)Tonoplast. d) plastids.

9.adenine pairs with thymine by

a)single hydrogen bond. b)double hydrogen bond. c)triple hydrogen bond

d)no hydrogen bond is present.

10.numbers of Histone molecule present in Nucleosome is

a)five. b)six. c)seven. d)eight.

11. The cell component visible only during cell division is

a)Chloroplast. b)Mitochondria. c)Chromosome d)Chromatin.

A:Type:[9] Answer:

1.	c. Telophase.	7.	b. G1,S,G2
2.	b. Chiasmata.	8.	a. Mitochondria.
3.	b. Idiogram.	9.	b. Double hydrogen bond.
4.	a. Metaphase.	10.	d. Eight.
5.	d. G2phase.	11.	c. Chromosome.
6.	b. S phase.		

Q:Type:[10] Fill the blanks according to relation as indicated in first case:

1.crossing over : variation : : uncontrolled cell division:______.
2.RNA: Uracil: : DNA: ________.
3.Dark strain: Heterochromatin: : light strain:_______.
4.Mitosis: two daughter cell::Meiosis:________.
5.Interphase:G1+S+G2: : Mitosis: ________.
6.Cristae:Mitocondria::Tonoplast: ________.
7.Plastid: Photosynthesis::Ribosome:________.
8. Animal cell: Golgi apparatus::Plant cell:________.

9.Longest human cell:Nerve::Largest human cell: _________.

10.Smallest cell: PPLO::largest cell:____________.

A:Type:[10] Answer& Explanation:

1.crossing over : variation : : uncontrolled cell division:**Cancer.**

Exp: crossing over leads to mixing of two different genes and hence variation. Similarly, due to uncontrolled cell division cancer become the result.

2.RNA: Uracil: : DNA: **Thymine**.

Exp: DNA contains all the nitrogen bases except Uracil and similarly RNA contains all the nitrogen bases except thymine.

3.Dark strain: Heterochromatin: : light strain:**Euchromatin**.

Exp: the portion of chromosomes that strains dark are only condensed and called heterochromatin similarly the portion of chromosomes which lightly strains are partially condensed and known as Euchromatin.

4.Mitosis: two daughter cell::Meiosis:**Four haploid cells**.

Exp: Mitosis produces two diploid cells and Meiosis produces four haploid cells from the original diploid cell.

5.Interphase:G1+S+G2: : Mitosis: **Karyokinesis + Cytokinesis.**

Exp: Phases G1,S and G2 combined are known as interphase. Similarly,thesum of Karyokinesis and Cytokinesis is called Mitosis.

6.Cristae:Mitocondria::Tonoplast: **vacuoles.**

Exp: crossing over leads to mixing of two different genes and hence variation. Similarly, due to uncontrolled cell division cancer become the result.

7.Plastid: Photosynthesis::Ribosome:**Protein synthesis**.

Exp: Plastid (chloroplast) is related to photosynthesis. Similarly, protein synthesis in the cell is carried out by ribosomes.

8. Animal cell: Golgi apparatus::Plant cell:**Dictyosomes**.

Exp: dictyosomes are Golgi apparatus of plant cells.

9.Longest human cell: Nerve::Largest human cell: **Ovum**.

Exp: largest human cell is the ovum cell of a human female.

10.Smallest cell: PPLO::largest cell:**Ostrich egg**.

Exp: world largest cell is the Ostrich egg.

SECTION-II

Question: 1

(a) Give the reason:
1) Gametes have a haploid number of the chromosome.
2) Lysosomes are termed as suicidal bags of a cell.
b) What is the importance of Meiosis in creating variation.

Answer:

1)Due to meiosis cell division gametes are having a haploid number of chromosome.It is the reason behind the strict maintains of a definite and constant number of chromosomes in the organisms.

2)Enzymesthat are present in the Lysosome takes part in destroying foreign substances,injured organelles and intracellular digestion.This makes it suicidal bags of a cell.

Question: 2

(a) What is the cell cycle?
(b)When cell could exit from the cell cycle?
(c) Differentiate chromosomes according to the position of the centromere.
(d) What are called Nucleolar chromosome?
(e) Differentiate between the mitosis cell division of plant and animal cell.

Answer:

a)Cell cycle: it is the sequence of events by which a cell duplicates its genome,synthesises the other constituents of the cell and finally divides into two daughter cells is called the *cell cycle.*

b)Cell cycle consists of three transition points G1,S and G2.If a cell does not pass the G1-S transition then it will exit from the cell cycle.

c)According to the position of centromere chromosomes are four types:

1)Telocentric 2)Acrocentric 3)Meta-centric 4) Sub-metacentric.

d)In some chromosomes,a secondary constriction may be present at its length.This plays an important role in the formation of the nucleolus.In a nucleus, only two chromosomes posses such a nuclear zone and are therefore called a nucleolar chromosome.

e)Difference of mitosis in animal and plant cell:
1. In an animal cell, spindle formation takes place through asters but in a plant cell, it takes place through microtubules.

2. In animal cell Cytokinesis is a centripetal type but it is centrifugal in a plant cell.

3.furrow is formed in an animal cell but not in a plant cell.

Question: 3

(a) Briefly describe the structure of a chromosome.
(b) Briefly describe the G1 phase of the cell cycle.?
(c) Where do you find DNA in a cell?
(d) What is called Kinetochore?
(e) What is called the G_0 phase.

Answer:

a) Chromosome has the following structures

Chromatid: A chromosome consists of two symmetrical structures called chromatids. The chromatids are attached to each other by a centromere.

Chromonema:A Chromonema represents a chromatid in the early stages of condensation.

Chromomeres: the chromomeres are bead-like accumulations of chromatin material. Chromatin materials are regions of tightly-folded DNA.

Centromere and Kinetochore: the centromere lies within a thinner segment, called primary constriction.

b)G1:This is called the growth phase. This is a preparatory phase for oncoming divisions. In this phase cell grows in size, synthesizing RNA and proteins.DNA content does not change at this stage.

c) Nucleus and mitochondria.

d) During metaphase small disc-shaped structure at the surface of the centromeres serve as the sites of attachment of the spindle is called Kinetochore.

e)G_0: it is the inactive stage of the cell when it remains metabolically active but no longer proliferate unless called on
to do so depending on the requirement of
the organism.

Question: 4

(a) The diagram given below represents a stage during mitotic cell division in an animal cell.

(i) Identify the stage. Give a

reason to support your answer.

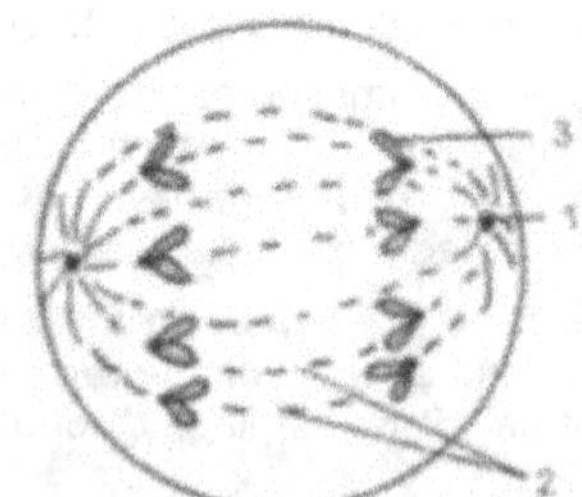

(ii) Name the parts labelled 1, 2 & 3.

(iii) What is the chromosome number of the cell?

(iv) Draw a neat labelled diagram of the cell as it would appear inthe next stage. Name the stage.

Answer:

(i) This picture depicts the *anaphase* of mitosis cell division.

***Supporting events*:**

a) Centromere splits here and chromatids are separated at this phase.

b) Chromatids are starts moving to opposite poles.

(ii) 1-centrioles; 2-spindle fiber; 3-chromatid.

(iii) in the given picture there are four pairs of chromosomes present.

(iv) the next stage is **Telophase**.

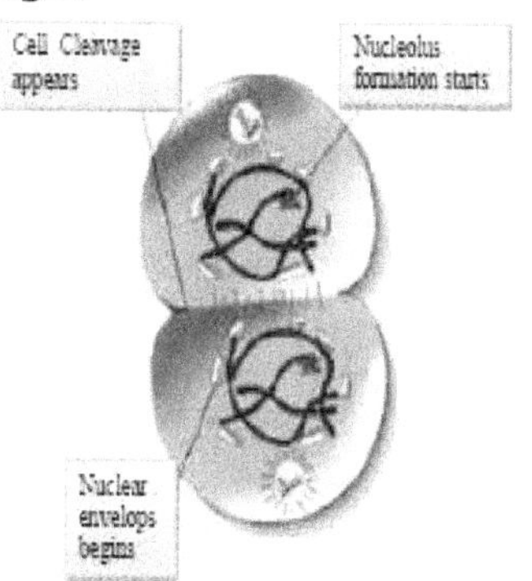

Telophase

Question: 5

(a) The diagram given below represents a stage during mitotic cell division in an animal cell.

(i) Identify the stage. Give a reason to support your answer.

(ii) Name the parts labelled 1, 2 and 3.

(iii) Where in the body this type of cell division occurs?

(iv) Draw a neat labelled diagram of the cell as it would appear in the previous stage. Name the stage.

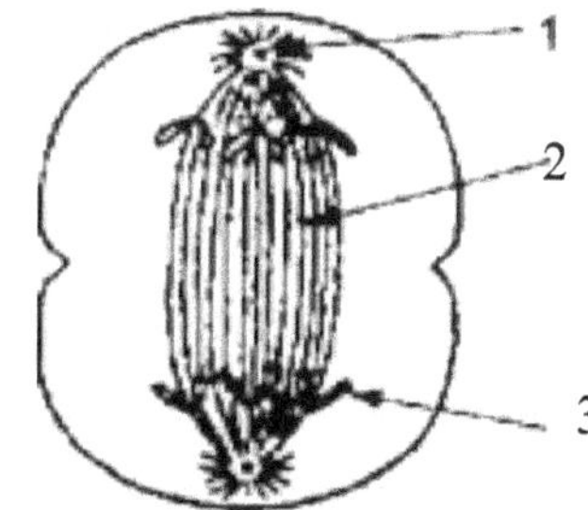

Answer:

(i) This picture depicts the *anaphase* of mitosis cell division.

***Supporting event*:**

a) Centromere splits here and chromatids are separated at this phase.

b) Chromatids are starts moving to opposite poles.

(ii) 1-aster; 2-spindle fibers; 3-sister chromatids.

(iii) this type of cell division(mitosis) occurs in the somatic cells of the body.

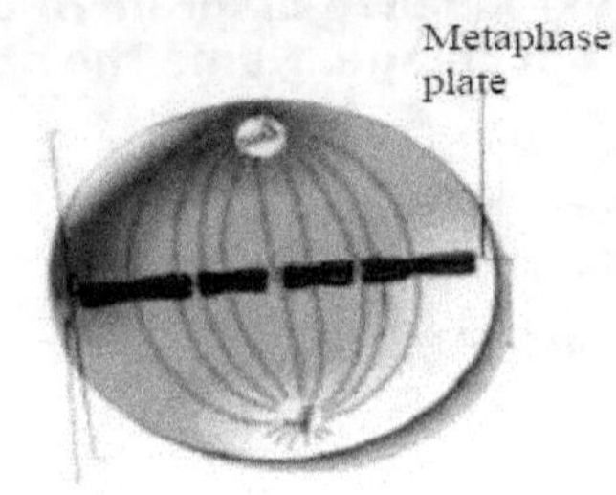

Metaphase

Question: 6

(a) The diagram given below represents a stage during mitotic cell division in an animal cell.

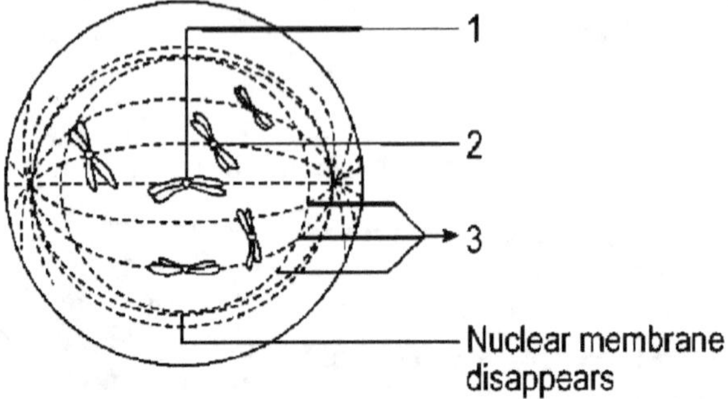

(i) Identify the stage. Give a reason to support your answer.

(ii) Name the parts labelled 1, 2 and 3.

(iii) What changes are occurring at this stage?

(iv) Name the cell organelle that forms the aster.

(v)Name the stage which follows this stage of mitosis. How can this stage be identified?

Answer:

(i) This picture depicts the *Prophase* of mitosis cell division.

Supporting evenst:

the nuclear envelope is broken down and long strands of chromatin condensed to form shorter more clearly visible chromosomes.

(ii) 1-centromere; 2-sister chromatids; 3-spindle fibers.

(iii) Changes occurs at this stage:

a) Chromosomes condense and thicken.
b)The homologous chromosomes undergo a break in their double-stranded DNA at the same location.
c) The mitotic spindles begin to form.
(iv)_Centrosome_.
(v)_Metaphase_ is the next stage.

**Event to identify the stage**:
The chromosomes are assembled at the equator.

Question: 7

(a) The diagram shows a schematic representation of the start of a certain phenomenon in cell division

(i) Name the phenomenon.

(ii) In which type of cell division this phenomenon occurs?

(iii) Name the parts labelled 1 & 2.

(iv) What changes are occurring in this process and what is its significance?

(v) Name the next stage.

Answer:

i)   This picture depicts the starts of crossing over.

ii)   In reproductive cells, this cell division phenomenon occurs.

iii) **1-**Chromatid;**2-**centromere.

iv) Crossing over is the exchange of genetic materials between two homologous chromosomes and this leads to a new combination of genes in the sex cells hence variation occurs.

v)   The next stage is prophase-I and it's also called Diakinesis.

GENETICS

SECTION-I

Q:Type:[1] Name the followings:

1. The two alternative forms of a gene.
2. Progeny of parents who are unlike in at least one character.
3. Genetically identical individuals.
4. A cross in which two characters are taken into consideration.
5. An allele that expresses itself only when present in homozygouscondition.
6. When a character exists in many alternative forms.
7. When first-generation individuals are crossed with one of the two parents from which they are derived.
8. Another name for the law of segregation of gametes.
9. Transmits characteristics from parent to offspring.
10. The traits are determined by the combined effect of more than one pair of genes.
11. Exchange of chromatid segments between the homologous chromosomes.
12. A single gene is responsible for a variety of traits.
13. Sudden change in certain characters of an organism.
14. The method of understanding history and also to predict the future of family by gene analysis.
15. The operation of removal of anthers from the flower in the bud stage.
16. The scientific name of the plant used by Mendel for his experiment.
17. The genes which exclusively occur in the Y chromosome are called.
18. The genes which exclusively occur in the X chromosome are called.
19. Individuals suffering from this disease lack of factor responsible for clotting of blood.
20. When first-generation individuals are crossed with only the recessive parent is called.
21. The cross between two individuals having one pair of contrasting characters.

A:Type:[1] Answer :

1.	Allele.	8.	Purity of gametes.	15.	Emasculation.
2.	Hybrid.	9.	Heredity	16.	*Pisum Sativum.*
3.	Clones.	10.	Polygenic traits.	17.	Holandric genes.
4.	Dihybrid cross.	11.	Crossing over.	18.	Sex-linked genes.
5.	Recessive allele.	12.	Pleiotropy.	19.	Hemophilia.
6.	Multiple alleles.	13.	Mutation.	20.	test cross.

7.	Back cross.	14.	Pedigree.	21.	Monohybrid cross.

Q:Type:[2] Fill in the blanks:

1) The genetic make –up or constitution of an individual is known as ___________.
2) Recessive character is masked in _________ condition.
3) A man with excessive development of hairs on pinna is an example of the _______ gene.
4) Defective tooth enamel is an example of X linked __________ inheritance.
5) Color blind peoples are unable to distinguish between ________ and ______ color.
6) Mutation causes change in ________ structure.
7) World first cloned animal was named as _________.
8) The genes which exclusively occur in Y-chromosome are called _________ genes.
9) X-linked genes are commonly known as _________ genes.
10) The skin colour of a human is an example of _______ traits.
11) Variation in heredity is observed in ________ produced offspring's.
12) Thalassemia is an example of ______ disease.
13) When the cross takes place between the parents and differing in a single pair of contrasting characters is known as __________.
14) An individual or cell with a single complete set of chromosomes is called _________.
15) The fundamental physical and functional unit of heredity is known as ___________.

A: Type:[2] Answer :

1.	Genotype.	6.	DNA.	11.	Sexually.
2.	Heterozygous.	7.	Dolly.	12.	Genetic.
3.	Holandric.	8.	Holandric.	13.	Backcross.
4.	Dominant.	9.	Sex-linked.	14.	Haploid.
5.	Red , Green	10.	Polygenic.	15.	Gene.

Q:Type:[3] Match the column:

Sl. No	Column A	Sl. No	Column B
1	Y-linked.	A	Male.
2	X-linked.	B	Codominance.
3	Hemizygous.	C	Holandric genes.
4	XY linked inheritance	D	3:1
5	Law of segregation.	E	Genes are localized in homologous section.
6	Single gene responsible for variety of traits	F	Sex-linked genes.
7	Phenotype is not result of intermediate	G	RBC.
8	Sickle cell trait	H	Hypo-phosphatemic rickets.
9	Mendelian phenotype ratio for a monohybrid cross	I	9:3:2:1
10	Mendelian phenotype ratio for a Dihybrid cross .	J	Straight hair.
11	X-linked dominant disease.	k	Pleiotropy
12	Recessive trait	L	Purity of gametes.

A:Type:[3] Answer& Explanation :

Sl. No	Column A	Sl. No	Column B
1.	Y-linked.	C	Holandric genes.
Expl.	The genes which exclusively occur in the Y chromosome are called Holandric genes.		
2.	X-linked.	F	Sex-linked genes.
Expl.	The X linked type sex-linked inheritance is performed by those genes which are localized in the non-homologous section of the X-chromosome and they have no corresponding allele in the Y chromosome.		
3.	Hemizygous	A	Male.
Expl.	Males are termed hemizygous for genes of the X-chromosome.		

Sl. No	Column A	Sl. No	Column B
4.	XY linked inheritance	E	Genes are localized in the homologous section.
Expl.	The XY-linked type sex-linked inheritance is performed by those genes which are localized in the homologous section.		
5.	Law of segregation.	L	Purity of gametes.
Expl.	During segregation since the gametes always contain one factor for a character, it is called the law of purity of gametes.		
6.	A single gene is responsible for a variety of traits.	K	Pleiotropy
7.	Phenotype is not a result of intermediate	B	Codominance.
Expl.	For some traits, both the allele are expressed in heterozygous individuals.		
8.	Sickle cell trait	G	RBC
Expl.	RBC bend like a sickle and restrict the blood flow.Sickle-cell versions ofhemoglobin stick tothemselves, stacking to form fibers that distort the shape of red blood cells carrying the protein.These sickle-shaped cells no longer flow smoothly through blood vessels, having a tendency to clogor degrade, causing the medical problems associated with this disease.		
9.	Mendelian phenotype ratio for a monohybrid cross.	D	3:1
10.	Mendelian phenotype ratio for a Dihybrid cross.	I	9:3:3:1
11.	X-linked dominant disease.	H	Hypophosphatemic rickets.
12.	Recessive trait	J	Straight hair.

Q:Type:[4] True or False:

1) When F1 individuals are crossed with only the recessive parent, it is called a back cross.
2) Tt is an example of true breeding.
3) Genetically identical individuals are called twins.
4) Holandric genes are exclusively occurs in X chromosome.
5) In AB type blood Co-dominance property of allele is observed.
6) Skin colour of human is an example of polygenic traits.
7) Attached earlobe is an example of a dominant hereditary trait.

8) People with colour blindness are unable to distinguish two colour blue and green.
9) Cloning is an example of asexual reproduction method.
10) Mutation cause changes in cell structure.
11) There are six pea plant traits that Mendel had examined.
12) When F1 individual is crossed with one of the two parents from which they are derived,then such cross is called a back cross.
13) Pea plants require less area to grow-this is a reason behind the selection of pea plant by Mendel.
14) Flower colour available in pea plants are red and white.
15) The number of pairs of autosomes in man is 22.
16) Chromosomes other than the pair of sex chromosomes are called alleles.
17) Hypertrichosis is X-linked.
18) Snapdragon gives the example of intermediate expression.
19) Pea plant can't be self-pollinated.
20) Colour of eye is an example of a polygenic trait.

A:Type:[4] Answer& Explanation :

1) **[False]** When F1 individuals are crossed with only the recessive parent, it is called **test cross**.
2) **[False]**. **TT** or**tt** is an example of true breeding.
3) **[False]** Genetically identical individuals are called **clones**.
4) **[False]**Holandric genes are exclusively occurs in **Y-chromosome**.
5) **[True]**. In AB type blood Codominance property of allele is observed.
6) **[True]**. Skin color of human is an example of polygenic traits.
7) **[False]**. Attached earlobe is an example of **recessive** hereditary trait.
8) **[False]**. People with color blindness are unable to distinguish two color **red**and green.
9) **[True]**. Cloning is an example of asexual reproduction method.
10)**[False]**. Mutation cause changes in **DNA** structure.
11)**[False]**. There are **Seven** pea plant traits that Mendel had examined.
12)**[True]**. When F1 individual is crossed with one of the two parents from which they are derived ,then such cross is called back cross.
13)**[False]**.Though information is correct but it was not the reason behind selection of pea plant.
14)**[False]**. Flower color available in pea plants are **blue** and white.
15)**[True]**. The number of pairs of autosomes in man is 22.
16)**[False]**. Chromosomes other than the pair of sex chromosomes are called autosomes.
   **A pair of genes that controls the two alternative expressions of the same character and has the same loci in the homologous chromosomes is called allele.
17)**[False]**.Hypertrichosis is **Y**-linked.

18) **[True]**.Snapdragon gives the example of intermediate expression.
19) **[False]**.Pea plant are *normally*self-pollinated.
20) **[False]**.*Color of skin* is an example of polygenic trait.

Q:Type:[5] Choose the Correct answer:

1.Who is known as the father of Genetics?

a)Mendel.   **b)**Brown. **c)**De Vries **d)** Morgan.

2.Who is known as the father of Mutation principle?

a)Mendel.   **b)**Brown. **c)**De Vries **d)** Morgan.

3.Reason behind selection of pea plant by Mendel were:

a)Variation.**b)**Bisexual. **c)** Non self-pollinating **d)** both a & b.

4. Pedigree analysis is useful to predict

a)   Mutation. **b)**genehistory. **c)**sex of fetus. **d)**None of the above.

5.Removal of anthers from flowers artificially is known as

a)   Castration. **b)**Emasculation. **c)**Cutting. **d)**Cross-pollination.

6.Sickle cell anemia could possible by

a)   **C**loning. **b)**mutation. **c)**sex linked inheritance. **d)**still no cause found by scientist.

7.When a single gene is responsible for a variety of traits , it is called

a)Pleiotropy. **b)**Mutation. **c)**Polygenic traits. **d)**none of the above.

8.Variation of heredity is observed in

a)sexualreproduction. **b)**Asexual reproduction.**c)**both a and b**d)**none of the above.

9.Following type of inheritance genes did not have corresponding allele in Y-chromosome.

a)sex linked genes. **b)**Holandric genes. **c)**XY-linked genes. **d)**Mutated genes.

10. The autosomal genes whose phenotypic expression is determined by the presence or absence of sex chromosome

a)Sex limited genes.**b)**sex influenced genes. **c)** Holandric genes. **d)**Mutated genes.

11. The recessive gene is the one that expresses itself in a)heterozygous condition. **b)**Homozygous condition. **c)** F2 generation **d)**Y-linked inheritance.

A:Type:[5] Answer:

1.	**a.** Mendel.	**6.**	**b.** Mutation.
2.	**c.** De Vries.	**7.**	**a.** Pleiotropy.
3.	**d.** Both (a) & (b).	**8.**	**a.** Sexual Reproduction.
4.	**b.** Gene History.	**9.**	**a.** Sex linked genes.
5.	**b.** Emasculation.	**10.**	**a.** Sex limited genes.
		11.	**b.** Homozygous condition

Q:Type:[6] Write One difference of pair(on the given parameter):

01	Test cross & Back cross	*Function*
02	Clones & offspring.	*Formation*
03	X-linked a& Y-linked inheritance.	*Transfer function*
04	Sex limited genes and sex influence genes.	*Structure*
05	Pure and hybrid strains.	*Structure*
06	Phenotype and genotype.	*appearance*
07	Dominant & recessive traits.	*Function*
08	Monohybrid & Dihybrid.	*Function*
09	Polygenic traits & Pleiotropy.	*Function*
10	Law of segregation and law of independent assortment.	*Function*

A:Type:[6] Answer:

1) **[Function]**When F1 individuals are crossed with only the recessive parent , it is called test cross. When F1 individuals are crossed with one of the two parents from which they are derived, such a cross is called back cross.

2) **[Formation]** Clones are genetically identical individuals produced by artificial asexual reproduction . offspring are progenies produced as a result of sexual reproduction.

3) **[Transfer function]**X-linked genes are never transferred from father to son but Y-linked inheritance genes are directly transfer from father to son.

4) **[Structure]**Sex limited genes are autosomal genes but sex influenced genes are influence by sex of the organism.

5) **[Structure]** In Pure strains two allelomorphic genes representing the same character but in Hybrid strain two allelomorphic genes are representing the alternatives of a character come together.

6) **[Appearance]**Phenotypes are the external appearance of the character and genotypes are the constituents of an individual with regard to a character of genes.

7) **[Function]** An allele which express itself even in the presence of its alternate allele is called dominant trait and an allele which expressed itself only when present in homozygous condition.

8) **[Function]**A cross in which only one character is taken into consideration is called monohybrid and if a cross occurs with two characters then it is called Dihybrid.

9) **[Function]** When some traits are determined by the combined effect of more than one pair of genes are called polygenic traits. When a single gene is responsible for a variety of traits then it is called Pleiotropy.

10) **[Function]** Law of segregation states that the paired factors responsible for a character segregate into gametes and are recombine in fertilization. Law of independent assortment says when more than one pair of contracting characteristics are brought together in an individual, the entry of one pair of alleles separates independently and assorted independently of any other pair of alleles.

11) **[Appearance]** Intermediate expression occur when there is an apparent bending in the phenotype due to incomplete dominance. Codominance occurs when both the genes are individually expressed their character without suppressing each other.

12) **[Structure]** Holandric genes are exclusively occurs in X-chromosomes but Sex linked genes don't have any corresponding allele in Y-chromosome.

Q:Type:[7] Define the terms:

1.	Pedigree analysis.	6.	Codominance.
2.	Mutation.	7.	Polygenic genes.

3.	X-linked inheritance.	8.	Law of independent assortment.
4.	Sex influenced genes.	9.	Law of Dominance.
5.	Pleiotropy.	10.	Law of segregation.

A:Type:[7] Answer& Explanation:

1) **Pedigree analysis:** It is a family tree which describing the inheritance of particular characteristics across the generations. It is the method to understand the history of the genes and also to predict the future of a family and the location of a genome associated with the genetic disease.

2) **Mutation:**Mutation is sudden change in certain characters or traits due to changes in the DNA structure .Mutations occasionally occur within cells in the body as they divide. Although these mutations will not be inherited by any offspring.

3) **X-linked inheritance:** X-linked type sex linked inheritance is performed by those genes which are localized in the non-homologous section of X-chromosome, and that have no corresponding allele in Y-chromosome.

4) **Sex influenced genes:**These are those traits which are influenced by the sex of the organisms.

5) **Pleiotropy:**A single gene may be responsible for a Varity of traits , this is called Pleiotropy.

6) **Codominance:** For some traits two alleles can be codominant. Here both expressed in heterozygous individuals. People who have AB type blood they actually have the characteristics of both type A and type B blood.

7) **Polygenic genes**: Some traits are determined by the combined effect of more than one pair of genes. these are referred to as polygenic genes.

8) **Law of independent assortment:** it says when more than one pair of contracting characteristics are brought together in an individual, the entry of one pair of alleles separates independently and assorted independently of any other pair of alleles.

9) **Law of dominance:**When a pair of contrasting characteristics are present together, only one is able to express itself while the other remains suppressed.The character which is expressed is called dominant and the suppressed character is called recessive character.

10) **Law of Segregation:**It states that the paired factors responsible for a character segregate into gametes and are recombine in fertilization.

SECTION-II

Question: 1

1) **What is heredity?**
2) **Gametes are always pure-Comment.**
3) **Name the unit of heredity.**
4) **Red-green colour blindness is a sex-linked inherited character. Gene b for colour blindness is recessive to gene B for normal vision. This gene b is carried only on the X chromosome.**

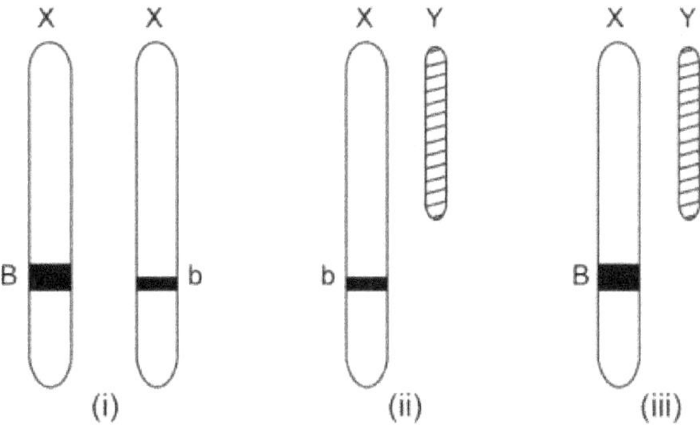

a) **Describe the phenotypes of (i), (ii) and (iii).**
b) **Explain why red-green colour blindness is more likely to occur in men than women.**

Answer:

1. **Heredity:** Heredity is the transmission of traits from one generation to the following generation.
2. Since the gametes always contain one factor of a character, it is called gametes are always pure.
3. The unit of heredity is Gene.
4. a. (i) Normal woman bur carrier of colour blindness.
       (ii) Colour blind man.
       (iii) Normal man.

b. As colour blindness is a defects due to recessive genes which occur on the X-chromosome so it is more likely to occur in men than women.In female it is less likely that both X chromosome carry the defective gene.So, if either of the X-chromosome carries the defective genes, the gene being receissive and its influence will be masked by the normal gene which is present on the other X-chromosome. As in male XY chromosome is present so, if one X-chromose carry defective gene so no other normal gene of Y chromosome could mask it.As a results the recessive gene gets expressed and the colour blindness defects occurs.

Question: 2.

1. **Give any 2 reasons why Mendel selected pea plant for his experiments.**
2. **Explain Back cross & Test cross.**
3. **Suggest two ways in which mutation could happen in human cells.**
4. **What is emasculation?**
5. **Copy and complete the following table of contrasting characters given by Heredity traits of human.**

S. No.	Character	Dominant	Recessive
1	Lips.		
2	Cheek shape		
3	Eye color.		
4	Hair		
5	Earlobe		

Answer:

1. **Reasons:1.** Many varities with pure form are available in alternative forms of character. **2.** Being bisexual , pea plant are normally self polinated but cross polination could be done artificially because the size of flower is very convenient.
2. **Back cross:** When F1 individuals are crossed with one of the two parents from which they are derived , such a cross is called back cross.

Test cross: When F1 individuals are crossed with only the recessive parent, it is called test cross.

3. A. Radiation exposure.

B. certain change in DNA structure.

4. **Emasculation**: It is the process of removal of anthers from the flower bud for the hybridisation technique and for the required cross pollination.

Sl. No.	Character	Dominant	Recessive
1	Lips.	Thick	Thin
2	Cheek shape	Dimpled.	Normal.
3	Eye color.	Brown.	Blue.
4	Hair	Curly.	Straight.
5	Earlobe	Free.	Attached.

Question: 3.

1. **Explain the following terms:**
   a. Homologous chromosomes.
   b. Alleles.
2. **Give the Dihybrid ratio. Name and state the law which explains the same.**
3. **With the help of a Punnett square show a monohybrid cross up to the F2 generation between plants having purple and white flowers. Also, write the genotypic and phenotypic ratio of the F2 generation.**
4. **State Mendel's First law of heredity.**

Answer:

1. **a)Homologous chromosome:**These are the pair of chromoses with same shape and size, each of which is obtained from either of the parents.
   b) Allele: A pair of genes that controls the two alternative expressions of the same character and has the same loci in the homologous chromosomes is called allele.
2. **Dihybrid ratio:** 9:3:3:1
   [Third] Law of independent assortment: When more than one pair of contrasting characters are brought togather in an individual, the entry of one pair of alleles seperates independently and assorts indepndently of any other pair of alleles .
3.

$$P1 \quad\quad PP \quad \times \quad\quad pp$$
[purple flower, male]   [White flower, female]

Gametes   **P**   **P**   p   p

Punnet square F1:

Gametes	P	P
P	[purple]	[purple]
P	[purple]	[purple]

Note: F1 generation have all purple flower but whole progeny is heterozygous for the traits.

$$P2 \quad\quad Pp \quad\quad \times \quad\quad Pp$$
[purple flower, male]   [Purple flower, female]

Gametes   **P**   p   **P**   p

Punnet square F2:

Gametes	P	p
P	PP [purple]	Pp [purple]
p	Pp [purple]	pp [White]

Note: Phenotype is   3[purple flower] : 1 [White flower]
Genotype is 1 [Homozygous purple flower] :2 [Heterozygous purple flower] : 1 [Homozygous White flower]

4.   **First law of heredity:** When a pair of contrasting characters present together , only one is able to express itself while the others remain suppressed.

Question: 4

1. **Explain the following terms:**
   a. Sex limited genes.
   b. Criss-cross inheritance.
c. Law of purity of gametes.
2. Name the two sex linked disease in male.
3. State Mendel law of segregation.

Answer:

1.   **a.Sex limited genes**: these are autosomal genes whose phenotypic expression is determined by the presence of absence of sex chrosome.E.g. beard development in human being.

   b.Criss cross inheritance: It is a type of inheritance in which a X-;onked recessive gene is transmitted from P1 male parent to F2 male progeny through its F1 heterozygous females and different F1 and F2 results in the reciprocal crosses.

2.   **Law of purity of gametes:** Law of segression is called law of purity of gametes. As per this law paired factors responsible for a character segregate into gametes and are recombined at fertilisation.

3.   **Two sex linked disease in male:**Colour blindness and Haemophilia.

4.   Refer part 3 of Q-4.

Question: 5

1.   **A homozygous tall plant (T) bearing red coloured flowers (R) is crossed with a homozygous dwarf plant (t) bearing white flowers(r):**
a.   **Give the genotype and phenotype of the F1 generation.**
b.   **Give the possible combinations of the gametes that can be obtained from the F1 hybrid.**

c. Give the Dihybrid ratio and the phenotype of the offspring of the F2 generation when two plants of the F1 generation above are crossed.

2. Write two applications of Mendel's law.

Answer:

1. **a. Genotype of F1 generation**is TtRr i.e. heterozygous tall plant with red colour flower.

   b. Possible combination of gametes are: TR, Tr, tR, tr

   c. Dihybrid ratio:

   Phenotype:9:3:3:1

   Genotype:1:2:2: 2:2:1: 2:1:2:1

2. **Application of Mendel's law:**

   1: Gives a new idea about the new combination of hybrids and genetic diseases.

   2: important for plant and animal breeding to produce new and best breed.

Question: 6

1) Why is haemophilia more common in males than females?

2) The given pedigree chart shows tongue rolling.

 a. Is this trait dominant or recessive?

 b. Give reason for the above answer.

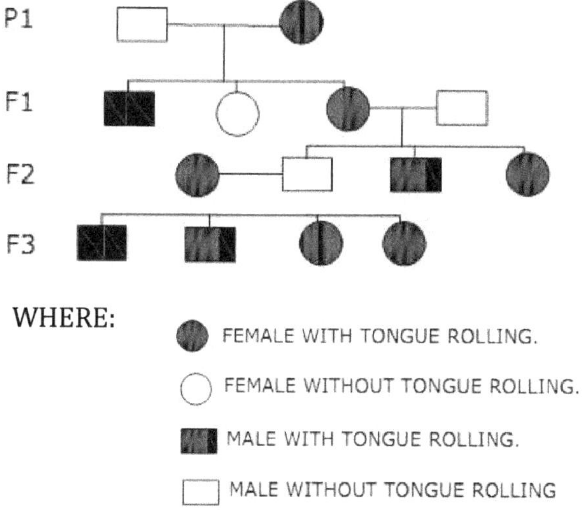

Answer:

1. Haemophilia is a sex-linked dominant disease of male.
2. **a.** Here the trait tongue rolling is dominant.
   b. Explanation: Here in the given chart out of two parents, the female shows tongue rolling and the male member is a non-tongue roller.In the F1 progeny, a son and a daughter are tongue rollers and another daughter is a non-tongue roller.This indicates that the female carries heterozygous genes. If the female was a homozygous parent then all the three offsprings would have got at least one gene for the tongue rolling and making them all tongue rollers.

Question: 7

A family consists of two parents and their four children, and the pedigree chart below shows the inheritance of the trait polydactyl.

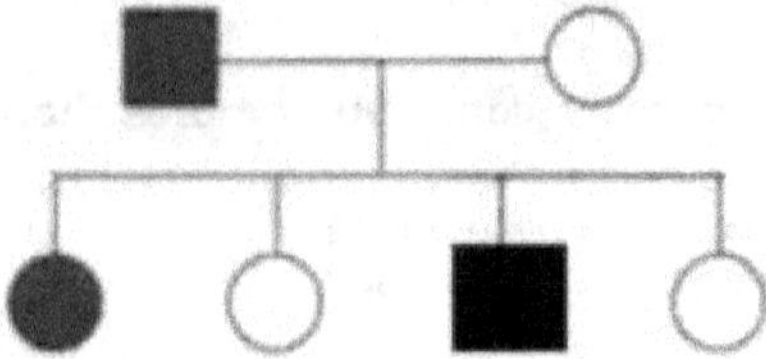

(i) Who is a polydactyl parent?
(ii) How many daughters and sons have been born in the family?
(iii) What does child 1 and 3 indicate about this trait?
(iv) Complete the depiction of all probabilities of the trait in child 2 and 4.
(v) What is polydactyl?

Answer:

i)   The father is polydactyl.
ii) Two daughters and two sons have born in the family.
iii) Here child 1 and 3 shows polydactyl.
iv) Child 2 and 4 have hand with normal number of fingers.
v)   Polydactyl: it is the condition of genes due to which a person has extra fingers in hand or toe.

Question: 8

Given below is a diagram of a double helical structure of DNA.

a. **Name the four nitrogen bases which form a DNA molecule.**
b. **Give the full form of DNA.**
c. **Name the unit of heredity.**
d. **Mention two point differences between mitosis and meiosis.**

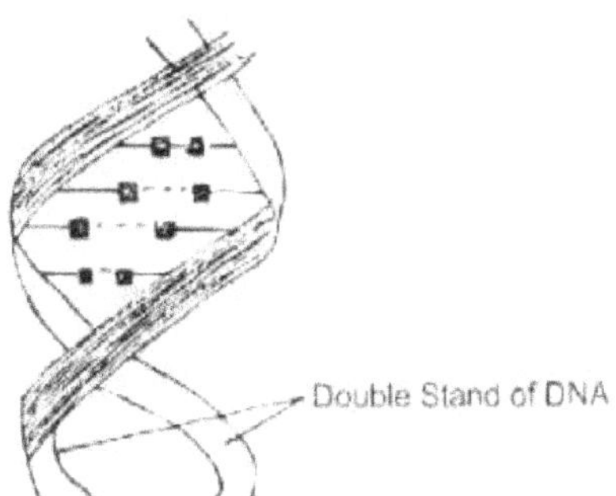

Answer:

a. **Nitrogen bases are:** Guanine, Thymine, adenine and Cytosine.
b. Deoxyribonucleic acid.
c. Gene is the unit of heredity.
d. **Difference:**

Mitosis	Meiosis
Two daughter cells are produced.	Four daughter cells are produced.
Diploid cells are produced.	Haploid cells are produced.

ABSORPTION BY PLANTS

SECTION-I

Q:Type:[1] Name the followings:

1. The minimum pressure required to stop the flow of pure water into a solution across a partially permeable membrane.
2. A solution with greater solute concentration.
3. A process of getting pure water from the concentrated solution is called.
4. oozing of cell sap from an injured part of the plant is called.
5. The phenomenon in which living or dead cells of plants in their dry or semi-dry state absorb water by surface tension is called.
6. Part of the root protects the root tip as it grows through the soil.
7. The condition of a cell when it is fully stretched.
8. The shrinkage of the protoplasm of a cell when it was kept in hypertonic solution is called.
9. The stage where plasmolysis just starts.
10. The reverse of the turgidity condition is called.
11. The reverse of the plasmolysis condition is called.
12. Turgor movement is generally called.
13. Transports water from the soil to other parts of the plant.
14. Large quantity of water passed out as vapor.
15. Pressure through which water can rise to some feet.
16. The movement of water molecules from the region of higher solvent concentration to lower solvent concentration through a semi-permeable membrane.
17. The movement of molecules of a substance from a region of higher concentration to lower concentration.
18. The pull produced in the uppermost xylem cells in the leaves.
19. The mutual attraction with each other of water molecules is called.
20. Absorption takes place along the gradient of what?
21. A pressure developed in a solution when it is separated from pure water by a semi-permeable membrane.
22. The condition of a cell in which the cell contents are shrunken.
23. The process by which a hydrophilic substance absorb water.
24. The pair of cells surrounding the stomata.

A:Type:[1] Answers:

1.	Osmotic Pressure.	8.	Plasmolysis.	15.	Root Pressure.
2.	Hypertonic Solution.	9.	Incipient Plasmolysis	16.	Osmosis.
3.	Reverse Osmosis.	10.	Flaccidity.	17.	Diffusion.

4.	Exudation/Bleeding.	**11.**	De-plasmolysis.	**18.**	Transpiration pull.
5.	Imbibition.	**12.**	Sleeping movement.	**19.**	Cohesive force.
6.	Root cap.	**13.**	Transportation.	**20.**	Concentration.
7.	Turgidity.	**14.**	Transpiration.	**21.**	Osmotic Pressure.
22.	Flaccid.	**23.**	Imbibition.	**24.**	Guard cells.

Q: Type:[2] Fill in the blanks:

1) __________ method is used to kill the weeds by weedicides.
2) Due to ________ in guard cells their osmotic pressure increases.
3) The shrinkage of the protoplasm of a cell is called _________.
4) __________ movement is also called sleeping movement.
5) The root cap acts as a _________ tissue.
6) The apparatus used to demonstrate osmosis is called ___________.
7) ________ is a rating of the maximum potential pressure that can be developed in the solution as a result of osmosis.
8) Osmosis is the diffusion of ________ molecules only.
9) During active transport cell energy is supplied from ______.
10) ______ funnel is used to demonstrate Osmosis.
11) Most of the water absorbed by the plant is done by________absorption.
12) A fully stretched cell is known as ______ cell.
13) In ______ solution, a living cell remains normal.
14) When the solute concentration of cell sap is ______ than that of soil water, the water enters the root hairs.
15) The cell wall is a ______ membrane.

A:Type:[2] Answers:

1.	Plasmolysis.	**6.**	Osmometer.	**11.**	Passive.
2.	Photosynthesis.	**7.**	Osmotic pressure.	**12.**	Turgid.
3.	Plasmolysis.	**8.**	Water.	**13.**	Isotonic.
4.	Turgor.	**9.**	ATP.	**14.**	Higher.
5.	Meristem.	**10.**	Thistle.	**15.**	Preamble.

Q:Type:[3] match the column:

Sl. No	Column A	Sl. No	Column B
1.	Photosynthesis	**A.**	Xylem cells.
2.	Imbibition.	**B.**	Epiblema.

Sl. No	Column A	Sl. No	Column B
4.	Mineral absorption.	D.	Transpiration.
5.	Turgidity.	E.	Phloem.
6.	Root hair.	F.	Passive absorption.
7.	Helps to make new cells at the root tip.	G.	Glucose.
8.	Guard cells.	H.	Sleeping movement.
9.	Water vapour.	I.	Fully stretched cell.
10.	Folding & Unfolding of leaves.	J.	Chloroplast.

A:Type:[3] Answers & Explanation :

Sl. No	Column A	Sl. No	Column B
1	Photosynthesis	G	Glucose.
Expl.	By photosynthesis method plant produce glucose.		
2	Imbibition.	F	Passive absorption.
Expl.	Imbibition does not require energy from ATP.		
3	Transpiration pull.	A	Xylem cells.
Expl.	Due to transpiration water deficit condition takes place and a sort of pull is produced in the uppermost xylem cells which are called transpiration pull.		
4	Mineral absorption.	C	Active absorption.
Expl.	Mineral absorption is required energy from ATP.		
5	Turgidity.	I	Fully stretched cell.
Expl.	Turgidity is the state when a cell cannot accommodate further any more water.		
6	Root hair.	B	Epiblema.
Expl.	Root hairs are thin, delicate unicellular prolongation of the Epiblema.		
7	Helps to make new cells at the root tip.	E	Phloem.
Expl.	Phloem brings food from the leaves to the root which is used to make new cells at the root tip.		
8	Guard cells.	J	Chloroplast.
Expl.	Guard cells consist of chloroplast.		

Sl. No.	Column A	Sl. No.	Column B
9	Water vapour	D	Transpiration.
Expl.	A large quantity of water is passed out as vapour during transpiration.		
10	Folding & Unfolding of leaves.	H	Sleeping movement.
Expl.	Folding and unfolding of leaves take place due to turgor movement and it is also called sleeping movement.		

Q:Type:[4] True or false:

1) Root hairs are thin, delicate prolongation of the cortex.
2) Root hairs are multicellular.
3) Osmosis regulates the opening and closing of stomata.
4) Transpiration pull is essential to conduct water in herbs.
5) Turgor movements are seen in many monocot plants.
6) The shrinkage of protoplasm is called De-plasmolysis.
7) Large quantity of water is passed out as vapour during imbibitions.
8) Imbibition's property is not observed in proteins but it observed in fat.
9) At least 95% of the mass of a plant is composed of water.
10) Osmometer is used to demonstrate osmosis.

A:Type:[4] Answers :

1) **[False]**Root hairs are thin, delicate prolongation of *Epiblema*.
2) **[False]**Root hairs are *uni-cellular*.
3) **[True]**Osmosis regulates the opening and closing of stomata.
4) **[False]**Transpiration pull is essential to conduct water in *plants.*
5) **[False]**Turgor movements are seen in many *leguminous* (dicot) plants.
6) **[False]**The shrinkage of protoplasm is called *plasmolysis.*
7) **[False]**Large quantity of water is passed out as vapour during *transpiration.*
8) **[False]**Imbibition property is not observed in proteins but it's*not* observed in fat.
9) **[False]**At least *75%* of the mass of a plant is composed of water.
10) **[True]**Osmometer is used to demonstrate osmosis.

Q:Type:[5] Choose the correct answer [MCQ]

1.Outward movement of water through a semi-permeable membrane is called

a) Exosmosis. **b)**pyrolysis. **c)** plasmolysis. **d)**transpiration.

2.Movement of the molecules of solute and solvent both take place in

a) Diffusion. **b)**reverseosmosis. **c)**Osmosis. **d)**Active transport.

3.Which of the following is always a rapid process?

a) Diffusion.**b)**reverse osmosis. **c)**Osmosis.   **d)** Active transport.

4.The minimum pressure required to stop the flow of water into a solution across a partially permeable membrane is called

a)transpirationpull. **b)**Osmoticpressure. **c)**turgity. **d)** None of the above..

5.Which cells provide mechanical supports to the non-woody tissues?

a)turgidcells.**b)**cambium. **c)**dead cells. **d)**Xylem.

6.Growing zone of the root is located by

a) Near root cap.**b)**just after steam. **c)**between steam and zone of elongation.**d)**all over the root.

7.Approximately 98% of the water is absorbed through

a)active absorption. **b)** passive absorption   **c)**either (a) or (b)**d)** none of the above.

8.Guard cells are become flaccid at night due to

a) Diffusion.**b)**reverse osmosis.**c)** inter Osmosis.**d)**Exosmosis.

9.The cell wall of a root is made of

a) Single-layer. **b)** two-layer. **c)**Multi-layer. **d)**varies according to the type of the plant.

10. Pectin found in
a)outer layer of cell wall. **b)** Inner layer of cell wall. **c)** both in inner & outer layer. **d)**not found in cell wall.

A:Type:[5] Answers [MCQ] :

1.	a. Exosmosis.	**6.**	a. near root cap.
2.	a. Diffusion.	**7.**	b. Passive absorption.
3.	d. Active Transport Pressure.	**8.**	a. Exosmosis.
4.	b. Osmotic.	**9.**	b. Two-layer wall.
5.	a. Turgid cells.	**10.**	a. Outer layer of cell.

Q:Type:[6] Write One difference of pair(on the given parameter):

01	Xylem & phloem.	**Function.**
02	Stomata & root hair.	**Formation.**
03	Root hair & root cap.	**Function.**
04	Isotonic and hypertonic solution.	**Density.**
05	Active transfer & Passive transfer.	**Function.**
06	Root pressure and transpiration pull.	**Formation.**

07	Zone of maturation & growing zone of the root.	Location.
08	Imbibition& exudation.	Occurrence.
09	Osmosis & Diffusion	Medium of function.
10	Turgidity & flaccidity	Formation.
11	Plasmolysis & De-plasmolysis.	Effect.

A:Type:[6] Answers [MCQ] :

1) **[Function]**Xylem carries water and mineral salts up to the stem and Phloem brings food from the leaves to all the parts of a plant.

2) **[Formation]** Stomata found in leaves and it is formed by guard cells. Root hair is thin, delicate unicellular prolongation of the Epiblema of the root.

3) **[Function]**Root hair helps to hold the plant with soil and also helps to absorb water from the soil. The root cap protects the root tip as it is growing through the soil.

4) **[Density]**A solution with equal solute concentration outside and inside the cell is called an isotonic solution. A solution with greater solute concentration compared to the cell is called a hypertonic solution.

5) **[Function]**Active transfer is the movement of molecules against a concentration gradient which uses some cell energy from ATP. Passive transfer is the movement of molecules from a region of higher concentration to lower concentration, either with the use of a semi-permeable membrane or without presence of it.

6) **[Formation]**The pressure which developed in the roots due to the inflow of water, which helps in pushing the plant sap upwards is called root pressure. Due to the transpiration from the leaves, a great water deficit takes place in its cells and as a result of this a sort of pull is produced in the uppermost Xylem cells and it is called transpiration pull.

7) **[Location]**Zone of maturation is located just after the end of the stem towards the root where root cells are completely grown and the growing zone of the root is located just before the root cap where cells are getting multiplied.

8) **[Occurrence]** The phenomenon in which living or dead cells of plants in their dry or semi-dry state absorb water by surface tension is called imbibition. The oozing of cell sap from an injured part of the plant is called exudation or bleeding.

9) **[Medium of function]** Osmosis takes place in water but diffusion is taking place in liquid and gas medium.

10) **[Formation]** turgidity is the condition of a cell when it is completely absorbed water through endosmosis and water cannot be accommodated. Flaccidity is the shrinkage of protoplasm and it's just opposite to turgidity.

11) **[Effect]** During plasmolysis cells shrink when placed in a hypertonic solution. During de-plasmolysis cells distend and become turgid when placed in a hypotonic solution.

Q:Type:[7] Define the followings:

1.	Turgidity.	6.	Osmosis.
2.	Flaccidity.	7.	Imbibition.
3.	Plasmolysis.	8.	Diffusion.
4.	Root pressure.	9.	Turgor movement.
5.	Transpiration pull.	10.	Passive adsorption.

A:Type:[7] Answer :

1) **Turgidity:**Turgidity is the condition of a cell when it is completely absorbed water through endosmosis and more water cannot be accommodated

2) **Flaccidity**: Flaccidity is the condition of a cell when it is shrink due to plasmolysis.

3) **Plasmolysis:**When a cell is placed in a hypertonic solution, its protoplasm will shrink and this phenomenon is called plasmolysis.

4) **Root pressure:**The pressure developed in the roots due to the inflow of water, which helps in pushing the plant sap upwards is called root pressure.

5) **Transpiration pull:** Due to the transpiration from the leaves, a great water deficit takes place in its cells and as a result of this a sort of pull is produced in the uppermost Xylem cells and it is called transpiration pull.

6) **Osmosis:** it is the net movement of water molecules from a region of their higher concentration to a region of their lower concentration through a semi-permeable membrane.

7) **Imbibition:**The phenomenon in which living or dead cells of plants in their dry or semi-dry state absorb water by surface tension is called imbibition.

8) **Diffusion:**it is the movement of particles within a gas or liquid from a region of their higher concentration to their lower concentration region.

9) **Turgor movement:** it is the movement of plants body parts e.g. folding and unfolding of leaflets or drooping of leaflets of sensitive plant etc. due to change in turgidity of cells.

10) **Passive absorption:**It is the method of absorption that happens due to a change in concentration and it does not use cell energy during its happening.

Q:Type:[8] Explain Why?

1. Why do leaves of touch-me-not plant droop when touched?
2. Why Grass is killed if salt is sprinkled on it?
3. Why freshwater fish cannot survive in seawater but seawater could?
4. Why resins swell up when kept in water?
5. Why wilted lettuce leaves become crisp/firm when placed in cold water for a while?

A:Type:[8] Answer :

1. It is due to the turgor pressure difference between the upper and lower halves of the base of petiole (pulvinus). Stimulus of touch leads to lower half cells lose water and upper half cells of leaves become turgid due to transfer of water from lower cells.

2. Grass killed because adding salt results in loss of water from the grass cells due to exosmosis. Due to loss of water pressure decreases to that extends that the protoplasm of the cells goes away from the cells away.

3. Freshwater fish can't survive in the ocean or saltwater because the seawater is too salty for them. The water inside their bodies would flow out their cells, and they will die of dehydration/Exosmosis.All fish, whether they live in salt water or fresh water, must maintain a certain level of salinity in their bloodstream to survive. Most are restricted to one environment because they cannot change the way they regulate this salinity, but some species spend periods of their life in both environments.

4. The water molecules pass the cell membrane of the raisins and the raisins thus get swollen and this process is called Osmosis.

5. Wilted lettuce leaves become crisp/firm when placed in cold water for a while because they take up water due to endosmosis in a hypotonic solution.

SECTION-II

Question: 1.

Given below is the diagram of an apparatus set-up to study a very important physiological process:

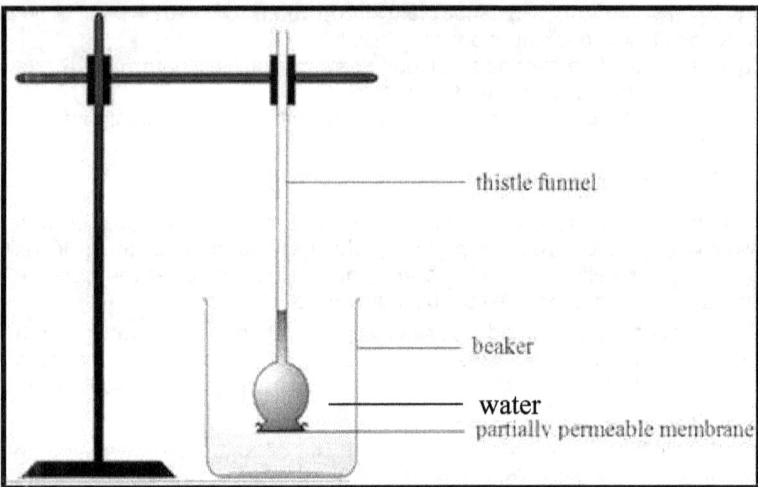

1. Name the process being studied?
2. Explain the process.
3. What change would you observe in the thistle funnel containing sugar solution after about 10 minutes?
4. Is sugar solution hypertonic or hypotonic?
5. Name the part of the plant cell which is represented by the sugar solution.
6. Explain why much salt is added to the pickles?

Answer.

1. Osmosis.

2. It is the diffusion of water molecules through a semi-permeable membrane from a low concentration solution to a high concentration solution.

3. After 10 minutes the sugar solution of the thistle funnel rises up to endosmosis.

4. The sugar solution is hypertonic as its concentration is very high.

5. Cell sap.

6. When added salt in a pickle a hypertonic medium is created due to which water is drawn out of the bacterial cells, and thus, the cells are killed by plasmolysis. Therefore, much salt is added to the pickles for their preservation.

Question: 2.

The given figure is the cross section of the root in the root hair zone. Answer the following question according to this picture.

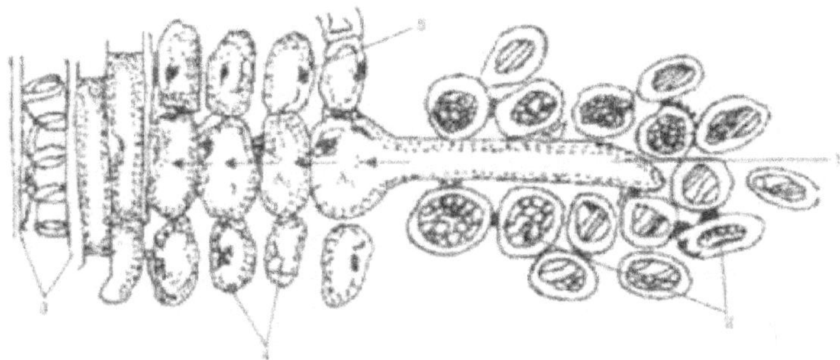

a. Name the parts labelled 1 to 5.

b. How many cells are present in each root hair?

c. Draw the labelled diagram of root hair cell when it is close to soil consist of fertilizers.

d. What pressure is responsible for the movement of water in the direction given in the picture?

e. How this pressure is developed?

Answer:

a) Lebel:
1. Root hair.
2. Soil particles.
3. Xylem.
4. Cortex.
5. Nucleus.

b) Root hairs are made of a single cell.

c)

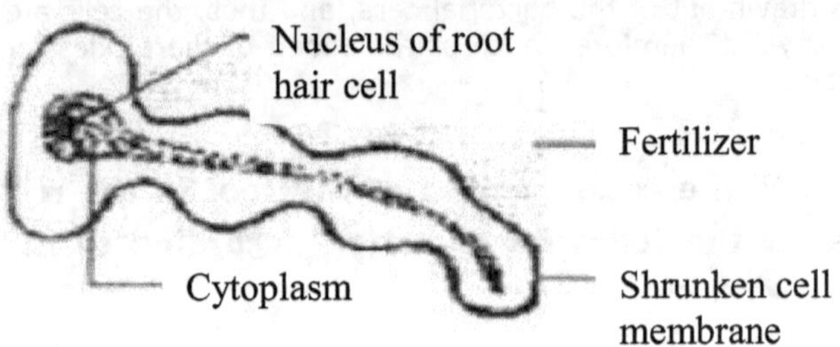

d) Osmotic pressure and root pressure are responsible for the movement of water.

e) Due to the absorption of water by root hair cortex cells become turgid. The elastic wall of those cells exerts osmotic pressure on the fluid and force them towards Xylem and become flaccid.Again it absorbs water and turgid. Alternat turgidity and flaccidity creates the roots pressure and ultimately helps to absorb water.

Question: 3

Study the diagram given below and answer the questions that follow:

a) Explain the physiological process being studied.

b) What will be observed in the two test tubes after two to three days?

c) Give a reason for your answer in (b) above.

d) Why is the surface of water covered with oil?

e) State the purpose of setting up test tube Q.

Answer:

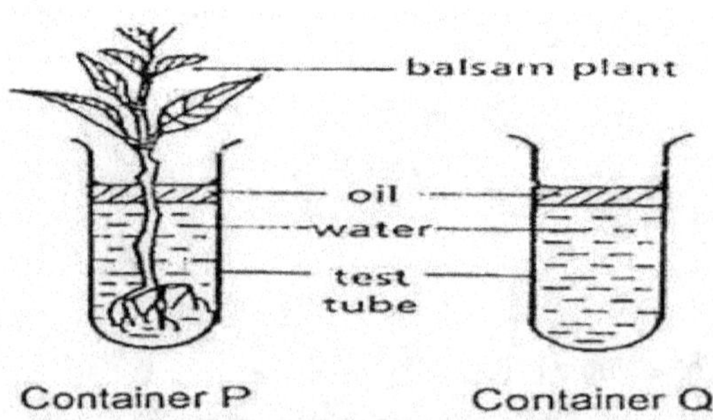

a) Here the process studied is transpiration. It is the process by which plant loses water in the form of water vapour through their aerial parts. Transpiration helps plants to maintain their body temperature.It also cools the regions around the plants.

b) **Observation:** Water level of Container P will reduce after 2-3 days but in container Q water level will remain the same.

c) Due to transpiration water will transfer through root to leaves of the plant.Then due to transpiration water will vaporise and reduce water level in container P.But, in container Q as oil has placed on the surface so water will not vaporise and level will be maintained.

d) Oil is placed on the water surface of container Q to prevent any water loss due to evaporation from the water surface other than transpiration.

e) Test tube Q placed to show that water level reduced only due to transpiration and not by any other means.

Question: 4

Given below are diagrams of plant cells of plant cells as seen under the microscope after having been placed in two different solutions:

a. **What is the technical term for the condition of**
   1. **Cell A.**
   2. **Cell B.**

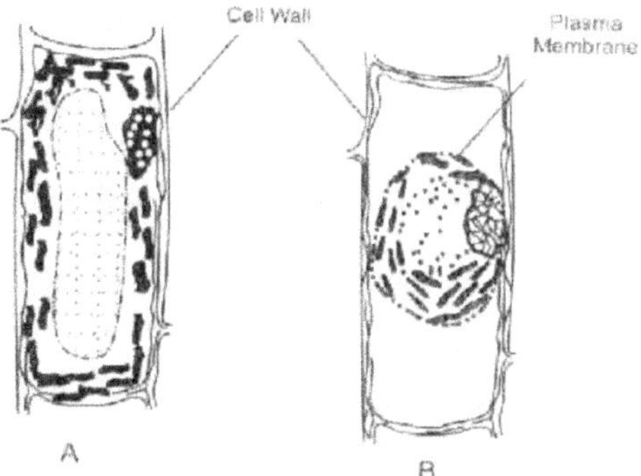

b. **From the solutions given in brackets (water, strong sugar solution, 1% salt solution) name the solution into which:**

1. **Cell A.**
2. **Cell B was placed before being viewed under the microscope.**

c. **Under what conditions in the soil will the root hair cell resemble:**
1. **Cell A. 2. Cell B**
d. **Name the pressure responsible for the movement of water from the root hair cell to the xylem of the root. How is it set up?**

e. **Name the pressure that helps in the movement of water up the xylem of the root.**

Answer:

a)   Cell A: turgid cell. Cell B: Plasmolysed cell.
b)   In Water: Cell A.
 In Strong Sugar solution: Cell B.
 In 1% salt solution: Cell B.
c)   1.   Root hair cell will resemble with cell A when the soil is well watered.
2.   Root hair will resemble cell B when soil containing high
 amount of fertiliser but less water in it.
d)   The pressure responsible for the movement of water from root hair cell to xylem is called root pressure.
   Root pressure:Due to the absorption of water by root hair cortex cells become turgid. The elastic wall of those cells exerts osmotic pressure on the fluid and force them towards Xylem and become flaccid.Again it absorbs water and turgid. Alternat turgidity and flaccidity creates the roots pressure and ultimately helps to absorb water.
e)   Transpiration pull.

Question: 5

Answer briefly:
(i) State the importance of turgidity and plasmolysis in plants (any 4 points).
(ii) State the significance of osmosis. (any 3 points).
(iii) State the significance of Diffusion (any 3 points).
(iv) Define osmosis.

Answer:

i)   **a.** Turgid cells provide mechanical support in non-woody tissues e.g. sugarcane.
b. Turgidity is essential for maintaining rigidity in leaves.
c.   The opening and closing of stomata are depended on the turgidity of guard cells.
d. Plasmolysis is used to kill weeds in lawns and in preserving food items.

ii) a. It helps in the absorption of water and minerals by the plants.
b. It develops turgidity and so maintains turgor pressure in the plant cells.
c. It allowsthe movement of water from one cell to another.

iii) a. It helps in the transpiration of water vapour.
b. It keeps the walls of the internal plant tissue moist.
c. Ions and other molecules spread into the protoplast through diffusion.

iv) **Osmosis:** It is the net movement of water molecules from a region of their higher concentration to a region of their lower concentration through a partially permeable membrane.

TRANSPIRATION

SECTION-I

Q:Type:[1] Name the followings:

1. Oozing out of water droplets from the edge of the leaf.
2. When the amount of water lost through transpiration exceeds absorption through roots causing this in a plant leaf.
3. Two parts of the leaf which allowing transpiration.
4. The instrument measuring transpiration.
5. This of the steam which allowing transpiration.
6. This type of plants leaves contains stomata on both the surface.
7. This paper is used in the transpiration experiment to show the presence of moisture.
8. Presence of these materials on the stem and leaf reduces transpiration.
9. This type of transpiration accounts for minimum transpiration.
10. Structure through which most of the transpiration takes place.
11. The plant with sunken stomata.
12. The loss of water from injured parts of a plant.
13. The plant in which stomata are absent.
14. The special marginal structure in a leaf through which guttation occurs.
15. This method helps to cool the plant body.
16. The force that helps in the conduction of water.

A:Type:[1] Answer:

01	Guttation.	07	Cobalt chloride Paper.	13	Hydrilla.
02	Wilting.	08	Anti-tranpirants.	14	Hydathode.
03	Cuticle & Stomata.	09	Cuticular transpir.	15	Transpiration.
04	Ganong's Photometer.	10	Stomata.	16	Cohesive force.
05	Lenticels.	11	Nerium.		
06	Monocots.	12	Bleeding.		

Q:Type:[2] Fill in the blanks:

1) Leaves with thick _________ over the epidermis help to reduce the loss of water by transpiration.

2) Sunken stomata found because of increased evaporation due to _____ _______.

3) __________ helps in the translocation of water and minerals through xylem.

4) _____________ is an instrument to measure the rate of transpiration.

5) Transpiration is highest during___________.

6) About _______ % of the total water is lost through stomata.

7) About _______ % of the total water is lost through cuticle.

8) Water lost through stem is by _________.

9) Stomata are present on the ___________ surface of the leaves in di-cots.

10) The rate of transpiration is directly proportional to ____________ ratio.

A:Type:[2] Answer:

01	Cuticle.	05	Summer.	09	Lower.
02	Air movement.	06	90%.	10	Root shoot.
03	Transpiration.	07	10%.		
04	Photometer.	08	Lenticels.		

Q:Type:[3] Write One difference of pair(on the given parameter):

01	Wilting and abscission.	Cause of occurrence.
02	Hydathodes and stomata.	Function
03	Guttation and Bleeding.	Cause of occurrence
04	Translocation and transpiration.	Purpose.
05	Cuticle and lenticels.	Structure.
06	Photometer and Photometer.	Function.
07	Evaporation and transpiration.	Function
08	Evaporation and transpiration.	Process.
09	Dicot leaf stomata and monocot leaf stomata.	Location
10	Deep root and shallow root.	Function.

A:Type:[3] Answer:

1) [*Cause of occurrence.*]When the amount of water lost through transpiration is more than the amount of water absorbed through roots wilting of leaves occurs. When very little water is available to plants transpiration results in the closing of stomata following the production of Abscisic acid which causes premature leaf fall and this called abscission.

2) [**Function**] Hydathodes helps in Guttation and stomata helps in transpiration.

3) [*Cause of occurrence*]Guttation happens when root pressure is high and transpiration is low. Bleeding is the exudation of cell sap from the injured parts of the plants.

4) [**Purpose**]translocation helps to transfer water and minerals through Xylem after entering into the root hair. Transpiration helps to loss of excess water through aerial parts of the plants to keep them cool.

5) [**Structure**] Cuticle is the thin layer of wax on the leaf. Lenticels are the special openings that develop in the older steam in place of stomata.

6) [**Function**]photometer is used to measure the rate of transpiration in plants. A photometer is used to measure light.

7) [**Function**] Evaporation is the loss of water from only the free surface of plants. Transpiration is the loss of water from aerial parts of the plants.

8) [**Process**] Evaporation is a physical process but transpiration is a physiological process.

9) [**Location**] In dicot leaf stomata is present on the lower surface of the leaves. In Monocot leaf stomata found on both lower and upper surface of the leaf.

10) [**Function**] Deep roots penetrate to a very low water table and shallow roots absorb water from the lightest rainfall of the upper surface of the soil.

Q:Type:[4] True or false:

1) Gaseous exchange occurs in all body cells.
2) Photolysis is the process of splitting water molecules in presence of grana and temperature.
3) At very low temperature no guttation takes place.
4) Transpiration could occur at night.
5) Guttation occurs at noon.
6) The wall of guard cells towards the stomata is thin.
7) Transpiration takes place only in green plants.
8) Lenticels are minute opening on the steam.
9) In a dicot leaf, most transpiration takes place from the lower surface.
10) Moist cobalt chloride paper is blue.
11) Stomata are absent in the submerged hydrophytes.
12) Monocots leafs having stomata on both surfaces.
13) Transpiration is a physical process.
14) Transpiration is a faster process than evaporation.
15) Transpiration is controlled by the osmosis process.
16) Watertight condition should be maintained in a photometer.
17) The rate of transpiration is inversely proportioned to the root-shoot ratio.

18) The presence of cuticle on the leaf surface reduces transpiration.
19) Sunken stomata are found where air movement over the surface of the leaf is very low.
20) The vascular bundle is consists of Xylem and Phloem.
21) Leaves are reduced to spines in xerophytic plants.
22) Guttation is the exudation of plant sap from the injured parts of the plant.

A:Type:[4] Answer:

1) **[True]**Gaseous exchange occurs in all body cells.
2) **[False]**Photolysis is the process of splitting water molecules in presence of Grana and light.
3) **[True]**At very low temperature no guttation takes place.
4) **[False]**Transpiration could occur during the day time.
5) **[False]**Guttation occurs intheearly morning/night.
6) **[False]**The wall of guard cells towards stomata is thick.
7) **[False]**Transpiration takes place only in all plants.
8) **[True]**Lenticels are minute opening on the steam.
9) **[True]**In a dicot leaf most transpiration takes place from the lower surface.
10) **[False]**Moist cobalt chloride paper is pink in colour.
11) **[True]**Stomata are absent in the submerged hydrophytes.
12) **[True]**Monocots leafs having stomata on both surfaces.
13) **[False]**Transpiration is a physiological process.
14) **[False]**Transpiration is a slow process than evaporation.
15) **[True]**Transpiration is controlled by the osmosis process.
16) **[True]**Water tight condition should be maintained in a photometer.
17) **[False]**The rate of transpiration is directly proportioned to the root-shoot ratio.
18) **[True]**Presence of cuticle on leaf surface reduce transpiration.
19) **[False]**Sunken stomata are found where air movement over the surface of the leaf is very high.
20) **[True]**Vascular bundle is consists of Xylem and Phloem.
21) **[True]** Leaves are reduced to spines in xerophytic plants.
22) **[False]** Bleeding is the exudation of plant sap from the injured parts of the plant.

A:Type:[5] Match the column:

Sl. No	Column A	Sl. No	Column B
1	Transpiration.	A	Leaf cells become flaccid.8
2	Translocation.	B	Abscisic acid.
3	Sunken stomata.	C	Loss of water as vapour from the surface of plant.
4	Potometer.	D	Cobalt chloride.

Sl.No	Column A	Sl.No	Column B
5	Guttation.	E	A factor of transpiration.
6	Evaporation.	F	Evaporation of water from areal parts of plants.
7	Abscission.	G	Water lost in the form of water droplets.
8	Wilting.	H	Transpiration.
9	In moisture transfer to pink colour.	I	Water and mineral.
10	Lenticels.	J	Measuring water transpiration rate.
11	Root-shoot ratio.	K	Nerium.

A:Type:[5] Answer:

Sl. No	Column A	Sl. No	Column B
1.	Transpiration.	F	Evaporation of water from aerial parts of plants.
Expl.	transpiration is the loss of water from aerial parts of the plant.		
2.	Translocation.	I	Water and mineral.
3.	Sunken stomata.	K	Nerium.
Expl.	Because of increased airflow over the leaf, the evaporation increases and stomata of leaves in a dry environment sink into the leaf and get covered with hair to produce pockets of still air. It is called sunken stomata and found in Nerium.		
4.	Photometer.	J	Measuring water transpiration rate.
Expl.	Plant lose some weight due to transpiration.		
5.	Guttation.	G	Water lost in the form of water droplets.
6.	Evaporation.	C	Loss of water as vapour from the surface of plant.
7.	Abscission.	B	Abscisic acid.
Expl.	When very little water is available to plants, transpiration results in the closing of stomata following the production of Abscisic acid. It causes premature falling of a leaf.		

Sl. No	Column A	Sl. No	Column B
8.	Wilting.	A	Leaf cells become flaccid.8
Expl.	When the amount of water lost through transpiration is more than absorption through roots, leaf cells and it becomes flaccid and causing wilting of a leaf.		
9.	In moisture transfer to pink colour.	D	Cobalt chloride.
10.	Lenticels.	H	Transpiration.
11	Root-shoot ratio.	E	A factor of transpiration.
Expl.	Transpiration is proportionate to the root-shoot ratio.		

Q:Type:[6] Choose the correct answer[MCQ]:

1. Photometer is an instrument to measure the rate of

a)translocation. **b)**transpiration.**c)**Growth of the plant.**d)** Photosynthesis.

2. loss of water as droplets from hydathodes is observed in

a)Banana tree.   **b)** Tomato trees.**c)** Pea plants.**d)** All of the above.

3. Which of the following is an anti-transpirant? :

a)Auxins. **b)** Cytokinin **c)** Abscisic acid.**d)** both b & c.

4. Which of the following tree leaf have stomata on both surfaces

a)Mango. **b)**Orisasativa. **c)**Pea **d)** None of the above..

5. The thin layer of wax present on some plant leaf is called

a)stomata. **b)**lenticels **c)**cuticle **d)** exudation.

6. About 90% of the total water is lost through

a)Stomata. **b)**Lenticels.**c)**Cuticle.**d)** none of the above.

7. in which of the following plant stomata is absent?

a)   Hydrilla.**b)**Fern. **c)**papaya. **d)** none of the above.

8.Guard cells concave wall is

a)   Thin. **b)**thick. **c)**either(a) and (b) and it depends on the cotyledon number. **d)** none of the above.

9.Abscission is observed where the water content in soil is

a)veryhigh.**b)**very little. **c)**no water at all. **d)**normal.

10. Guttation occurs

a) At night. **b)** At dawn **c)** in presence of light. **d)** both (a) and (b).

A:Type:[6] Answer[MCQ]:

1.	b. Transpiration.	6.	a. Stomata.
2.	b. Tomato tree.	7.	a. Hydrilla.
3.	c. Abscisic acid.	8.	b. Thick.
4.	b. *Orisa Sativa.*	9.	b. Very little.
5.	c. Cuticle.	10.	d. Both (a) and (b)

Q:Type:[7] Write the main functions of the followings:

1.	Stomata.	7.	Sunken stomata.
2.	Cuticle.	8.	Photometer.
3.	Abscisic acid.	9.	Root hair.
4.	Leaf Spines.	10.	Evaporation.
5.	Hydathodes.	11.	Transpiration.
6.	Lenticels.	12.	Guttation.

A:Type:[7] Answer:

1) **Stomata:** Transpiration.
2) **Cuticle:** prevent evaporation.
3) **Abscisic acid:** to remove leaf when very little water is present.
4) **Leaf spines:** to terminate loss of water in the desert.
5) **Hydathodes:** to lose excess water as water droplets.
6) **Lenticels:** to lose water as vapour.
7) **Sunken stomata:** to produce pockets of still air.
8) **Photometer:** to measure water uptake by the cut shoots.
9) **Root hair:** imbibitions and osmosis.
10) **Evaporation:** to lose water from the free surface.
11) **Transpiration:** to lose water from aerial parts.
12) **Guttation:** to lose excess water from hydathodes.

Q:Type:[8] Explain:

1. How guard cells open stomata?
2. Why transpiration on the two sides of a dorsiventral leaf is different on a different side?
3. Why cactus leaves are modified to spines?
4. Why plant in dry soil started abscission first before die?

5. Why water droplets found at the edges of tomato leaf in early morning.
6. Why the rate of transpiration increases in hot and dry weather?
7. How transpiration cool plant.
8. Why anti-transpirant used to keep cut flowers fresh for a long time.
9. Why in hot summer most herbaceous plants wilt at noon and recover in the evening?

A:Type:[8] Answer:

1. The Wall of guard cells towards the stomata opening is thick while the outer convex wall is thin. The inflow of water in the guard cells causes them to bulge outwards, thus widening the stomata opening.

2. There is more transpiration takes place from the lower surface of the leaf due to the presence of numerous stomata there.

3. Cactus grow in the desert area. Due to the lack of water present, it is obvious to protect the plant from transpiration as well as evaporation lose thus leaves are modified to spines.

4. When very little water is available to plants. Transpiration results in the closing of stomata following the production of Abscisic acid. It causes the premature fall of the leaf to control the loss of water.

5. When the root pressure is high and transpiration is low water drops ooze out through the margin of tomato leaves due to the presence of hydathodes.

6. Transpiration could make plant cool during hot and humid air.

7. Transpiration loses some energy by means of losing water vapour.

8. Anti-transpiranthelps to reduce the rate of transpiration.

9. The rate of transpiration during mid-day exceeds the rate of absorption of water by the roots. The cells, therefore, lose turgidity. In the evening of during the absence of light, there is no loss of water through transpiration and the turgidity of the leaves re-acquired and they stand erect.

SECTION-II

Question: 1

1) **Name the three types of transpiration. Which of these accounts for maximum transpiration in the plant?**
2) **What are the advantages of transpiration to the plants?**
3) **What is an anti-transpirant? Name some anti-transpirant.**
4) **List five adaptation found in desert plants to reduce transpiration.**

5) Mention the disadvantages of transpiration to the plants.

Answer:

1. Three types of transpiration are :
          a. Stomatal transpiration.
          b. Cuticular transpiration.
          c. lenticular transpiration.
Stomatal transpiration accounts for maximum transpiration in the plant.

2. **Advantages are** :
a. Transpiration helps plants to maintain their body temperature.
b. It helps in the translocation of food.

3. Anti-transpirant: These are some chemical substances that are used to reduce the rate of transpiration.
Example: Abscisic acid. , Silicon emulsions.

4. Adaptations found in desert plants are :
          a. Leaves with a thick cuticle.
          b. Reduced number of stomata.
          c. Sunken stomata.
          d. Spongy parenchyma is replaced with palisade parenchyma in many leaves.

5. Disadvantages of transpiration are:
          a. Wilrting of the plant.
          b. Stunted growth.
          c. Excess energy expenditure.
          d. Premature leave fall.

Question: 2

Given below is an apparatus used to study a particular process in plants. Study the same and answer the questions of the followings:

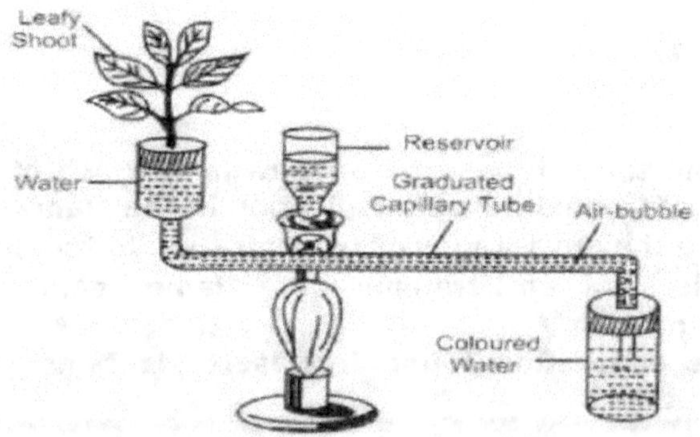

1) Name the apparatus.
2) Mention some limitations of this apparatus.
3) Which phenomenon is studied with the help of this apparatus?
4) What is the function of the part marked "Reservoir"?
5) What is the role of the air bubble in the experiment?

Answer:

1. Ganong's photometer.
2. This photometer does not measure the water loss by the plant transpiration but it measures water taken up by the plant. A portion of water is used by plant cells and some water is lost due to transpiration.
3. Transpiration.
4. Reservoir is used to bring the air bubble to its original position and this is done by releasing some water from the reservoir into the capillary tube.
5. The movement of the bubble in the graduated tubes gives the volume of water lost in a given time which is equivalent to the rate of transpiration of the leafy shoot.

Question: 3

Given below is an experiment set up to study a particular process:

1) **Name the process being studied.**
2) **Explain the process.**
3) **Why is the pot covered with a plastic sheet?**
4) **Mention one way in which this process is beneficial to the plant.**
5) **Suggest a suitable control for this experiment.**

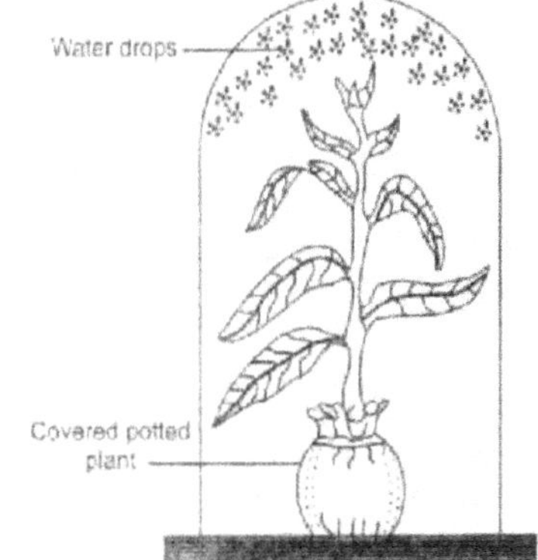

Answer:

1. Transpiration.
2. **Transpiration:** it is a process of loss of water vapour from the surface of the plant [stomatal, cuticular & Lenticular] mainly from the leaves. Only a very small quantity of water is used by the plant and most of the water is lost through this method.

3. Plastic sheet will prevent the escape of water vapour from the pot which will help to carry out the test without any error.
4. Suction force created due to transpiration helps in the secent of the sap in the plant. More and more transpiration means more and more water and minerals absorption from the soil.
5. A suitable control for this experiment would be a pot without a plant covered with a plastic sheet and kept in the bell jar.

Question: 4

The diagram below represents a structure found in a leaf. Study the same and answer the questions that follow:

1) **Name the parts labelled A and B.**
2) **What is the biological term for the above structure?**
3) **What is the function of the part labelled A?**
4) **Mention two structural features of A; which help in the function as mentioned in question 3.**
5) **Where is this structure likely to be found in a leaf.**
6) **How does the above structure help the plant?**
7) **How many other cells are found surrounding the structure as seen in the diagram?**

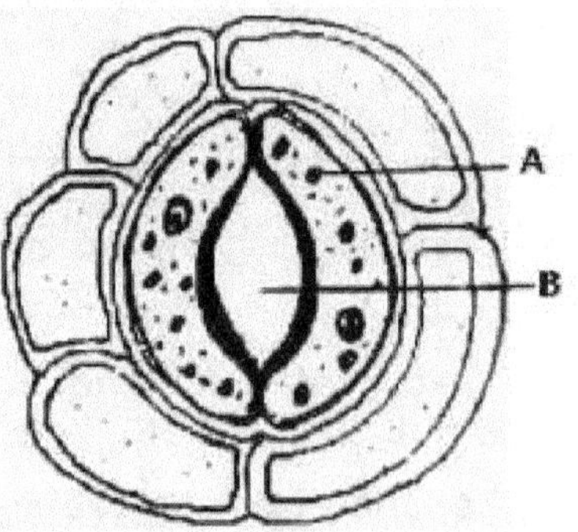

Answer:

1. Label A: Guard cell.   Label B: Stoma
2. Stomatal apparatus.
3. Guard cell regulates the opening and closing of the stoma.
4. Structural features: Guard cells have a thick outer wall and thin inner walls. The turgidity and flaccidity of guard cells help to regulate the opening and closing of stomata.
5. Stomata are found on the upper and lower epidermis of the leaf.
6. Stomata help to do transpiration and exchange of gases. Transpiration keep plant cool and exchange of gases is required to do photosynthesis and respiration of plant.
7. Five epidermal cells are found surrounding the structure and they are called accessory cells.

Question: 5

The followings are diagrams of certain structure in plants in two conditions

1. **Identify the structure shown.**
2. Name the parts labelled 1 to 5.
3. What is the most apparent difference between picture A & B?
4. Describe the mechanism which brings such structural change?
5. Mention the time when structure B is generally observed in a plant?

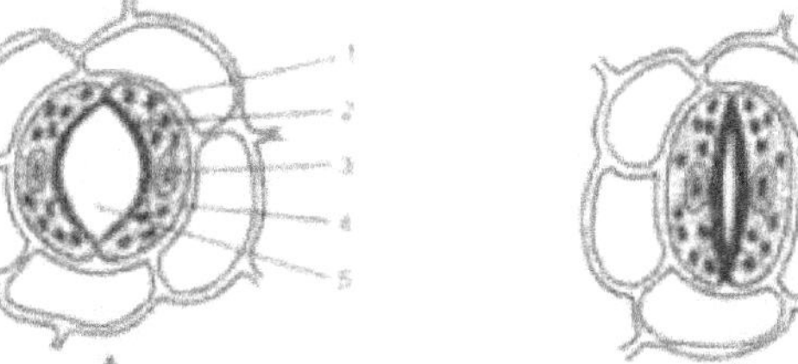

Answer:

1. A: Open Stoma.   B: Closed stoma.
2. Label: 1. Chloroplast. 2. Inner thin wall of guard cell.   3.Nucleus
   4. Outer thick wall of guard cell.   5. Open stoma.
3. Guard cell regulates the opening and closing of the stoma.
4. Guard cells in Picture A are turgid and the stoma is open. Guard cells are flaccid in picture B and the stoma is closed.
5. During day time concentration of carbohydrates rises, leading to osmotic uptake of water and guard cells are swell up. Since guard cells, inner walls are thin and outer walls are thick, thus widening the stomata opening. When the osmotic pressure of guard cells become lower, the water leaves these cells and guard cells become flaccid .this results closing of the stoma.

Question: 6

An experimental set-up showing a certain phenomenon in plants is shown below. Study the diagram and answer the questions that follow:

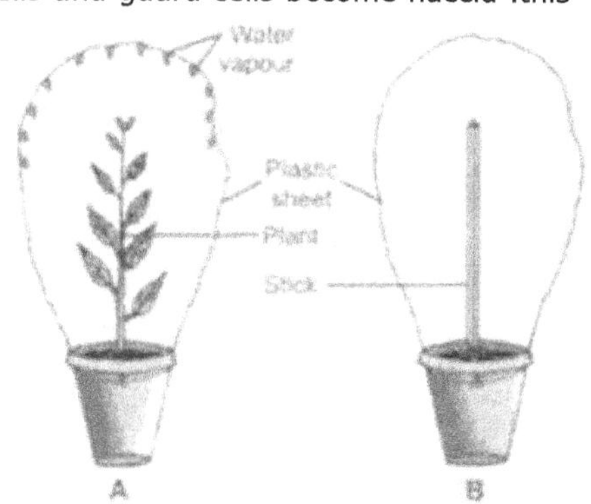

1) Which phenomenon is represented in the above set-up?

2) **What is the purpose of pot 'B'?**
3) **Certain xerophytes plants have a thick cuticle on their leaf surface. Give reasons.**
4) **What is bleeding?**

Answer:

1. This experiment set up aims to demonstrate the phenomenon of transpiration of plant.
2. Pot B demonstrate the control for this experiment which explained that the evaporated water comes from leaves only.
3. A thick waxy cuticle develops over the epidermis to reduce the loss of water by transpiration.
4. **Bleeding**: It is the exudation of sap from the injured parts of the plants. When an incision is made in the stem of the plant growing in the well-watered soil, Xylem sap starts oozing out due to root pressure or bleeding.

Question: 7

The given figure shows a section through a part of a leaf of Nerium.

a. Label the parts numbered 1–4.
b. What is the figure depicting?
c. Mention any two disadvantages of transpiration.
d. State any two differences between transpiration and evaporation.

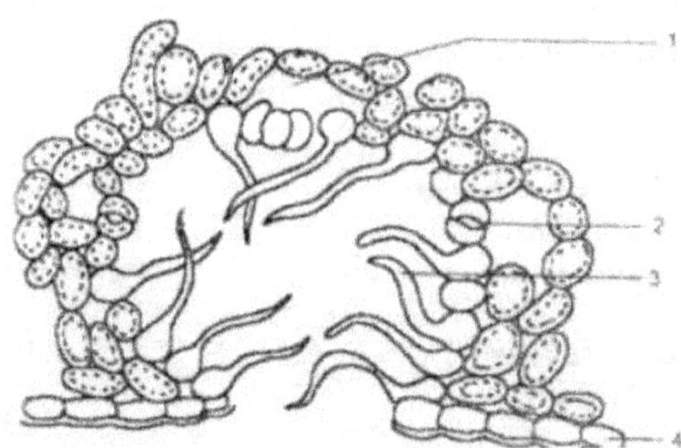

Answer:

a) Label: 1. Sub stomatal air space. 2. Stoma   3. Hair.   4.Lower epidermis.

b) This is a figure of a shrunken stoma covered by hair of the leaf of Nerium.

c) Disadvantages of transpiration are:

    a. Wilrting of the plant.
    b. Stunted growth.
    c. Excess energy expenditure.
    d. Premature leave fall.

d) **Difference:**

	Transpiration	**Evaporation**
01	Loss of water from aerial parts of the living plants.	Loss of water from the surface of water bodies.
02	Formation of vapour continues after saturation of surrounding air.	Evaporation stopped completely when the surrounding air is completely saturated.

PHOTOSYNTHESIS

SECTION-I

Q:Type:[1] Name the followings:

1. The organism that produces food by using energy from a chemical reaction (not from sunlight) is called.
2. The main element for the formation of chlorophyll is.
3. The site of the light-independent reaction in the chloroplast.
4. The chemical reaction in which O_2 is given out.
5. Light of a particular wavelength is called.
6. By this reaction, CO_2 is converted to carbohydrates.
7. The most common storage form of plant food.
8. The presence of a Light-induced reaction that leads to splitting of water is called.
9. One of the pigments found in all mammals.
10. The process of conversion of ADP to ATP during the first phase of photosynthesis.
11. The chemical that absorbs CO_2 during the dark reaction.
12. The first stable product from carbon dioxide is produced during photosynthesis.
13. The ground substance present in a chloroplast.
14. The most abundant pigment found on earth.
15. The process of conversion of several molecules of glucose to one molecule of starch.
16. The principal site of Photosynthesis in a green leaf.

A:Type:[1] Answer:

01.	Chemoautotroph.	09.	Haemoglobin.
02.	Magnesium.	10.	Phosphorylation
03.	Stroma.	11.	RUDP. [Ribulose Di Phosphate]
04.	Photosynthesis.	12.	Phosphoglycericacid. [PGA]
05.	Monochromatic light.	13.	Chlorophyll.
06.	Dark reaction.	14	Chlorophyll.
07.	Starch.	15.	Photosynthesis.
08.	Photolysis.	16.	Chloroplast.

Q:Type:[2] Fill in the blanks:

1) By Photophosphorylation __________ is converted to ____________.

2) The opening of the stomata usually depends upon the ________ of the guard cell.
3) During photosynthesis, light energy is trapped by __________.
4) During photorespiration plant takes in __________ and releases ____________ gas to atmosphere.
5) CO2 enters into the __________ par of chloroplast from atmosphere by __________.
6) Dark reaction is also known as __________ or ____________ reaction.
7) Light energy is used in splitting the ________ molecule, into ________.
8) Other than starch, __________ is another form of storage product in plants.
9) The end product of photosynthesis are ________, __________ & __________.
10) The best temperature range for photosynthesis is ________ to ________ degree C.
11) Light reaction takes place in ________ of chloroplast.
12) Reduction of NADP takes place in _________ reaction.
13) Oxygen released during photosynthesis comes from ______.
14) Potassium pyrogallol could absorb ________ gas.
15) The number of carbon atoms present in one molecule of Fructose is ________.
16) K+ ion concentration theory is related to _________ part of leaves.
17) ATP stands for _________.
18) The end product of fermentation is _________.

A:Type:[2] Answer:

01.	ADP, ATP.	10.	5, 35
02.	Turgidity.	11.	Thylakoid.
03.	Chlorophyll.	12.	Light.
04.	Oxygen, carbon-di-oxide.	13.	Water.
05.	Stroma, diffusion.	14	Oxygen.
06.	Calvin cycle, Bio-synthesis.	15.	6.
07.	Water, H+ & OH- ions.	16.	Stomata.
08.	Sucrose.	17.	Adenosine tri-phosphate.
09.	Oxygen, Water, Glucose.	18.	Lactic acid/ethyl alcohol

Q:Type:[3] True or False:

1) The mode of nutrition exhibited by plants is called heterotrophic.
2) The thylakoid membrane is a phospholipids bi-layer.
3) Stomatal opening and closing occur due to active transport of Ca+ ion.
4) Dark reaction means this reaction occurs when it is night.
5) The thylakoids are the stacks of granum.

6) Photo systems are three types.
7) ADP to ATP synthesis is called Photophosphorylation.
8) Dark reaction reducing carbon dioxide.
9) Calvin cycle takes place is grana.
10) Photosynthesis occurs in all cells of the plant.
11) The first stable product made from CO_2 during photosynthesis is PGA.
12) In photosystem-1 solar energy absorbs and supplied energies electrons to the cytochrome system.
13) Starch is the chief constituents of the cell wall.
14) Maximum photosynthesis takes place in the red light.
15) Etiolated trees leave colour is green.
16) Starch colour becomes red when iodine solution is added to it.
17) Potassium hydroxide absorbs Oxygen.
18) The dark reaction of photosynthesis is light-independent.
19) The source of Oxygen that comes out as a byproduct during photosynthesis is CO_2.
20) With the increase of CO2 concentration, during medium light intensity rate of photosynthesis is highest.
21) The plant that manufactures their food is termed heterotrophs.

A:Type:[3] Answer:

1) **[True]**The mode of nutrition exhibited by plants is called heterotrophic.
2) **[True]** The thylakoid membrane is a phospholipids bilayer.
3) **[False]** Stomatal opening and closing occur due to active transport of K+ ion.
4) **[False]** Dark reaction means this reaction occurs when it is day but the light is not required.
5) **[True]** The thylakoids are the stacks of granum.
6) **[False]**Photo systems are two types.
7) **[True]** ADP to ATP synthesis is called Photophosphorylation.
8) **[True]** Dark reaction reducing carbon dioxide.
9) **[False]** Calvin cycle takes place is Stroma.
10) **[False]** Photosynthesis occurs in all cells of the plant which contains chlorophyll.
11) **[True]** First stable product made from CO_2 during photosynthesis is PGA.
12) **[False]** In photosystem-1 solar energy absorbs and supplied energies electrons to NADP.
13) **[False]** Cellulose is the chief constituents of the cell wall.
14) **[True]** Maximum photosynthesis takes place in the red light.
15) **[False]** Etiolated trees leaves colour is yellow.
16) **[False]** Starch colour becomes blue when iodine solution is added to it.
17) **[False]** Potassium hydroxide absorbsCO_2.
18) **[True]** The dark reaction of photosynthesis is light-independent.

19) **[False]** The source of Oxygen that comes out as a byproduct during photosynthesis is H_2O.
20) **[False]** With the increase of CO2 concentration, during high light intensity the rate of photosynthesis is highest.
21) **[True]** Plant that manufactures their food are termed as heterotrophs

Q:Type:[4] Match the column:

Sl. No	Column A	Sl. No	Column B
1	Photosystem-1	A	ATP generation.
2	Photosystem-2	B	A reducing agent in photosynthesis.
3	PGA.	C	Absorbed solar energy supplied energized electrons to NADP.
4	Dark reaction.	D	Stomata.
5	Starch.	E	$NADPH_2$
6	RUDP.	F	The most common storage form of food.
7	Thylakoid.	G	Absorbed solar energy supplied energized electrons to the cytochrome system.
8	K+ theory.	H	releasing O_2.
9	Magnesium.	I	Reduction of CO_2.
10	Photorespiration.	J	Release CO_2.
11	Dark reaction energy supplier.	K	Chlorophyll.
12	Photosynthesis.	L	Stable Carbon compound.

A:Type:[4] Answer & Explanation:

Sl. No	Column A	Sl. No	Column B
1.	Photosystem-1	C	Absorbed solar energy supplied energized electrons to NADP.
Expl.	In Photosystem-1 the absorbed solar energy supplied energized electrons to NADP.		
2.	Photosystem-2	G	Absorbed solar energy supplied energized electrons to the cytochrome system.
Expl.	In Photosystem-1 the Absorbed solar energy supplied energized electrons to the cytochrome system.		

Sl. No.	Column A	Sl. No.	Column B
3.	PGA.	L	Stable Carbon compound.
Expl.	RUDP reduced CO2 to PGA and its first stable compound of carbon during photosynthesis.		
4.	Dark reaction.	I	Reduction of CO_2.
Expl.	Please refer explanation for part 3 of this table.		
5.	Starch.	F	The most common storage form of food.
6.	RUDP.	B	A reducing agent in photosynthesis.
Expl.	Please refer explanation for part 3 of this table.		
7.	Thylakoid.	A	ATP generation.
Expl.	The thylakoid chlorophyll molecules absorb light energy and then transfer it to other protein molecules. This stage of photosynthesis generates ATP.		
8.	K+ theory.	D	Stomata.
Expl.	An increase in K+ ion concentration in guard cells makes them hypertonic and increase turgidity. This helps in the opening of stomata.		
9.	Magnesium.	K	Chlorophyll.
Expl.	Magnesium present in the centre of chlorophyll.		
10.	Photorespiration.	J	Release CO_2.
Expl.	It is the respiration of plant during day time where light is not required.		
11	Dark reaction energy supplier.	E	$NADPH_2$
Expl.	During the dark reaction of photosynthesis, the energy supplied by ATP and $NADPH_2$.		
12	Photosynthesis.	H	releasing O_2.
Expl.	During photosynthesis, O_2 is released from water.		

Q:Type:[5] Choose the correct answer[MCQ]:

1.Energy required for Dark reaction is supplied by

a)ATP. **b)**ADP. **c)**$NADPH_2$**d)**Both (a) & (c).

2.During photosystem-1 the energized electrons are supplied to

a) NADP. **b)**Cytochrome. **c)**Nucleus.**d)**none of the above.

3.Oxygen released as a by-product after photosynthesis comes from

a) Absorbed water.**b)** Absorbed CO_2. **c)**Starch. **d)**RUDP.

4.Calvin cycle takes place during

a)daytime. b)Night. **c)** both (a) and (b). **d)** Only when the intensity of light is high.

5.RUDP combined with CO2 and produces

a)Starch. **b)**Glucose. **c)**PGA. **d)**ADP.

6.most common form of food storage is

a)Starch. **b)**Cellulose. **c)**Fructose. **d)**Glucose.

7.Arrange the colour of a light ray from a low to high rate of photosynthesis: Green, Red, Blue.

a)   Red, green, Blue, White. **b)** Blue, Red,White green.**c)**White, Red, Blue, green .**d)**Green, Blue, Red, White.

8.Color of etiolated trees leaves are

a) Green. **b)** any colour other than green. **c)**Yellow.**d)** none of the above.

9.The assimilatory powers for the dark reaction are:

a) ATP and O2.**b)**ADP and ATP.**c)**ATP and NADP. **d)**ATP and NADPH$_2$.

10.nitrifying bacteria like *Nitrosomonas* derived energy by

a)   Photosynthesis.**b)** Chemosynthesis. **c)** Saprophytic mode of nutrition.**d)** both (b) & (c).

A:Type:[5] Answer & Explanation:

1.	d. Both (a) & (c)	**6.**	a.Starch.
2.	a.NADP.	**7.**	d. Green, Blue, Red White.
3.	a. Absorbed water.	**8.**	c.Yellow.
4.	a. Day time.	**9.**	d. ATP & NADPH2.
5.	c. PGA.	**10.**	c. Saprophytic mode.

Q:Type:[6] Define the following terms:

1.	Thylakoid.	**6.**	Etiolated plants.
2.	Photolysis.	**7.**	Photorespiration.
3.	Compensation point.	**8.**	Calvin cycle.
4.	Photosynthesis.	**9.**	Photophosphorylation.
5.	De-starched plants.	**10.**	Chemoautotroph.

A:Type:[6] Answer:

1) **Thylakoid:**it is the stacked arrangement of granum present in chloroplast.
2) **Photolysis:**it is the process of breaking water molecules by the light energy absorbed by chlorophyll.
3) **Compensation point:**it is the time when photosynthesis rate and rate of respiration become equal for a tree.
4) **Photosynthesis:** it is the process of preparation of food with the help of CO_2,Water and sunlight and also produces O_2 gas as a byproduct equal to the amount of CO2 absorbed.
5) **Destarched plants:** it is the plant that has been kept in complete darkness for about 48 hours and which does not contain any reserve food.
6) **Etiolated plants:**It is the plant condition when its leaves are become yellow and the stem long and pale due to the absence of light over a prolonged period.
7) **Photorespiration:** it is the respiration of a plant during day time when the plant takes oxygen and release CO2.
8) **Calvin cycle:**it is a cyclic process during photosynthesis when RUBP first converted CO_2 to PGA and then again regenerated to RUBP with the help of energy provided by ATP and $NADPH_2$.
9) **Photophosphorylation:**it is the process of formation of energy-rich compound ATP from ADP and inorganic phosphate by utilizing light energy.
10) **Chemoautotroph:**the organism that produces food by using energy from the chemical reaction are called chemoautotroph.

Q:Type:[7] Explain the followings:

1. All life would come to an end if there were no green plants.
2. Sleeping under a tree is not advisable at night.
3. Why it is necessary to place a plant in dark before starting an experiment on photosynthesis.
4. What do you understand by the principle of limiting factors?
5. Why it is called that Oxygen is a waste product of photosynthesis?
6. Why the reduction in the water content of leaves reduces photosynthesis?
7. Why dark reaction is not actually happening in dark?
8. The rate of photosynthesis is low at high temperature-why?

A:Type:[7] Answer:

1. All consumers depend on the food produced by green plants. If there were no green plants then there will be no food will available for other living organisms. Green plants also released oxygen and that is necessary for the respiration of living organisms to release energy. So, all life will come to an end if there were no green plants.

2. During the day Carbon dioxide is used by the plant to do photosynthesis hence no CO2 is released. T night plant stops photosynthesis and releases CO2 due to respiration and that will concentrate below the tree. Higher concentration of CO2 is harmful to us so it is not advice able to stay below a tree during the night.

3. The presence of starch is evidence of photosynthesis. Hence before starting an experiment for photosynthesis the plant should be kept in a dark place for about 24 to 30 hrs. to destarch the leaves. During this period, all the starch from the leaves will be sent to the storage organs and the leaves will not show the presence of starch. So the various experiments on photosynthesis can be carried out effectively.

4. According to the principle of limiting factors proposed by Blackmann, when a process is controlled by several factors, the rate of the process is determined by the factor which is in the shortest supply.

5. Oxygen is released by plants after photosynthesis is a waste product as carbon-di-oxide, water and sunlight are required to produce glucose.

6. Reduction in the water content of the leaves will progressively reduce the stomatal conductance of gases. As CO_2 concentration is a limiting factor of photosynthesis so photosynthesis also reduced.

7. Dark reaction is independent of light, hence it is called dark reaction but it's happening in the day time.

8. At high temperature, the rate of photosynthesis decreases as enzymes do not work efficiently.

SECTION-II

Question-1.

Complete the following by filling in the blanks numbered 1 to 10 with the appropriate word/term:

Photosynthesis involves light reaction and dark reaction. During (1)_____reaction, the chlorophyll present in the chloroplast gets activated by absorbing light energy. The energy splits (2) molecules to (3)_____ and Oxygen and releases two electrons. This process is called (4)__________.the (5)________ ions are picked up by NADP to form (6)________. The ADP is converted to (7) ________.This process is called (8) ________. During the dark phase , he compound produced at the end of light reaction reacts with CO2 to form (9)________.this product is converted to starch. The process is called (10) ________.

Answer:

Photosynthesis involves light reaction and dark reaction. During (1) *light* reaction, the chlorophyll present in the chloroplast gets activated by absorbing light energy. The energy splits (2) *water* molecules to (3)*hydrogen* and Oxygen and releases two electrons. This process is called (4)*photolysis*. The (5) *hydrogen* ions are picked up by NADP to form (6)*NADPH.* The ADP is converted to (7) *ATP.* This process is called (8) *Photophosphorylation*. During the dark phase, the compound produced at the end of light reaction reacts with CO_2 to form (9)*glucose.* This product is converted to starch. The process is called (10)*polymerization*.

Question-2.

Given below is a diagrammatic representation of the internal structure of an organelle found in a plant cell. Answer the question below

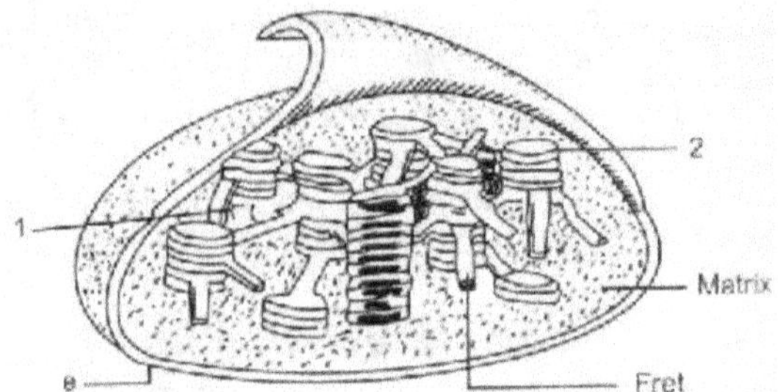

1) Identify the organelle.
2) Name the physiological process occurring in this organelle.
3) Mention one way in which this process is beneficial to man.
4) Name the phases of the process occurring in the part labelled "1" and "2".
5) A chemical substance NADP plays an active part in one of the phases. Give the expanded form of NADP and state its role in the above process.
6) Represent the physiological process mentioned in (2) above in the form of a chemical equation.

Answer:

1. Chloroplast.
2. Photosynthesis.
3. Photosynthesis is the only source of food for mankind.
4. 1. It is a stroma and here light-independent reaction takes place.
   2. It is Granum and their light-dependent reaction takes place.

5. **NADP**: Nicotinamide Adenine dinucleotide Phosphate.
NADP traps hydrogen which formed during the photolysis of water. It converted to NADPH and then NADPH2. This NADPH2 and ATP act as assimilator powers to provide energy for the dark reaction. The hydrogen of NADPH is used to combine with CO2 by utilizing energy to produce glucose.

6. **Equation of photosynthesis:**

$$6CO_2 + 12H_2O \xrightarrow[cholorophil]{light\ energy} C_6H_{12}O_6 + 6H_2O + 6O_2 \uparrow$$

Question-3.

The diagram below represents an experiment conducted to prove the importance of a factor in photosynthesis. Answer the followings:

1) Name the factor being studied in the experiment.
2) Why was the plant kept in the darkroom before conducting the experiment?
3) Why was the experimental leaf then kept in (i) boiling water (ii) methylated spirit?
4) Name the solution used to test for the presence of starch in the leaf.
5) What will we observe in the experimental leaf at the end of the starch test?
6) Give reactions of light-dependent part during photosynthesis.

Answer:

1. Photosynthesis requires light and here this light factor being studied in the experiment.
2. Plant was kept in the darkroom before conducting an experiment to destarch its leaves.
3. i) Boiling water used to kill the cells.
   ii) methylated spirit used to remove the chlorophyll.
4. Iodine solution. This solution-coloured starch to blue.
5. Due to the presence of starch produced during photosynthesis the exposed parts of the leaves will turn blue-black.The part which was covered with black paper will remain brown in iodine solution due to the absence of starch.
6. i) reduction of NADP: $2NADP + 4e + 4H^+ \longrightarrow NADPH_2$

ii) Photophosphorylation: ADP+Pi $\longrightarrow$ ATP
ii) methylated spirit used to remove the chlorophyll.

Question-4.

The figure alongside represents an experiment set-up to study a physiological process in plants:

1) Name the physiological process being studied.
2) Explain the process.
3) What is the aim of the experiment?
4) Give a well-balanced equation to represent the process.

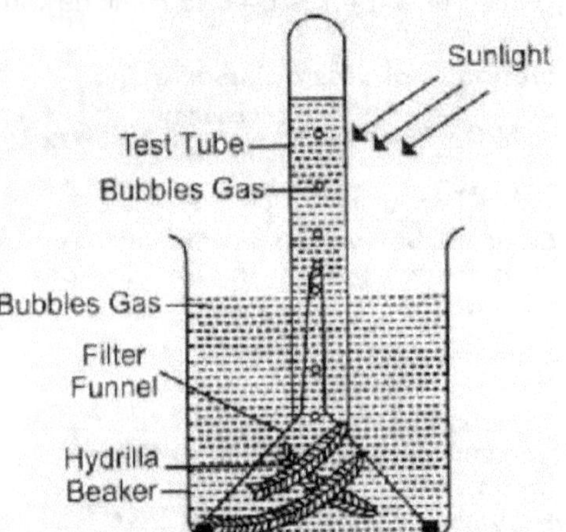

Answer:

1. Photosynthesis.
2. **Definition:** Photosynthesis is a process by which green plants manufacture carbohydrates from atmospheric carbon-di-oxide and water from the soil, in the presence of sunlight.
3. **Aim:** The aim of the experiment is to show that during the photosynthesis process Oxygen gas is produced and released by green plants.
4. **Equation of photosynthesis:**

$$6CO_2 + 12H_2O \xrightarrow[chol orophil]{light\ energy} C_6H_{12}O_6 + 6H_2O + 6O_2 \uparrow$$

Question-5.

1. **Draw a neat and well-labelled diagram of the chloroplast.**
2. **List the events taking place in the photochemical phase of photosynthesis.**
3. **Give the reason: Green leaves are thin and broad.**
4. **If you are planning an experiment to show the effect of light on photosynthesis:**
a. **Will you select white light or green light? Justify your answer.**
b. **Why would you select a Destrached plant?**

Answer:

1. **See the picture on the next page:**
2. **Events of photosynthesis:**

a.Light reaction: Absorption of light energy > Photolysis of water> Reduction of NADP>Photophosphorylation.

b.Dark reaction: Fixation of CO_2> Formation of sugar>regeneration of RUBP

3. Thinness of leaves helps to gas diffusion and broadness helps to get the maximum amount of sunlight.
4. **a.**Due to the green colour of leaves green light will be completely reflected out, no energy will be absorbed.So, we should use white light instead.

   b.Destarched plant will produce starch during photosynthesis in light and will establish that starch produced by photosynthesis as earlier no starch was present in leaves.

Question-6.

1. **Draw a diagram of the experimental set up to show that O_2 is evolved during photosynthesis.**
2. **With reference to photosynthesis, answer the following questions:**

(i) What is photosynthesis?
(ii) In what form is glucose stored in plants?
(iii) Name the two phases of photosynthesis.
(iv) What are the functions of the palisade parenchyma in a leaf?

Answer:

1. See the picture:

2. **i)Definition:** Photosynthesis is a process by which green plants manufacture carbohydrates from atmospheric carbon-di-oxide and water from the soil, in the presence of sunlight.
   ii) Starch.
   iii) two-phase: 1. Hill reaction/Photochemical reaction/light reaction 2. Dark reaction/Calvin cycle/Bio-synthetic reaction.
   iv) Palisade parenchyma reduce excessive transpiration.

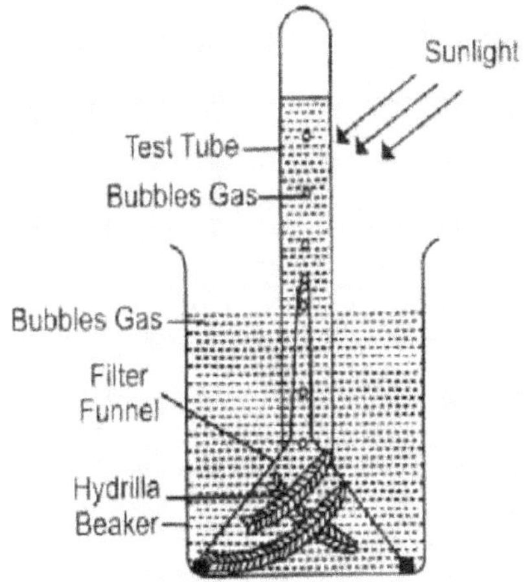

CIRCULATORY SYSTEM.

SECTION-I

Q:Type:[1] Name the followings:

1. The clotting within an intact blood vessel is called.
2. The elemental ion that helps in blood clotting.
3. Who developed ABO method.
4. The fluid that is occurring spaces between cells in the organs.
5. The largest lymphatic organ of the human body.
6. The pigment due to which blood is red.
7. The glycoprotein'son the surface of RBCs.
8. The purpose of gamma globulin protein in the blood plasma.
9. The protein present in Haemoglobin.
10. The vein that carries oxygenated blood.
11. The immediate treatment to replenish water in the blood.
12. Acidophils are the name of.
13. The outermost cover of the heart.
14. Plasma that is devoid of fibrinogen.
15. The organelles absent in mature RBCs.
16. By this deoxygenated blood from upper half of the body reach to heart right atrium.
17. The fluid that transports fatty acids and glycerol's.
18. The process by which WBCs engulf bacteria.
19. Prothrombin is formed by this organ.
20. The chemical that produced by WBC to prevent clotting of blood in the blood vessels.
21. A foreign body that induces the formation of antibodies in the body.
22. The instrument used to measure blood pressure.
23. This WBC act as scavengers.
24. The WBCs involved in eosinophilia.
25. Chest pain due to insufficient supply of blood to the heart muscles.
26. The site of the production of RBC in adult humans.
27. WBCs with nucleus having three to five lobes.
28. The vitamin required for the clotting of blood.
29. A universal donor is called to this blood group.
30. The blood cells whose deficiency causes Anemia.

A:Type:[1] Answer:

01.	Thrombosis.	05.	Spleen.
02.	Calcium.	06.	Haemoglobin.
03.	Karl Landsteiner.	07.	Antigen.
04.	Lymph.	08.	Respond to an antigen.

09.	Globin.	**20.**	Heparin.
10.	Pulmonary veins.	**21.**	Antigen.
11.	Oral rehydration solution.	**22.**	Sphygmomanometer.
12.	Eosinophils.	**23.**	Monocytes.
13.	Pericardium.	**24.**	Eosinophils.
14.	Serum.	**25.**	Angina Pectoris.
15.	Mitochondria.	**26.**	Megakaryocyte.
16.	Superior vena cava.	**27.**	Neutrophil.
17.	Lymph.	**28.**	Vitamin K.
18.	Phagocytosis.	**29.**	O
19.	Liver.	**30.**	RBC[Red Blood Cells]

Q:Type:[2] Find Odd terms:

1. Blood, tissue fluid, serum, Lymph.
2. Haemoglobin,Haemoerithrin,Haemocynanin,Chlorophyll.
3. Neutrophils, Basophils,Monocytes,Eosinophils.
4. Superior vena cava,Tri-cupsidvalve,Semilunarvalve,Pulmonary artery.
5. Haemophilia,Leucocytosis,Leucopenia,Leukemia.
6. Lymphocytes, Acidophils, basophils, Nutrophils.

A:Type:[2] Answer & Explanation:

1. Blood, tissue fluid, **serum**, Lymph.

Explanation: Serum is a protein less compound.

2. Haemoglobin, Haemoerithrin, Haemocynanin, **Chlorophyll.**

Explanation: Chlorophyll is found in the plant body.

3. Neutrophils, Basophils,**Monocytes**,Eosinophils.

Explanation: Monocytes are agranular WBCs.

4. Superior vena cava, Tri-cupsid valve, **Semilunarvalve**, Pulmonary artery.

Explanation: Except semilunar valve all are related to the right auriculo-ventricular system.

5. **Haemophilia**, Leucocytosis, Leucopenia, Leukemia.

Explanation: Haemophilia is an inherited blood disorder.

6. **Lymphocytes**, Acidophils, basophils, Neutrophils.

Explanation: Other than Lymphocytes all others are granular WBCs.

Q:Type:[3] Match the column:

Sl No.	Column A	Sl. No.	Column B
1	Lymph nodes.	A	120 days.
2	Thrombosis.	B	Basic dyes.
3	Plasma.	C	Neutrophils.
4	Platelets.	D	Prothrombin.
5	White blood cells.	E	Yellow-coloured.
6	Lymph.	F	Defence against disease germs.
7	Liver.	G	Blood clotting.
8	Phagocytosis.	H	Liquid part of blood.
9	Basophils.	I	Clotting within an unbroken blood vessel.
10	RBC.	J	Production of new white cells.

A:Type:[3] Answer & Explanation:

Sl. No	Column A	Sl. No	Column B
1.	Lymph Nodes.	J	Production of new white cells.
Expl.	White cells are produces in Lymph nodes.		
2.	Thrombosis.	I	Clotting within an unbroken blood vessel.
3.	Plasma.	H	Liquid part of blood.
4.	Platelets.	G	Blood clotting.
Expl.	Thrombokinase produced from platelets helps to clot.		
5.	White blood cells.	F	Defence against disease germs.
6.	Lymph.	E	Yellow-coloured.
7.	Liver.	D	Prothrombin.
Expl.	Prothrombin is formed by the Liver.		
8.	Phagocytosis.		Neutrophils.
9.	Basophils.		Basic dyes.
10.	RBC.		120 days.
Expl.	Life of RBC is 120 days.		

Q: Type: [4] Write the special functional activities of the followings.

1.	Neutrophils.	**6.**	Lymphatic nodes.	**11.**	Ca++ [related to blood]
2.	Monocytes.	**7.**	Lymph.	**12.**	Tricuspid valve
3.	Antibody.	**8.**	Vitamin K [related to blood]	**13.**	Eosinophil.
4.	Heparin.	**9.**	Hepatic portal vein.	**14.**	Fibrin
5.	WBCs.	**10.**	Haemoglobin.	**15.**	Aorta.

A:Type:[4] Answer:

1) **Neutrophils:** Protect the body from microbes by engulfing Phagocytosis.

2) **Monocytes:** Ingests microbes and foreign bodies.

3) **Antibody:** Protect the body from the antigen.

4) **Heparin:** Prevents clotting of blood in the blood vessels.

5) **WBCs:** Defend the body against germs and develop antibodies.

6) **Lymphatic nodes:** Produces white cells and antibodies.

7) **Lymph:** Ingest any bacteria which have gained access to the lymph.

8) **Vitamin K:** helps in the formation of prothrombin.

9) **Hepatic portal vein:** connect liver with stomach and intestine and moves blood from the spleen.

10) **Haemoglobin:** Helps to transport O_2 and CO_2 gas.

11) **Ca++:**Convert prothrombin to thrombin.

12) **Tricuspid valve:** Guards the opening between the right auricle and the right ventricle.

13) **Eosinophil**: Engulf particles formed by the antigen-antibody reaction.

14) **Fibrin:** fibrin network helps to clot blood.

15) **Aorta:** carries oxygenated blood to be distributed to all the body parts.

Q:Type:[5] True or False:

1) RBCs are of several kinds whereas WBCs are of one kind.
2) New RBCs are produced in the heart.
3) Monocytes act as scavengers.
4) Blood clotting is possible if Na+ is not present.
5) Systolic blood pressure in man varies from 70-60 mm Hg.
6) The light yellow fluid in the lymphatic vessels is called lymph.
7) The largest lymphatic gland is the spleen.
8) Monocytes are fighting against infection by the lymphatic system.
9) Thrombokinase and Ca++ convert plasma protein thrombin into prothrombin.
10) Thrombin threads are made the framework of the clot.
11) Calcium ion is a coagulation factor.
12) Thrombosis usually takes place in arteries.
13) Male children generally inherit Haemophilia from their mother.
14) Bicuspid valve guards the opening between the left auricle and left ventricle.
15) Pulse rate is different from heartbeat rate.
16) Mitochondria is not present in RBC.
17) RBCs are disintegrated in livery only.
18) Megakaryocyte cell is related to plasma.
19) Inferior vena cava carries oxygenated blood.
20) Heparin is produced by RBC.
21) Blood contains cells about 45% of the total blood volume.
22) Lymphocytes produceantibodies.
23) Pinocytosis is the method of engulfing the microbes by WBCs.
24) Vitamin E is essential for clotting.
25) Rh factor was first discovered in an American monkey.

A:Type:[5] Answer:

1) **[False]** WBCs are of several kinds whereas RBCs are of one kind.
2) **[False]**New RBCs are produced in the bone marrow.
3) **[true]**Monocytes act as scavengers.
4) **[False]**Blood clotting is possible if Ca+ is not present.
5) **[False]**Systolic blood pressure in man varies from 110-120 mm Hg.
6) **[True]**The light yellow fluid in the lymphatic vessels is called lymph.
7) **[True]**Largest lymphatic gland is the spleen.
8) **[False]** Lymphocytes are fighting against infection by the lymphatic system.
9) **[False]** Thrombokinase and Ca++ convert plasma protein prothrombin intothrombin.
10)**[False]**Fibrin threads are made a framework of the clot.
11)**[True]**Calcium ion is a coagulation factor.
12)**[False]**Thrombosis usually takes place in veins.
13)**[True]**Male children generally inherit Haemophilia from their mother.

14) **[True]**Bicuspid valve guards the opening between the left auricle and left ventricle.
15) **[False]**Pulse rate is the same as heartbeat rate.
16) **[True]**Mitochondria is not present in RBC.
17) **[False]**RBCs are disintegrated in livery or spleen.
18) **[False]** Megakaryocyte cell is related to RBC.
19) **[False]**Inferior vena cava carries deoxygenated blood.
20) **[False]**Heparin is produced by WBC[Basophils].
21) **[True]**Blood contains cells about 45% of the total blood volume.
22) **[True]**Lymphocytes produces antibodies.
23) **[False]** Phagocytosis is the method of engulfing the microbes by WBCs.
24) **[False]**Vitamin K is essential for clotting.
25) **[True]**Rh factor was first discovered in American monkey

Q:Type:[6] Fill in the blanks:

1) __________ is a WBC that prevent clotting of blood in blood vessels.
2) The process of engulfing and ingesting foreign particles is known as ____________.
3) In an adult human ________litres of blood is present and it makes up about _______ percent of body weight.
4) The outermost cover of heart is called ___________.
5) A portal vein carries blood from _________ to ________.
6) The largest blood cell is ________.
7) __________ is also called extracellular fluid.
8) The fluid matrix of blood is called__________.
9) Platelets helps in __________ formation.
10) ____________ artery carries deoxygenated blood.
11) Systemic circulation is the circulation of oxygenated blood from the left ventricle through ______.
12) _________ contains blood after the death of the organism.
13) A highly muscular chamber of the heart is the _________.

14) ______ produces antibodies.
15) Thrombokinase enzyme is formed from _______ cells.
16) Blood pressure is measured by ____________.
17) Number of circulation of blood from the heart is _______ per day.
18) Fibrinogen is converted into fibrin by ___________.
19) _________ blood group is called universal donor.
20) Myocardial infarction is commonly known as ________ __________.
21) The life span of RBCs is about _________ where as the life span of platelets is ______.

A:Type:[6] Answer:

1.	Basophils.	**8.**	Plasma.	**15.**	Platelets.
2.	Phagocytosis.	**9.**	Thromboplastin.	**16.**	Sphygmomanometer.
3.	5-6, 7-8%	**10.**	Pulmonary.	**17.**	100,000.
4.	Pericardium.	**11.**	Semilunar valves.	**18.**	Thrombin.
5.	Spleen, Liver	**12.**	Veins.	**19.**	O.
6.	Monocytes.	**13.**	Ventricles.	**20.**	Heart attack.
7.	Lymph.	**14.**	WBC	**21.**	120 days,5 days.

Q:Type: [7]Write one difference of pair (on the given parameter).

01	Antigen & Antibody	*Appearance.*
02	Serum and heparin	*Formation*
03	Eosinophils &Basophils.	*Staining.*
04	Vit. K and Ca++	*Function*
05	Monocytes & Neutrophils	*Structure*
06	AV node & SA node	*Function*
07	Blood Group O and AB	*Structure.*
08	Afferent arteriole & Efferent arteriole.	*Structure.*

A:Type: [7]Answer & explanation.

1) **[Appearance]**Antigen appears on the surface of RBC and antibody in the blood plasma.

2) **[Formation]** Serum formed after clotting of blood and heparin produced by basophils to prevent clotting blood.

3) **[Staining]**Eosinophils-stained orange-red and Basophils stained blue-black.

4) **[Function]**Vitamin K helps to form prothrombin and Ca++ convert it to thrombin.

5) **[Structure]** Monocytes are kidney-shaped and Neutrophils are polymorphic with three to five lobes.

6) **[Function]**AV node-connect the electrical system of the atria and ventricle. SA node generates an electrical pulse.

7) **[Structure]** O blood is antigen free and AB group is antibody free.

8) **[Structure]** Afferent arteriole is the blood vessel with a wider lumen that transports blood to the glomerulus. An efferent arteriole is a blood vessel with a narrow lumen that carries blood from the glomerulus.

Q:Type: [8]Choose the correct answer(MCQ).

1.Lymph has

a) Only WBCs. **b)**OnlyRBCs. **c)**Only platelets. **d)**more protein and calcium than blood.

2.Relaxation mode of the heart is called

a) Beat. **b)**Systole. **c)**Diastole. **d)** Pulse.

3. a diagrammatic representation of heartbeat is called

a)EEG   **b)**ECG   **c)**Polygraph. **d)** Monogram.

4. Portal veins are carries blood from

a)capillary at the gut wall to capillary at the liver. **b)** Capillary to heart. **c)**capillary at the gut wall to the heart. **d)**None of the above is correct.

5.Tricuspid valve is present between

a)right atrium and ventricle. **b)** the two atria. **c)**the two ventricle. **d)** Left atrium and ventricle.

6.The heart is covered by

a)meninges. **b)** Conjunctiva **c)**Pericardium **d)**Pleural membrane.

7. Hardening of arteries with ageing is called

a)Arteriosclerosis **b)**Clumping reactions. **c)**Silicosis **d)**None of the above.

8.Clamping reaction will take place when a person infused following blood

a) A   **b)**O   **c)**B   **d)**None of the above.

9.Which blood cells are nucleus less?

a)RBCs   **b)**WBCs   **c)**Platelets **d)**None of the blood cells is nucleus free.

10. The colour of serum is

a)Yellow. **b)**pale yellow. **c)** Dark brown. **d)**Colorless.

11.pH of blood is

a)6.3 to 7.5 **b)**7 to 8 **c)** 6.5 to 7 **d)** 7.3 to 7.5

12. Old WBCs are destroyed like

a) RBCs   b)WBCs c) Platelets d) other cells.

13.WBCs count is higher in

a)Adult b)Children. c) Middle-aged person. d)All having the same ratio throughout life.

14.An increase in the number of leucocytes, is called

a)Jaundice b)Leukeria c) Leucopenia. d)Leucocytosis.

15.Acidophils are another name of

a) Eosinophils. b)Basophilsc) Neutrophils. d) None of the above.

16. Pulse wave is mainly caused by the

b) Systole of atria b) Diastole of atria c) Systole of left ventricle d) Systole of the right ventricle.

A:Type: [8]Choose the correct answer(MCQ).

1.	**a.** Only WBCs.	7.	**b.** Arteriosclerosis.	13.	**b.** Children.
2.	**c.** Diastole.	8.	**c.** B.	14.	**d.** Leucocytosis.
3.	**b.** ECG.	9.	b. RBCs.	15.	**a.** Eosinophils.
4.	**a.** capillary at the gut wall to capillary at the liver.	10.	**d.** Pale yellow.	16.	**c.** Systole of the left ventricle
5.	**d.** right atrium and ventricle	11.	**d.** 7.3 to 7.5		
6.	**b.** Pericardium.	12.	**d.** Other cells.		

Q : Type: [9]Fill the blanks according to relation as indicated in the first case.

1. RBC :120days : : Platelets:______.
2.Basophils: Heparin: :Platelets: ________.
3.Arteries: small lumen: :Vein:______.
4.Arteries: Arterioles: : Veins:________.
5.RBC: Bone marrow: :WBC: _________.
6.Neutrophils: Neutral dyes::Eosinophils: ________.
7.Heparin: Anticoagulants:: Ca++:________.
8. Granulocyte: neutrophil::Agranulocyte:________.
9. Lymphocyte: Large nucleus::RBC: ________.
10. Blood: Red::Lymph:___________.

A: Type: [9] Answer:

1. RBC :120days : : Platelets:**3-5 days.**

*Exp:*The life of RBC is 120 days and the life of platelets is 3-5 days.

2. Basophils: Heparin: :Platelets: **thromboplastin.**

Exp: Platelets form thromboplastin.

3. Arteries: small lumen: :Vein:**wide lumen.**

Exp: veins havelessmuscular wall.

4. Arteries: Arterioles: :Veins:**venules.**

Exp: smaller arteries are arterioles and small veins are called venules.

5. RBC: Bone marrow: :WBC: **lymph node.**

*Exp:*WBC produced from bone marrow and lymph node.

6. Neutrophils: Neutral dyes::Eosinophils:**acidic dyes**.

Exp: Eosinophils have a strong affinity towards acidic dyes.

7. Heparin: Anticoagulants:: Ca++:**coagulants.**

Exp: Ca++ ion helps to produce thrombin to clot blood.

8.Granulocyte: neutrophil::Agranulocyte:**Monocytes/lymphocytes**.

9. Lymphocyte: Large nucleus::RBC: **no nucleus.**

Exp: RBC is a non-nucleus living cell.

10. Blood: Red::Lymph:**yellow.**

SECTION-II

Question-1.

1. List some of the important characteristics of blood.
2. What is plasma?
3. List functions performed by blood.
4. What are the two main circulatory fluids of our body?
5. What is called serum?

Answer:
1. **Characteristics of blood:**
   a. Blood is a connective tissue with 90-92% water in it.
   b. Blood pH is 7.3-7.5 i.e. slightly basic.
   c. Blood passed through blood vessels only.
   d. The Colour of blood is red due to the presence of Haemoglobin pigment.

2. **Plasma:**it is the pale-yellow coloured alkaline liquid that forms about 55% of the total blood volume.
3. **Functions of blood:**
a. Transportation of Oxygen and Carbon dioxide.
b. Transportation of nutrients and excretory materials.
c. Distribution of enzymes and hormones.
d. Distribution of heat and temperature control.
e. Prevention of infection and wound healing.
4. **Fluids in our body:** 1. Blood   2. Lymph.
5. **Serum:** it is the yellow-colouredblood plasma from which blood clotting material Fibrinogen has been removed.

Question-2.

1) **Briefly describe an RBC.**
2) **Why monocytes are called scavengers?**
3) **Briefly explain in steps how bold clot?**
4) **What is called thrombosis?**

Answer:

1. **RBC:**RBCs are circular disc-shaped blood corpuscles that have no nuclei at maturity.This cell does not contain mitochondria. In its cytoplasm, red pigment haemoglobin is present and coloured blood red. These corpuscles are responsible for the transportation of oxygen and carbon dioxide gas.This blood corpuscles are lasting for about 120 days and it is the highest among blood cells.RBCs are produced in the bone marrow i.e. megakaryocyte cells.

2. Monocytes are ingested microbes and other foreign bodies and remove dead cells so they are called scavengers.

3. **Steps of blood clotting**:
Step-1: Formation of thrombokinase enzyme by platelets and by the injured tissue.
Step-2: Plasma protein prothrombin converted to thrombin by thrombokinase and Ca++.
Step-3: Thrombin converts soluble fibrinogen into insoluble fibrin.This fibrin acts as a thread and form mesh at the wound.
Step-4: Blood cells are entangled in the mesh and together settle down as a clot or thrombus. Blood clot.

4. **Thrombosis**: Blood clotting within the intact blood vessels [usually in vein] is called thrombosis.

Question-3.

1) **What do you mean by ABO method?**
2) **What is the significance of the" Rh" factor?**
3) **What is a clumping reaction?**

4) What is called heartbeat?

5) Differentiate between Arteries and Veins.

Answer:

1. Based on the presence or absence of antigen and antibodies blood are divided into four categories and named as A, B, AB and O.this are called ABO method.
2. Rh stands for rhesus, a common monkey in which the factor was discovered.When the blood of Rh+ person is given to Rh- person, antibodies developed in the blood of Rh- recipient.In second transfusion of Rh+ blood to such a person, clumping of donors blood cells occurs, because Rh antibodies already developed in the recipient's blood react with Rh antigen.So Rh factor has been taken into account during a blood transfusion.
3. Clumping reaction occurs when two similar Rh+ or –ve blood infused and it destroys RBCs.
4. **Heartbeat:** one contraction or systole and one relaxation or diastole of the heart constitute one heartbeat.
5. **Difference:**

Artery	Vein
Arteries distribute blood from the heart to different parts of the body.	Vein collect blood from different parts of the body and pour it into the heart.
Arteries have a small lumen and no valves.	Veins have large lumen and valves to prevent backflow.
Arteries walls are thick and not collapsible.	Veins are collapsible as they have thin walls.

Question-4.

1) **Briefly explain the working of a heart.**
2) **Write differences between Lymph and blood.**
3) **Mention two structural difference between the Inferior vena cava and Dorsal aorta.**
4) **What happens if the coronary arteries get an internal clot?**
5) **What is called the cardiac cycle?**

Answer:

1. At the beginning let the heart is in a joint diastole state. Blood from the pulmonary vein and vena cava flow into the left and right auricle respectively. As the bicuspid and tricuspid valves are open, blood passes into the ventricle easily and then both the atrium undergo a simultaneous

contraction i.e. systole and increase the blood flow into the ventricles. When the ventricles are contracting, the auricles are relaxed. Ventricular systole increase pressure and causing closing of two cuspid valves due to attempt backflow of blood into the atria. As the ventricle pressure increases, the semilunar valve guarding the pulmonary artery and aorta are forced open and blood flows to these vessels. Now the ventricle relaxed and pressure falls causing the closer of semilunar valves which prevents backflow of blood into the ventricles. Due to declined ventricular pressure, tricuspid and bicuspid valves are pushed open by the pressure in the atria. The blood is now once again moves freely to the ventricle.

2. Difference:

Blood	Lymph
It is a red coloured tissue.	It is a yellow coloured tissue.
It contains platelets.	Platelets are not presents.
Contains more proteins, calcium and phosphorus.	Contains fewer proteins, calcium and phosphorus.
Flows rapidly through arteries and veins.	Flows slowly through lymphatic vessels.
It requiresthe heart to pump.	Lymph node act as a pump.

3. Difference:

Inferior vena cava	Dorsal aorta.
It carries deoxygenated blood from the lower half of the body.	It carries oxygenated blood to all parts of the body.
It is entering the heart.	It is leaving the heart.

4. If coronary arteries get an internal clot then deadening of the corresponding area of the heart muscle occurs, causing myocardial infarction and which commonly known as a heart attack.

5. The sequentially repeated event in the heart which is cyclically repeated is called the cardiac cycle.

Question-5.

The diagram below shows the human circulatory system. Answer the following questions.

1. Name the blood vessels 1,3,6 & 7?

2. Name the blood vessels supplying blood to the walls

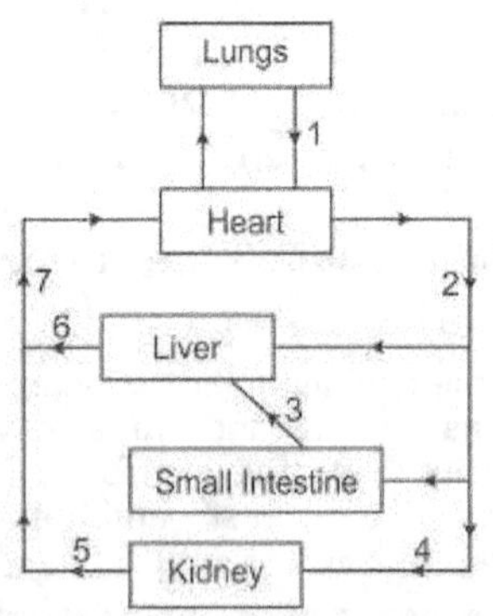

of the heart with oxygen.

3. Draw a neat sketch of blood vessel-2 with cross-section.

4. Mention one structural difference between blood vessels number 4 and 5.

Answer:

1. **Label: 1:** Pulmonary vein. **2** is Aorta. **3.** Hepatic portal vein. **6.** Hepatic vein. **7.**Inferior vena cava.
2. Coronary arteries supply blood to the heat with oxygen.
3. **See the sketch:**

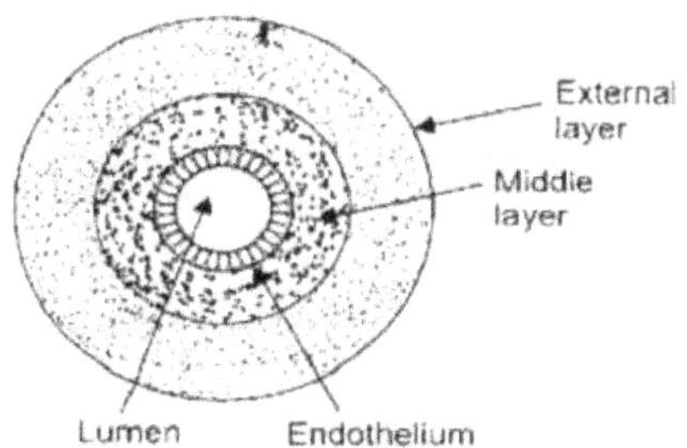

4. Difference: supply blood to the heart with oxygen.

4.Renal Artery	5. Renal Vein
Its have a thick muscular wall.	It hasa thin muscular wall.
It has a narrow lumen.	It hasa wide lumen.
Valves are absent.	Valves are present to prevent backflow.

Question-6.

1. **Why RBCs are called that it's having the most suitable oxygen transport system?**
2. **How the Rh factor could affect pregnancy?**
3. **When a person is called to having Leukemia?**
4. **What is called sickle cell anemia?**

Answer:

1. RBCs are called the most suitable oxygen transporter because it's havingmore surface to volume ratio to absorb oxygen and due to absence of mitochondria they can not use oxygen themselves and able to transfer all oxygen to the tissues without loss.

2. Rh factor plays a crucial role in childbirth where the couple have different Rh factors. During pregnancy, the Rh+ foetus stimulates the formation of antibodies in the Rh- mother blood.During the first pregnancy, enough antibodies are not produced to herm the foetus butin the case of the second pregnancy, the subsequent Rh+ foetuswill be exposed to the Rh- antibodies produced by the mother.A large number of RBCs produced by the mother will be destroyed due to clumping.This causes hymoplysis of blood in a foetus, resulting in haemolytic jaundice.This disease leads to the death of the foetus before or after birth.

3. Leukaemia is a type of blood cancer that develops when the number of WBCsincreases and affecting RBCs.

4. Sickle cell anaemia is a genetical disorder of RBCs. Due to this RBCs shape is found as a sickle in place of a circular disc. Due to this hook RBcs are mostly attached to the surface of the vessels and creates a restriction to flow which leads to less oxygen supply.The produces RBCs are also immatured.

EXCERTORY SYSTEM.

SECTION-I

Q:Type: [1]Name the followings.

1. Method of balancing the amount of water and ion in human beings
2. Kidney to urinary bladder is connected through
3. The dark-coloured outer zone of the kidney is called.
4. Pale coloured inner zone of the kidney is called.
5. The process of passing out urine from the body.
6. The fundamental unit of the kidney is called
7. Bowman's capsule and glomerulus together called
8. The acid which may found in urine
9. The blood vessels supplying blood to the kidney.
10. Accumulation of water in the body is called
11. The part of nephron present in the cortex of the kidney
12. The process of separating small molecules from larger ones using a semi-permeable membrane is called.
13. The branch of the renal artery enters the Bowman's Capsule.

A:Type:[1]Answer:

1.	Osmoregulation.	8.	Uric acid.
2.	Ureters.	9.	Renal artery.
3.	Cortex.	10.	Dropsy/Oedema
4.	Medulla.	11.	Bowman's capsule.
5.	Micturition.	12.	Ultrafiltration.
6.	Nephron.	13.	Afferent Arteriole.
7.	Malpighian capsule.		

Q:Type: [2] Find odd terms:

1. Ureter, Urethra, Uterus, Kidney.

2. Bowman capsule, Glomerulus, Henle loop, renal artery.

3. Lungs, Skin, Kidney, Pancreas.

4. Renal capsule, Proximal, Henle loop, Distal.

5. Dropsy, Haemophilia, Ketonuria, Proteinuria.

A:Type:[2]Answer:

1. Ureter, Urethra, **Uterus,** Kidney.

Explanation: Uterus is part of the reproductive system.

2. Bowman capsule, Glomerulus, **Henle loop**, renal artery

Explanation: Henle loop is present in the medulla part of a kidney.

3. Lungs, Skin, Kidney,**Pancreas**.

Explanation: Pancreas is not a part of the excretory system.

4. Renal capsule, Proximal, Henle loop, Distal

Explanation: the renal capsule is not a tubular part of the nephron.

5. Dropsy, Haemophilia, Ketonuria, Proteinuria.

Explanation: Dropsy problem occurs due to malfunction of kidney and others are a problem due to a metabolic problem.

Q:Type: [3] Define the terms:

1.	Ultrafiltration.
2.	Osmoregulation.
3.	Dialysis.
4.	Selective re-absorption.
5.	Tubular secretion

A:Type: [3] Answers and explanations:

1) **Ultra filtration:** Ultra filtration is a mechanical filtration method to filter very fine and small molecules from the blood in a glomerular capsule in the kidney.

2) **Osmoregulation**: The process of control of water content and the concentration of ions in the body is called Osmoregulation.

3) **Dialysis:** Dialysis is the process of separating small molecules from larger ones using a semi-permeable membrane.

4) **Selective re-absorption:** It is the process whereby certain molecules (e.g. ions, glucose and amino acids), after being filtered out of the capillaries along with nitrogenous waste products (i.e. urea) and water in the glomerulus, are reabsorbed from the filtrate as they pass through the nephron and retain back useful materials into the bloodstream.

5) **Tubular secretion:** It is the process where the proximal convoluted tubule removes waste materials from the blood and pass these into the filtrate by the process of secretion. Uric acid, ammonia, urea and some other molecules are removed by this process of tubular secretion.

Q:Type: [4] Match the column.

Sl. No	Column A	Sl. No	Column B
1	Water re-absorption	A	Nephron.
2	Renal capsule.	B	Uric Acid.
3	Dropsy.	C	Distal Convoluted tubule.
4	Tubular re-absorption.	D	Glomerulus.
5	Tubular secretion.	E	Bowman's capsule.
6	Metabolic waste.	F	Urea.
7	Fundamental unit of Kidney.	G	Concentration of blood plasma.
8	Hydrostatic pressure.	H	Henle loop.
9	Ammonia.	I	Proximal Convoluted tubule.
10	Osmoregulation.	J	Adulteration of edible oil.

A:Type: [4] Answers and explanations:

Sl. No	Column A	Sl. No	Column B
1.	Water re-absorption	H	Henle loop.
Expl.	Henle loop main function is to reabsorb water and sodium chloride from the filtrate.		
2.	Renal capsule.	E	Bowman's capsule.
Expl.	Bowman's capsule and glomerulus together are called renal capsule.		
3.	Dropsy.	J	Adulteration of edible oil.
Expl.	Adulteration of mustard oil with argemone seed oil causes dropsy.		
4.	Tubular re-absorption.	C	Distal Convoluted tubule.
5.	Tubular secretion.	I	Proximal Convoluted tubule.
6.	Metabolic waste.	B	Uric Acid.
Expl.	Uric acid created when the body breaks down chemicals called purines.		
7.	Fundamental unit of Kidney.	A	Nephron.

Sl. No	Column A	Sl. No	Column B
8.	Hydrostatic pressure.	D	Glomerulus.
Expl.	By using hydrostatic pressure glomerular filtration takes place.		
9.	Ammonia.	F	Urea.
Expl.	The urea cycle or ornithine cycle converts excess ammonia into urea in the mitochondria of liver cell.		
10.	Osmoregulation.	G	Concentration of blood plasma.

Q:Type: [5] True or false.

1) Bile pigments are formed from the breakdown of haemoglobin of blood.
2) Dialysis process used a permeable membrane.
3) The most poisonous waste by-products of metabolism is ammonia.
4) Uric acid found in urine comes from fat metabolism.
5) Henle loop shape is circular.
6) The skin plays an excretory role.
7) Tubular secretion takes place in proximal convoluted tubules.
8) The left kidney is placed slightly above the right kidney.
9) Osmoregulation controls the concentration of blood plasma.
10) Dropsy could cause by the adulteration of alcohol.
11) Liver, the largest gland in the body, is a detoxifying gland.
12) Bowman' capsule found in the medulla region of the kidney.
13) Medulla is the pale coloured inner zone of the kidney.
14) Human could run their normal life with the use of one good kidney.
15) Liver converts ammonia into the urine.

A:Type: [5] Answers

1) **[True]** Bile pigments are formed from the breakdown of haemoglobin of blood.
2) **[False]** Dialysis process used a semipermeable membrane.
3) **[True]** The most poisonous waste by-products of metabolism is ammonia.
4) **[False]** Uric acid found in urine is comes from protein metabolism.
5) **[False]** Henle loop shape is U.
6) **[True]** The skin plays an excretory role.
7) **[True]** Tubular secretion takes place in proximal convoluted tubules.
8) **[False]** The right kidney is placed slightly above the left kidney.
9) **[True]** Osmoregulation controls the concentration of blood plasma.
10) **[False]** Dropsy could cause by the adulteration of edible oil.
11) **[True]** Liver, the largest gland in the body, is a detoxifying gland.
12) **[False]** Bowman' capsule found in the cortex region of the kidney.
13) **[True]** Medulla is a pale coloured inner zone of the kidney.

14) **[True]** Human could run their normal life with the use of one good kidney.

15) **[False]** Liver converts ammonia into urea.

Q:Type: [6]Fill in the blanks.

1) Ureter runs from the inner side of each __________.
2) __________ muscle helps to urinate human beings.
3) The cleaned blood after the removal of waste is sent back through the renal ________.
4) The diameter of the Henle loop duct is ________ than the proximal convoluted tube.
5) Ultrafiltration in glomerulus takes place due to __________ pressure of blood.
6) __________ is converted to urea by liver.
7) __________ is the most dangerous metabolic waste in our body.
8) In our body ionic and water, balance is maintained by __________ method.
9) Accumulation of water in body tissue is commonly known as __________.
10) We pass urine ________ times in summer than in winter.
11) The dark colour outer zone of the kidney is called __________.
12) Each kidney receives oxygenated bold through __________ artery.
13) Level of mineral salts is balanced by __________ in our body.
14) Uriniferous tubules is the another name of __________.
15) Dialysis is a process of separating small molecules from larger ones by using ________ membrane.

A:Type: [6] Answers

1.	Kidney.	**9.**	Oedema/dropsy.
2.	Sphincter.	**10.**	Fewer.
3.	Vein.	**11.**	Cortex.
4.	Less.	**12.**	Renal.
5.	Hydrostatic.	**13.**	Kidney.
6.	Ammonia.	**14.**	Nephron.
7.	Ammonia.	**15.**	Semi-permeable.
8.	Osmoregulation.		

Q:Type: [7]Choose the correct answer(MCQ).

1. The process of removal of toxic wastes from the body of an organism is called

a) Intoxication.**b)** Excretion **c)** Metabolism.**d)** Osmoregulation.

2. Which of the following is not a waste produced in animals

a) Vitamins **b)**Uricacid.**c)** Ammonia **d)** None of the above.

3. Most dangerous by-product produced by our body due to metabolism is

a)Urea. **b)** Ammonia **c)** Ketone **d)** Uric acid.

4. Which of the following is not an excretory organ of human beings

a)Skin. **b)**Liver.**c)** kidney.**d)** Spleen.

5. Sphincter helps to do

a)Water re-absorption **b)** Renal secretion **c)**Urination **d)** None of the above.

6. The fundamental unit of the kidney is

a)Neuro-fibrils **b)** Uriniferous tubules **c)**Pericardium.**d)**renal capsule.

7. Tubular secretion takes place in

a)Distal convoluted tubule   **b)** Proximal convoluted tubule **c)**Henle loop **d)** None of the above.

8. Every minute our kidney could filter

b) 200 ml   **b)** 100ml **c)** 120 ml**d)** 140 ml

9.Water content [by weight] in urine is about

a)90%   **b)**96% **c)** 92% **d)** 99%

10. Dropsy is a disease due to failure of

a)Liver**b)**kidney **c)** both (a) and (b) **d)** None of the above.

11.the largest detoxifying gland in our body is

a)liver. **b)**Kidney**c)** Skin 7 **d)** lung

12. Bowman's capsule is a part of

b) Nephron.**b)**medulla. **c)** Cortex **d)** Liver

13. Mostly the following salt is present in the urine

a)Calcium Chloride **b)** Sodium Chloride **c)** Magnesium Sulphate **d)** Sodium Sulphate

14. Uric acids found in urine and its produced by the metabolism of

a)Fat**b)**carbohydrate **c)** Protein.**d)** Cellulose.

15. Bile pigment found in urine is form

a) Eosinophils **b)** Basophils **c)** platelets. **d)** RBC.

A:Type: [7] Answers

1	**b.** Excretion.	**9.**	**b.** 96%
2.	**d.** none of the above.	**10.**	**b.** kidney.
3.	**b.** Ammonia.	**11.**	**a.** liver.
4.	**d.** spleen.	**12.**	**b.** nephron.
5.	**c.** urination.	**13.**	**b.** sodium chloride.
6.	**b.** Uriniferous tubules.	**14.**	**c.** protein.
7.	**a.** Distal convoluted tubule.	**15.**	**d.** RBC
8.	**c.** 120 ml.		

SECTION-II

Question-1.

1. **Define excretion.**
2. **Name the excretory organs found in human.**
3. **Describe the functions of Glomeruli in the kidney.**
4. **What is Dialysis?**
5. **Give the principle involved in the functioning of an artificial machine to clean the blood.**

Answer:

1) The process of removal of toxic wastes from the body of an organism is called excretion.
2) Name of the excretory organs found in human beings are Lungs, Slin, kidneys and liver.
3) The blood flows through the glomerulus under greater pressure which is much greater than any other capillaries in the body because efferent arterioles are narrower than the afferent arteriole.This high pressure causes the smaller molecules of the blood to filter out through the glomerulus into the renal tubule.This infiltration under extraordinary forces is called ultrafiltration.
4) **Dialysis**: It is a process of separating small molecules from larger ones using a semipermeable membrane.
5) The dialysis machine receives blood through a tube connected to an artery in the arm.Inside the machine, blood flows through a cellulosic dialysis tubing which allows small molecules, including urea to pass through the walls. The cleaned blood is returned to the patient body through a tube connected to a vein in the same arm. The dialysis tubing is bathed in a liquid similar to blood plasma.

Question-2.

1) Why is excretion is necessary?
2) Name the process involved in the formation of urine.
3) List 5 excretory products of humans.
4) Name the common excretory products of animals.
5) What is the function of the Henle loop?

Answer:

1) **Necessity of excretion system:**
   a. To remove toxic wastes from the body.
   b. To maintain proper ionic balance within the body.
   c. To maintain water content in the body.

2) **The processes involved in the formation of urine is as follows:**
   Glomerular filtration >Tubular reabsorption>tubular secretion>reabsorbtion of water>excertion.

3) **Five excretory products of human:**
   1. Carbon dioxide.
   2. Bile pigments.
   3. Urea.
   4. Ammonia.
   5. Excess salts

4) Common excretory product of animals is ammonia.
5) Henle loop does reabsorption of water coming from glomeruli.

Question-3.

1) The elimination of water by the dialysis machine may be considered to be both excretion and osmoregulation-explain.
2) Why is osmoregulation is important?
3) Draw a labelled diagram of a nephron.
4) What remedial measures are followed if a person is showing a symptom of dehydration?
5) Why in the summer season less urination takes place compared to the winter season.

Answer:

1. Using the dialysis process we are separating small molecules from larger ones and remove excretion materials from the body. If we can't excrete waste materials then the concentration of blood will increase compared to blood cells which will imbalance osmoregulation. So we can say that elimination of water by dialysis machine may be considered to be both exertion and osmoregulation.

2. The process of control of water content and the concentration of ions in the body is called osmoregulation.It is done by the kidney.The blood plasmashould be maintained at the right concentration always. If the concentration of the blood is higher than body cells concentration then water will be drawn out from the body cells, which in turn, will shrink. If the blood has a lower concentration than body cells then body cells will absorb water from the blood and will enlarge.Both the situation is dangerous for health.

3. Nephron:

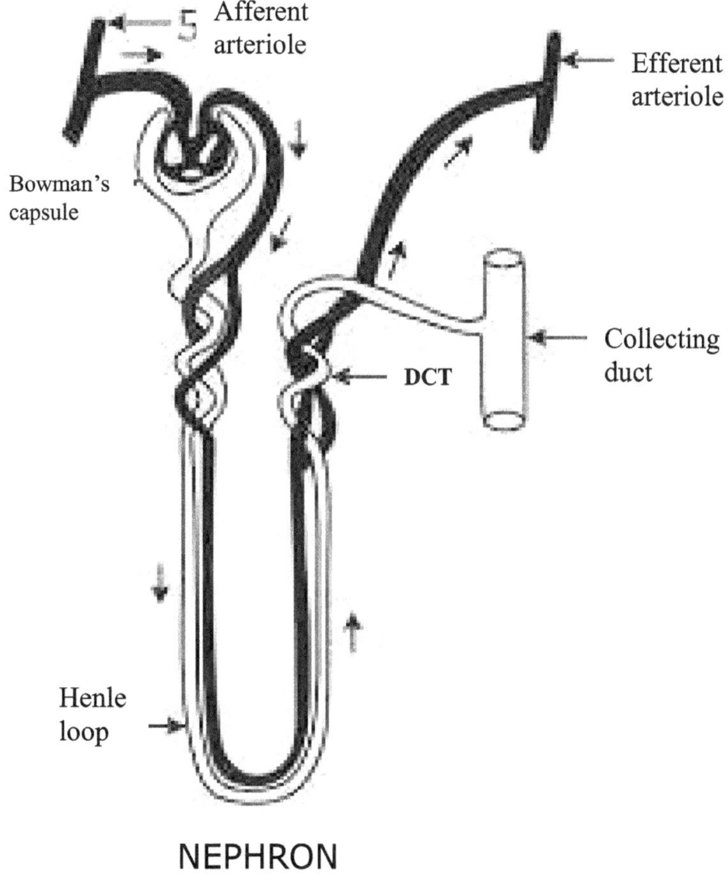

NEPHRON

4. During dehydration,a person should take more and more water with sugar and salt to maintain the concentration of blood.

5. In summer more water is lost by perspiration so there is more absorption of water from the kidney tubules into the blood.Thus the urine is more concentrated and thicker.In winter, perspiration is very less, so a smaller amount of water is reabsorbed by the kidney tubules, making the urine more frequent and diluted.

Question-4.

1) Briefly explain the formation steps of urine.
2) Draw structure of Malpighian corpuscles.
3) List the composition of a normal urine sample.

Answer:

1. **Steps of urine formation:**

Name of the part	Process
1.Glomerular filtration.	Blood pressure forces small molecules from the glomerulus into the glomerular capsule.
2.Tubular reabsorption.	Diffusion and active transport return molecules to blood at the proximal convoluted tubule.
3.Tubular secretion.	Active transport moves molecules from the blood into the distal convoluted tubule.
4.Reabsorbtion of water.	It happens across the length of the nephron and notably at the Henle loop and collecting duct.
5.Exertion.	Urine formation.

2. **Structure of Malpighian corpuscles:**

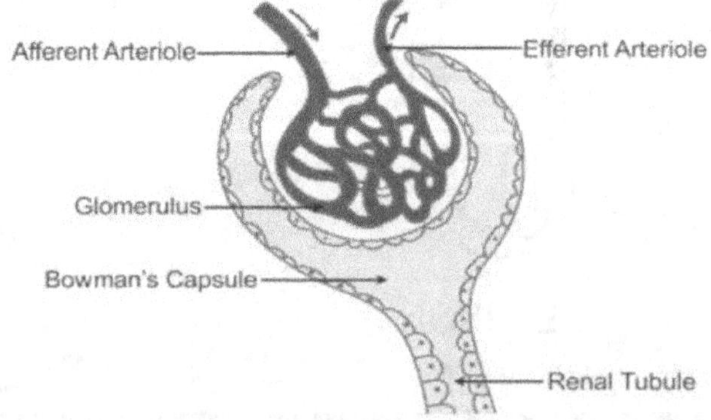

3. **Composition of normal urine:**
   Normal urine contains Water, Creatinine, uricacid, salts, urea, amino acids etc.

Question-5.

Observe the figure shown below and answer the followings.
1. Name the organ system shown in the figure.
2. Label the parts numbered 1 to 8.
3. Mention the function of part-1 and 2.

Answer:

1. The organ system is an excretory system.
2. Label:
   1. Vena cave.
   2. Aorta.
   3. Afferent arteriole.
   4. Efferent arteriole.
   5. Ureter.
   6. Urinary bladder.
   7. Sphincter muscle.
   8. Urethra.

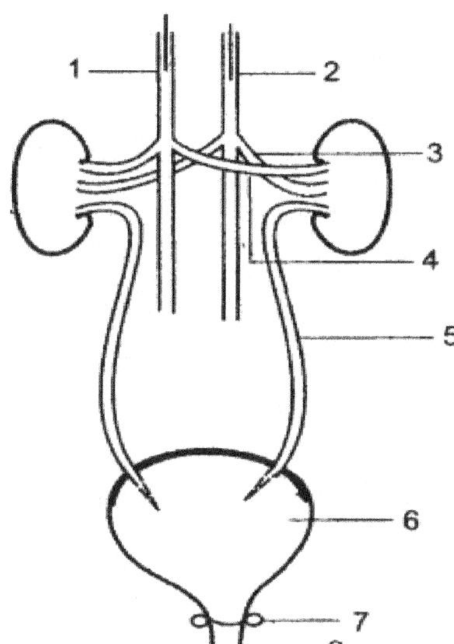

3. Vena cave: It carries deoxygenated blood from the upper and lower half of the body to the right atrium of the heart.
   Aorta: Its carry oxygenated blood to all part of the body.

NERVOUS SYSTEM & SENSE ORGANS.

SECTION-I

Q:Type: [1] Name the followings.

1. Perikaryon is the name of.
2. Nissl's granules are rich in.
3. The cation helps to conduct nerve pulse is.
4. The outermost layer of meninges is called.
5. The middle layer of meninges is called.
6. The inner two layers of the brain are filled with this fluid.
7. This nerve helps to identify the smell.
8. The medulla and cerebellum all together called.
9. The most affected part of the brain after alcohol consumption is.
10. Three bones in the ear are collectively known as.
11. The pigment present in rod cells.
12. The absence of electrical activity of the brain is called.
13. The knee jerk is an example of this action.
14. A fluid that occupies the larger cavity of the eyeball behind the lens.
15. Inflammation of meninges is called.
16. Matter present in the inner portion of the cerebrum.
17. The fluid that presents between the lens and the cornea.
18. The gland which produces tears.
19. White multi-layered sheathe found on Axon is called.
20. The organ that responsible for protecting the eyes from sweat.
21. A neurotransmitter stored at the terminal ends of the axon.
22. The largest part of the human brain is called.
23. The internal layer of the eye prevents the reflection of light.
24. The junction region between the two neurons is called.
25. The pigment present in cone cells.
26. This spot inside the eye is called the best area of vision.
27. Reissner's membrane is found in.
28. This helps to equalize air pressure on either side of the eardrum.
29. The part of the brain which maintains posture, equilibrium and muscular toning.
30. The muscle of the human eye is concerned with the focusing of objects at different distances.

A:Type:[1] Answer:

01.	Cell body of a neurone.	05.	Arachnoid.
02.	RNA.	06.	Cerebro-spinal fluid.
03.	Na+	07.	Olfactory nerve.
04.	Dura mater.	08.	Hindbrain.

09.	Cerebellum.	20.	Eyebrow.
10.	Ear ossicles.	21.	Cyanocobalamin.
11.	Rhodopsin.	22.	Cerebrum.
12.	Brain stem death.	23.	Choroid.
13.	Reflex action.	24.	Synapse.
14.	Vitreous humour.	25.	Iodopsin.
15.	Meningitis.	26.	Yellow spot/fovea centralis.
16.	White matters.	27.	Organ of Corti.
17.	Aqueous humour.	28.	Eustachian tube.
18.	Lacrimal glands.	29.	Cerebellum.
19.	Myelin sheath.	30.	Ciliary muscles.

Q:Type:[2] State the exact locations.

1	Papilla.	2	The receptors for the sense of thirst.	3	Basilar membrane.
4	Organ of Corti.	5	Yellow spot.	6	Pons varoli.
7	Medulla Oblongata.	8	Receptor for the sense of hunger.	9	Tympanic membrane.

A:Type: [2] Answer.

1) ***papilla***: Taste buds.
2) ***The receptors for the sense of thirst***: Pharynx.
3) ***Basilar membrane***: Cochlea
4) ***Organ of Corti***: Middle canal of the cochlea.
5) ***Yellow spot***: On retina and just opposite the lens.
6) ***Pons varoli***: Nerve fibers connecting two lobes of the cerebellum.
7) ***Medulla Oblongata***: the lowest part of the brain located at the base of the skull.
8) ***Receptor for the sense of hunger***: Stomach wall.
9) ***Tympanic membrane***: Between outer and middle ear.

Q:Type: [3] Find odd terms.

1. Myopia, Hypermetropia, Astigmatism, Colorblindness.
2. Myopia, Hypermetropia, Astigmatism, Meningitis.
3. Dendrite, Cyton, Axon, macula.
4. Cerebellum, Pons, cerebrum, medulla oblongata.
5. Dura mater, Pia mater, Arachnoid, C.S.F
6. Myelin sheath, Nissl's granule, endolymph, Perikaryon.

7. Pinna, Tympanum, Ossicles, Lacrimal gland.
8. Papilla, Pericardium, Organ of Corti, Olfactory epithelium.
9. Malleus, Utriculus, Stapes, Ossicles.
10. Cerebrum, Thalamus, Hypothalamus, Pons.
11. Incus, Steps, Malleus, Eustachian tube.
12. Pinna, Vestibular organ, Cochlea, semicircular canals.
13. Typing, tying shoelaces, knee jerk, Juggling.
14. Myelin sheath, Ranvier nod, Nissl's granule, Axontic nob

A:Type: [3] Answer:

1. Myopia, Hypermetropia, Astigmatism, **Colorblindness.**

Explanation: Color blindness is caused due to nerve whereas all other disorder I related to the lens.

2. Myopia, Hypermetropia, Astigmatism, **Meningitis.**

Explanation: Meningitis is related to the brain and others are related to the eye.

3. Dendrite, Cyton, Axon, **macula.**

Explanation: macula is not a part of the neuron.

4. Cerebellum, Pons, **cerebrum,** medulla oblongata.

Explanation: Cerebrum is part of the forebrain and others are parts of the Hindbrain.

5. Dura mater, Pia mater, Arachnoid, **C.S.F**

Explanation: CSF is aliquid.

6. Myelin sheath, Nissl's granule, **endolymp**h, Perikaryon.

Explanation: Endolymph is related to the ear and others are part of a neurone.

7. Pinna, Tympanum, Ossicles, **Lacrimal gland.**

Explanation: Other than the Lacrimal gland all are parts of Ear.

8. Papilla, **Pericardium**, Organ of Corti, Olfactory epithelium.

Explanation: Pericardium is not related to the sense organ and its outermost layer of the heart.

9. Malleus, **Utriculus**, Stapes, Ossicles.

Explanation: Other than Utriculus all are bone of the ear.

10. Cerebrum, Thalamus, Hypothalamus, **Pons.**

Explanation: Other than Pons all are parts of the forebrain.

11. Incus, Steps, Malleus, **Eustachian tube.**

Explanation: Eustachian tube is not an Ear ossicle.

12. **Pinna**, Vestibular organ, Cochlea, semicircular canals.

Explanation: Pinna is a part of the outermost ear and others are innermost
part of the ear.

13. Typing, tying shoelaces, **knee jerk**, Juggling.

Explanation: Knee jerk is an example of reflex action and others are voluntary action of muscles.

14. Myelin sheath, Ranvier nod, **Nissl's granule**, Axontic nob

Explanation: Nissl's granule is a part of the cell body of a neurone but others
are part of Axon.

Q:Type: [4]Match the column:

Sl.No	Column A	Sl.No	Column B
1	Stimulus.	A	Touch.
2	Lacrimal glands.	B	Lack of sensory cell.
3	Cone cells.	C	Magnification of vibration.
4	Ear canal.	D	Heat.
5	Sensory neuron.	E	Macula.
6	Stirrup.	F	Transmits impulses from receptors to the brain.
7	Blindspot.	G	Sense of smell.
8	Protective cover of the brain.	H	Ossicles.
9	Ruffini corpuscles.	I	Iodopsin.
10	Rod cell.	J	Change in the external and internal environment.
11	Eustachian tube.	K	Semuren.
12	Olfactory lobes.	L	Meninges.
13	Root hairs plexus.	M	Equalizing air pressure.
14	Yellow spot.	N	Tears.
15	Bones of ear.	O	Rhodopsin.

A:Type: [4] Answer:

Sl. No.	Column A	Sl. No	Column B
1.	Stimulus.	J	Change in external and internal environment.
2.	Lacrimal glands.	N	Tears.
Expl.	Secretion of lacrimal glands is called tears.		
3.	Cone cells.	I	Iodopsin.
Expl.	The pigment contains in the rod cell is Iodopsin.		
4.	Ear canal.	K	Semuren.
Expl.	Wax secreting glands in external auditory meatus prevents the entry of dust.		
5.	Sensory neuron.	F	Transmits impulses from receptors to the brain.
6.	Stirrup.	C	Magnification of vibration.
7.	Blindspot.	B	Lack of sensory cell.
8.	Protective cover of the brain.	L	Meninges.
9.	Ruffini corpuscles.	D	Heat.
10.	Rod cell.	O	Rhodopsin
Expl.	The pigment contains in the rod cell is Rhodopsin.		
11.	Eustachian tube.	M	Equalizing air pressure.
12.	Olfactory lobes.	G	Sense of smell.
13.	Root hairs plexus.	A	Touch.
14.	Yellow spot.	E	Macula.
15.	Bones of the ear.	H	Ossicles.

Q:Type: [5] Write the special functional activities of the followings:

1	Ear ossicles.	2	Cochlea.	3	Eustachian tube.
4	Semicircular canals.	5	Pinna.	6	Iris.
7	Fovea centralis.	8	Choroid.	9	Organ of Corti.
10	Aqueous humour.	11	Pons.	12	Medulla oblongata.

A: Type: [5] Answers:

1) Ear Ossicles: These are ear bones that magnified sound by vibration and set the fluid contained in the cochlear canal in vibrations.

2) **Cochlea:**It is a fluid-filled spiral tube, which transmits vibrations from the middle ear to the sensitive hair cells.

3) **Eustachian tube:** This equalizes air pressure on either side of the eardrum.

4) **Semicircular canals:** This containing sensory cells for maintenance of inner ear body position in response to movement.

5) **Pinna:**it collects and amplifies sound waves.

6) **Iris:**it controls the amount of light entering the eye.

7) **Fovea centralis:**It creates the brightest vision.

8) **Choroid:**It prevents light rays from reflecting and scattering inside the eye.

9) **Organ of Corti:** It is a sound reception system that transforms sound vibrations into a nerve impulse.

10) **Aqueous humour:**It supplies oxygen and nutrients and removes metabolic waste.

11) **Pons:**it transmits an impulse from one side of the cerebellum to the other and together with the medulla its controls breathing.

12) **Medulla Oblongata:** coordinates reflexes.

Q: Type: [6] True or false.

1) Nocturnal animals have more cones compared to rods.
2) Cones enable us to see three primary colours.
3) Cataract appears due to degeneration of protein fibres.
4) Human lens is a biconcave crystalline body.
5) Acetylcholine acts as a neurotransmitter.
6) Conditional reflexes are controlled by the cerebral cortex.
7) Number of human cranial nerves is 22.
8) In the brain, grey matters surround the white matter.
9) The most affected part after alcohol consumption is the cerebellum.
10) Two meninges cover the brain and the spinal cord.
11) The functional unit of the nervous system is a neuron.
12) The innermost layer of meninges is called the dura mater.
13) Cranial nerves arise from the brain.
14) Dilation of the pupil is brought about by the sympathetic nervous system.
15) Knee jerk is an example of involuntary action.
16) Our habits, likes, dislikes, prejudices and interest are unconditioned reflexes.
17) Lysozyme is present in tears.
18) Rods are responsible for vision in the dark.
19) Medulla oblongata controls all the involuntary activities of the body like heartbeats, respiration etc.

20) Area of the best vision in the eye is called the yellow spot.
21) Human ear consists of fourbones.
22) Receptors for the sense of hunger is located in the mouth.
23) All voluntary actions are controlled by the cerebellum.
24) Hypermetropia is a defect of the eyeball being elongated.

A:Type: [6]Answers:

1) **[False]**Nocturnal animals have more rods compared to cones.
2) **[True]** Cones enable us to see three primary colours.
3) **[True]** Cataract appears due to degeneration of protein fibres.
4) **[False]** Human lens is a biconvex crystalline body.
5) **[True]**Acetylcholine acts as a neurotransmitter.
6) **[True]** Conditional reflexes are controlled by the cerebral cortex.
7) **[False]** Number of human cranial nerves is 12.
8) **[True]**In the brain grey matters surrounds the white matter.
9) **[True]** He most affected part after alcohol consumption is cerebellum.
10) **[False]** Three meninges cover the brain and the spinal cord.
11) **[True]**The functional unit of the nervous system is a neuron.
12) **[False]** The innermost layer of meninges is called the pia mater.
13) **[True]**Cranial nerves arise from the brain.
14) **[True]**Dilation of the pupil is brought about by the sympathetic nervous system.
15) **[True]** Knee jerk is an example of involuntary action.
16) **[False]**Our habits, likes, dislikes, prejudices and interest are conditioned reflexes.
17) **[True]**Lysozyme is present in tears.
18) **[True]**Rods are responsible for vision in the dark.
19) **[True]** Medulla oblongata controls all the involuntary activities of the body like heartbeats, respiration etc.
20) **[True]**Area of best vision in the eye is called the yellow spot.
21) **[False]**Human ear consists of three bones.
22) **[False]**Receptors for the sense of hunger is located in the spinal cord.
23) **[True]**All voluntary actions are controlled by the cerebellum.
24) **[False]**Myopia is a defect of the eyeball being elongated.

Q:Type: [7]Fill in the blanks.

1) Highly branched extensions of Perikaryon is called ________.
2) The basic units of human brain is________.
3) Our tongue can perceive _________ basic tastes.
4) Nodes of Ranvier found in between ____________ ____________.
5) The junction region between the two neuron is called ____________.
6) Normally the outer surface of a neuron carries _________ charges.
7) Ascytyle colin in a ____________.
8) The largest region of brain is ____________.
9) _________ contracts or secrets on receiving the impulse.

10) Thalamus is concerned with relying on _________ impulses.
11) Calcium carbonate particles present in endolymph are called ____________.
12) The middle part of cochlea is filled with ___________.
13) Three bones of ear is collectively called _________.
14) Hypermetropia is also called ________sightedness.
15) Cataract is the problem related to ___________.
16) ______________ is called area of best vision.
17) Cones are sensitive to _________ light.
18) Metabolic waste of eye is removed by ____________.
19) ____________ are responsible for color vision.
20) The thin member of eye which is covering the entire front part of eye is __________.
21) The bone cavity where eye is located is called _________.
22) Peristaltic reflex is one type of _______ reflex.
23) Conditional reflexes are controlled by ____________ ____________.
24) Number of cranium nerves in human beings is ________pairs.
25) ______________ controls the activity of internal organs.
26) In spinal cord ______ matter is surrounds the _________ matters.
27) Short-sightedness can be corrected by using a _________ lens.
28) ___________ is a defect of the eye in which the optic axis of the eye becomes too short.

A:Type: [7] Answers:

01.	Dendrites.	15.	Lens.
02.	Neuron.	16.	Yellow spot.
03.	Four.	17.	Bright.
04.	Myelin sheath.	18.	Aqueous humour.
05.	Synapse.	19.	Cones.
06.	Positive.	20.	Conjunctiva.
07.	Neurotransmitter.	21.	Orbits.
08.	Cerebrum.	22.	Unconditional.
09.	Effectors.	23.	cerebral cortex.
10.	Sensory.	24.	12.
11.	otoliths.	25.	Medulla.
12.	Endolymph.	26.	White, Grey.
13.	Ossicles.	27.	Concave.
14.	Long.	28.	Myopia.

Q:Type: [8]Write One difference of pair (on the given parameter).

01	Colour blindness & Night blindness.	Cause.
02	Glaucoma & Cataract.	Formation.
03	Blindspot & Yellow spot.	Vision.

04	Rod cells & Cone cells.	Light Sensitivity.
05	Astigmatism & Presbyopia.	Cause.
06	Lacrimal gland & Wax gland of the ear.	Function.
07	Eyebrows and Eyelashes.	Function.
08	Myopia & Hypermetropia.	Glass type.
09	Dynamic balance & Static balance of ear.	Organ.
10	Choroid and Sclerotic layers of the eye.	Function.

A :Type: [8]Answer:

1) **[Cause]**Color blindness caused due to genetic disorder and night blindness is due to the non-formation of rhodopsin.

2) **[Formation]** Glaucoma formed at aqueous chamber of the eyes and cataract formed on the lens due to degeneration of protein fibre.

3) **[Vision]**Blind spot is the area of No Vision and Yellow spot is the area of best vision.

4) **[Sensitivity]**Rod cell is sensitive to dim light and cone cell is sensitive to bright light.

5) **[cause]** Astigmatism is due to uneven curvature of the cornea or the lens and Presbyopia is caused to loss of flexibility of the lens.

6) **[Function]**lacrimal gland lubricate eyelids and wash away dust particles. The Wax gland of the ear prevents dust entry and foreign particles in the ear.

7) **[Function]** Eyebrows protect the eye from raindrops and perspiration trickling to them and eyelashes prevent the falling of large particles in the eye.

8) **[Glass type]** Myopia required concave glass and Hypermetropia required biconvex lens.

9) **[Organ]** Dynamic balance done by Ampulla and static balance done by Cochlea.

10) **[Function]** Choroid prevent light rays from reflecting and scattering inside the eye and Sclerotic layers of the eye protect the eye from mechanical injuries.

Q:Type: [9]Choose the correct answer(MCQ).

1.The cerebral hemisphere in mammals are connected by

a)corpusluteum. **b)**hypothalamus.**c)**pons varolli.**d)** Corpus collosum.

2.A point of contact between two neurons is termed as

a)synopsis. b)neuromotor junction. **c)**synapse**d)**none of the above.

3.The photoreceptor cells of the retina sensitive to colour are

a)Cones**b)**rods**c)**organ of corti**d)**either (a) or (b).

4.White matter surrounds the grey matter in

a)brain**b)**spinal cord**c)**both (a) and (b)**d)**none of the above

5.Which of the following is not a reflex action?

a)salivation at the sight of food.**b)**knee jerk. **c)**blinking of eyes. **d)**secretion of sweat.

6.Astigmatism can be corrected by

a)convexlens. **b)**concave lens. **c)** cylindrical lens. **d)**none of the above.

7.Nearby objects cannot be seen clearly in

a)myopia.**b)**glaucoma**c)**astigmatism. **d)**Hypermetropia.

8.calcium carbonate particles present in endolymph are called

a)Ampulla**b)**cochlea **c)**otolith.**d)**None of the above

9.Meissner's corpuscles are the receptor of

a)heat)touch. **c)**cold **d)**vibration.

10. Diencephalon has a cavity called

a)thirdventricle. **b)**Corpus luteum. **c)** Medulla oblongata. **d)**pons.

11.which of the following helps to increase the speed of nerve impulse conduction.

a)axonnob. **b)**Ranvier nodes. **c)** Myelin sheath. **d)**None of the above

12.the fluid-filled gap between the nerve cells is called

a)synaptic cleft. **b)**synaptic nob. **c)** Myelin sheath. **d)**Ranvier nodes

13. Number of a human cranial nerve is

a)12**b)**12 pair**c)** 31 pair**d)**31

14. Number of the human spinal nerve is

a)12 **b)**12 pair. **c)** 31 pair. **d)**31

15. Optic nerve is a

a)motornerve. **b)**Sensory nerve. **c)** Mixed nerve**d)**None of the above.

16. The ventral root ganglion of the spinal cord contains axons of the

a)Motor neuron **b)**Sensory neuron **c)** Association neuron **d)**Intermediate neuron.

A :Type: [9]Answer:

01.	a. Corpus luteum.	09.	b. touch.
02.	b. synapse.	10.	d. third ventricle.
03.	b. cones.	11.	b. myelin sheath.

04.	**a.** spinal cord.	12.	**d.** synaptic cleft.
05.	**d.** secretion of sweat.	13.	**b.** 12 pair.
06.	**b.** cylindrical lens.	14.	**d.** 31 pair.
07.	**b.** Hypermetropia.	15.	**b.** sensory nerve.
08.	**a.** otolith.	16.	**a.** motor neuron.

SECTION-II

Question-1.

1. **Why does the deficiency of Vitamin A cause night blindness?**
2. **Briefly explain the process of seeing an object.**
3. **What happens when accidentally our hand touches hot objects?**
4. **Give a brief description of menninges.**
5. **Why old peoples are unable to perceive teste easily?**

Answer:

1. Rhodopsin which helps to see in the dim light is synthesized from Vitamin A.
2. Light rays from the object enter our eyes through conjunctiva, cornea, aqueous humour, lens and vitreous humour. The curvature of the cornea and lens bends the light rays to form an inverted and real image on the retina. The light energy of the image produces chemical changes in the sensitive cells of the retina and generate nerve impulses. These impulses are carried to the brain through the optic nerve and the nerve centers coordinate these impulses and then we are seeing an object through the brain. Superimposition of two images from the left and right eye gives us a sense of the depth of an object.
3. When we accidentally touch hot objects, the receptor perceives the stimulus and the sensory nerve carries a message from the receptor to the spinal cord. Relay neuron transmits impulses from the afferent neuron to the efferent neurons in the spinal cord. Then motor neuron carries impulses from the spinal cord to the effector. This impulse will remove the hand quickly.
4. Meninges is the protector of the brain and it is also continuous with the spinal cord. It consists of three layers. The outermost layer is called the duramater, the middle part is called arachnoid and the innermost layer is called piamater. The space between the inner two layers is filled with cerebrospinal fluid which serves as a shock absorber. This protects the brain from sudden jerk and jolts. This fluid also supplies the neurons in the brain with respiratory gases and nutrients and removes wastes.

5. With age, we lost some taste papilla and this leads to loss of taste at old age.

Question-2.

1) Why do you stop smelling the perfume on clothes while a person approaching you still perceives its smell?

2) Classify the following actions as a simple reflex or conditional reflex:

a. Playing the guitar.

b. Removing your hand suddenly when pricked by a thorn.

c. Sucking capacity developed in newborn babies.

d. Blinking of eyelids.

3) What is the role of three semicircular canals in the vestibule apparatus?

4) Can you reason why we feel dizzy for a short while as if going in circles, even after we stopped spinning round and round?

Answer:

1. Perception involves the interpretation of sensory information. Prolong exposure to a particular smell leads to its gradual weakening and finally disappearance. These olfactory adaptations are due to change in the receptor and olfactory centers of the brain.

2. Types of reflex

a) **Playing the guitar:** Conditional reflex.

b) **Removing your hand suddenly when pricked by a thorn:** unconditional reflex.

c) **Sucking capacity developed in newborn babies:** unconditional reflex.

d) **Blinking of eyelids:** unconditional reflex.

3. Role of three semicircular canals: These three semicircular canals are enlarged into swelling called the ampullae which contain sensory cells for the maintenance of body position in response to movement.

4. When we halt the rotation of semicircular canal also halted. But because of inertia, the endolymph keeps spinning, resisting change yet again. As the fluid continues to move, it once again deflects the cupula this time in the direction in which you were spinning moments before and as the oozing cupula bends those hair cells, a signal of movement is transmitted to the brain. This sense that we are still moving, but you're not.

Question-3.

1) **How do we perceive sound?**
2) **Draw a labelled diagram of a myelinated neuron.**
3) **In the above-drawn figure show the following parts: Perikaryon, Dendrites, Axon, Nodes of Ranvier Nissl's granules.**
4) **State the function of sensory neuron and motor neuron.**
5) **Differentiate between voluntary and involuntary action.**

Answer:

1. We perceive sound by the following 6 steps:
a. Sound transfers into the ear canal and causes the eardrum to move.
b. The eardrum will vibrate with vibrates with the different sounds.
c. These sound vibrations make their way through the ossicles to the cochlea.
d. Sound vibrations make the fluid in the cochlea travel like ocean waves.
e. Movement of fluid in turn makes the hair cells. The auditory nerve picks up any neural signals created by the hair cells. Hair cells at one end of the cochlea transfer low pitch sound information and hair cells at the opposite end transfer high pitch sound information.
f. The auditory nerve moves signals to the brain where they are then translated into recognizable and meaningful sounds. It is the brain that "hears".

2. A Diagram of a neuron is shown below

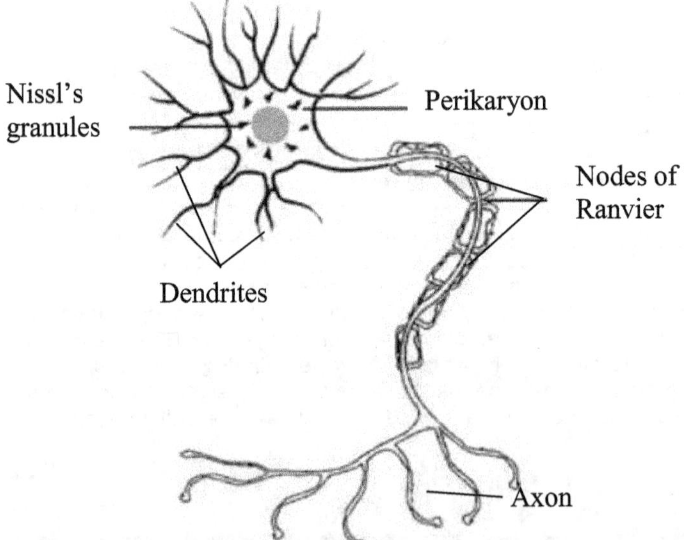

3. **Sensory neuron**: Its carries messages from the receptor to the spinal cord/brain.
   Motor neuron: It carries impulses from the spinal cord/brain to the effectors[muscles, gland or organs].

4. **Difference**:

Voluntary Action	Involuntary Action
Actions are under the will.	Action is not under the will.
May or may not have information from receptor.	Respond against the information from receptor.
Impulse originates in the brain.	Impulse originates in receptors or sense organs.
Involve brain.	Involve spinal cord.

Question-4.

Given below is a diagram depicting defects of the human eye. Study the same and then answer the questions below:

1) **Draw a labelled diagram to show how the above-mentioned defect is rectified?**
2) **Identify the defect.**
3) **Name the parts labelled as 1, 2 and 3.**
4) **Give two possible reasons for this eye defect.**

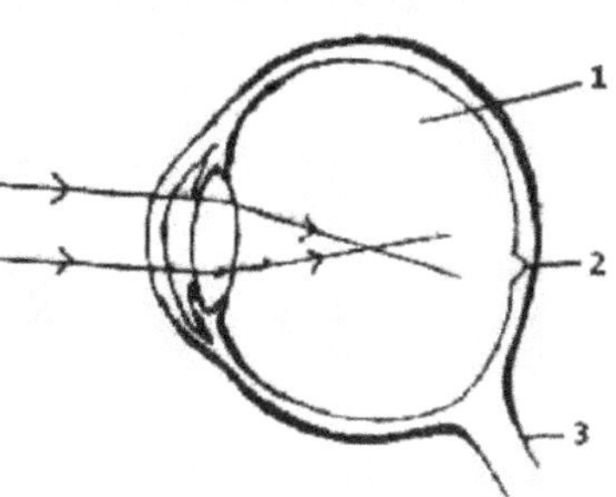

Answer:

1. **Labelled diagram is shown below:**

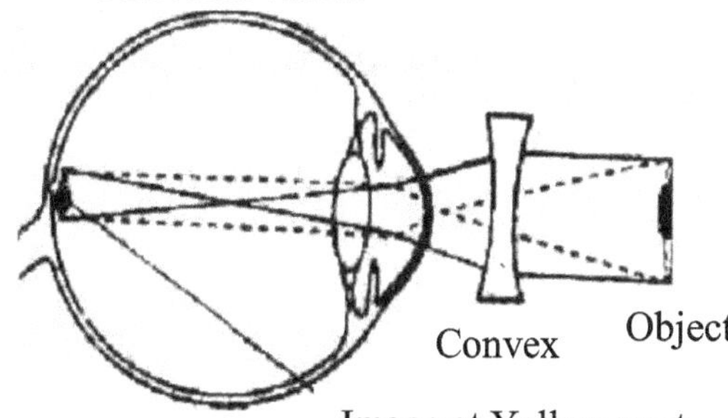

2. Myopia.
3. **Parts are** 1. Vitreous humor chamber. 2. Yellow spot. 3. Optic nerve.
4. Causes of these defects:
   1. Lengthening of the eyeball from front to back.
   2. Too curved lens.

Question-5.

The diagram below represents the structure found in the inner ear. Study the same and then answer the questions below:

1. **Name the parts labelled A,B,C and D.Name the part of the ear responsible for transmitting impulses to the brain.**
2. **Name the part labelled above which is responsible for :**
a. **Static equilibrium.**
b. **Dynamic equilibrium.**
c. **Hearing.**
3. **Name the audio receptor cells which pick up vibrations.**
4. **Name the fluid present in the inner ear.**

Answer:

1. **label:** A: Semicircular canal. B: Utriculus.   C: Sacculus.   D: Cochlea.
2. Auditory nerve of the ear.
3. a. **Static equilibrium:** Sacculus and Utriculus.
c. **Dynamic   equilibrium:** Semicircular canal.
d. **Hearing:** Cochlea.

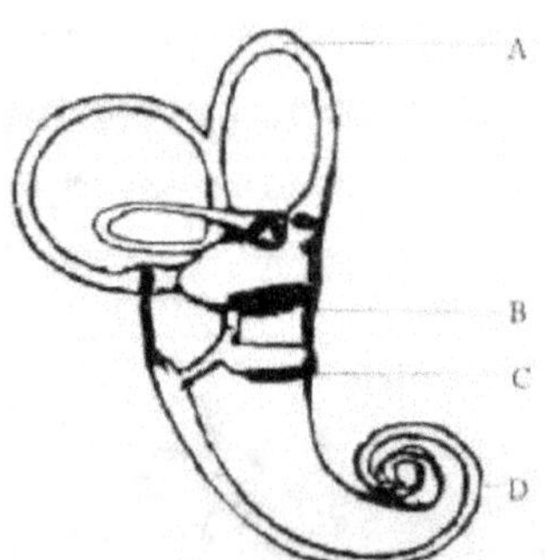

4. Receptor hair cells of Organ of Corti.
5. Endolymph.

Question-6.

The diagram shows a section of the human brain. Answer the questions that follow:

1. **Name the part labelled as A,B and C.**
2. **Give the main function of each parts A,B and C.**
3. **Name the three protective membranes covering the brain.**
4. **Name the basic unit of the brain.**

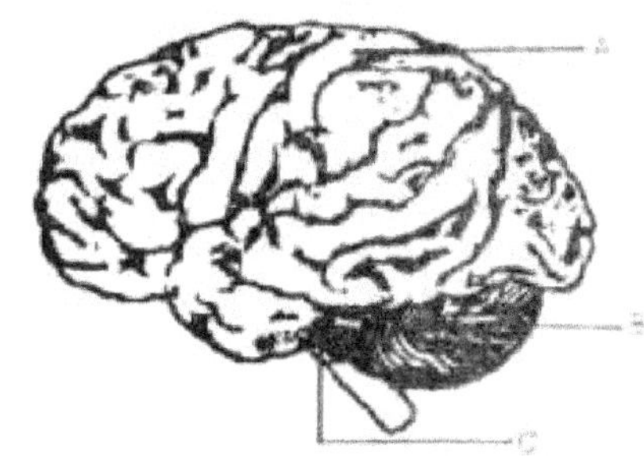

Answer:

1. **Label:** A: Cerebrum. B: Cerebellum C: Medulla Oblongata.

2. **Function:**
A:Cerebrum: It controls Consciousness, thinking, memory, reasoning, perception and stimulus interpretation.
B: Cerebellum: It maintains posture, equilibrium and muscle toning.

C: medulla Oblongata: It coordinates reflexes like swallowing, coughing, sneezing and vomiting etc.
3. **Three protective membranes:**
A:Dura mater at outside.
B: Arachnoid in the middle.
C:Pia mater at the innermost layer.
4.   The basic unit of the brain is the Neuron.

Question-7.

The diagram given below depicts the cross section of the spinal cord. Study the same and then answer the questions that follow:

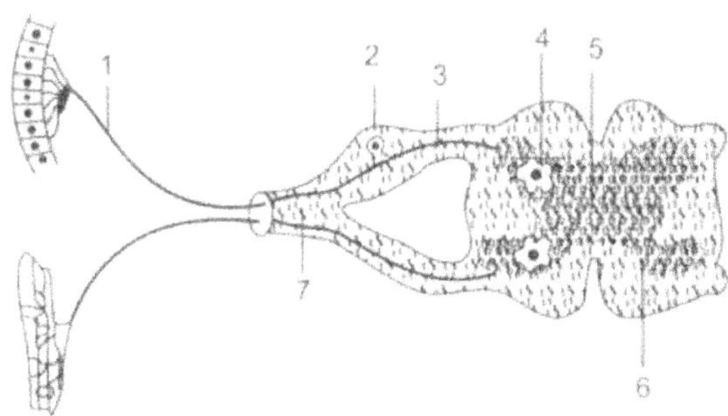

1) Name the process that is being depicted.
2) Name the parts labelled as 2,5 and 6.
3) Name the cells in contact with the part labelled as 1.
4) What is the function of the parts labelled 3,4 and 7? What is the technical term given to the pathway represented by 3,4 and 7?
5) How does the arrangement of cells in the spinal cord differ from that in the brain?

Answer:

1. Nerve pathways with spinal reflex.
2. Label: 2: cell body in dorsal root ganglion. 5: Central canal 6: Grey mater.
3. 1.Receptor cell.
4. **Function:**
a.: Sensory neuron-It carries sensory impulses from the receptor towards the spinal cord.

b. Association neuron- It receives impulses from the sensory neuron and passes them to the motor neuron.
c.Motor neuron- it carries response impulses towards the effectors' organ.
The technical term used to the pathway represented by 3,4 & 7 is *Reflex arc.*
5.In the spinal cord, the cell bodies of the neurons lie on the inner side i.e. grey mater, axons of neurons lie in the outer region i.e. white mater. In the brain, the arrangement is exactly the opposite and here grey matter lies outside and white matter lies the inner side.

Question-8.

Draw a diagram of the human eye as seen in a vertical section and label the part which suits the following functions/descriptions:

1) The layer which prevents reflection of light.
2) The structure that alters the focal length of the lens.
3) The region of distinct vision.
4) The part which transmits the impulse to the brain.
5) The outermost transparent layer in front of the eye lens.
6) The fluid present in the anterior part of the eye in front of the eye lens.

Answer:

1. The layer which prevents reflection of light: Choroid.
2. The structure that alters the focal length of the lens: Ciliary muscle

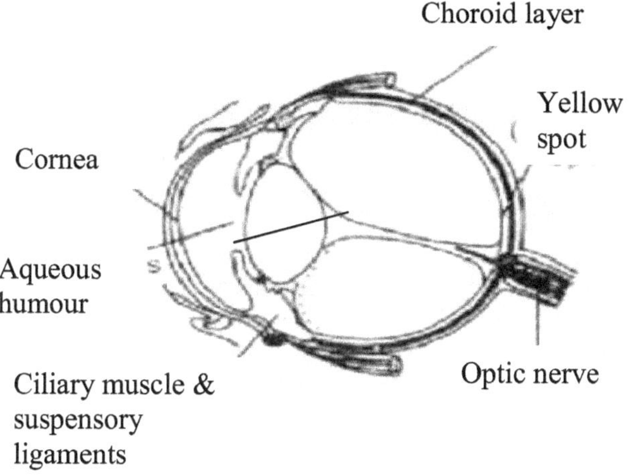

and suspensory ligaments.

3. The region of distinct vision: Yellow spot.
4. The part which transmits the impulse to the brain: Optic nerve.
5. The outermost transparent layer in front of the eye lens: Cornea.
6. Fluid present in the anterior part of the eye in front of the lens: Aqueous humor.

Question-9.

Given below is the diagram of the human ear. Study the same and answer the questions that follow:

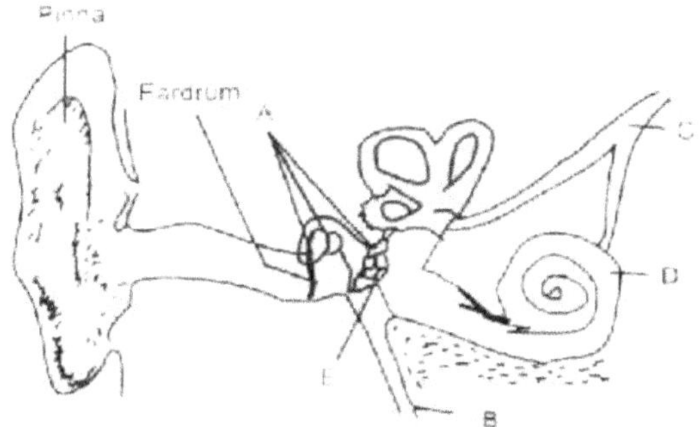

1) Give the biological term for the part labelled 'A" and state its function.
2) Name the part labelled "B" and state its function.
3) Name the part labelled "C" and state its function.
4) Give the function of ear wax.

Answer:

1. Biological term for part A is **Ear ossicles**. Ear ossicles receive vibration from the ear drum[tympanum] and magnify them. The vibration of the last bone i.e. stapes is transmitted to the membrane of the oval window to transmit vibration to the cochlea.
2. Name of the label B is the **Eustachian tube** and its function is to equalize air pressure on either side of the eardrum so that it could freely vibrate.
3. Name of the label C is **Auditory nerves**. It transmits nerve impulses from the cochlea to the brain when nerve impulse generates due to sound and transmits nerve impulse from semicircular canals incase of balancing to the brain.
4. Function of ear wax: **a**. Wax of the ear has insect repellant properties and hence prevents the entry of insects into the auditory canal and also prevent the entry of dust particles. **b**. It lubricates and protects the eardrum.

Question-10.

Given below is the diagrammatic presentation of a defect of the human eye.

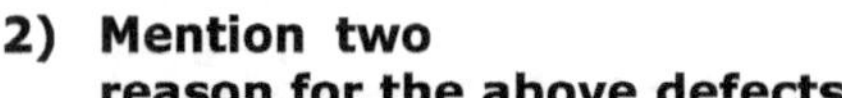

1) **Identify the defects.**
2) **Mention two reason for the above defects.**
3) **State how the defect can be rectified.**
4) **Name the part responsible for maintaining the shape of the eyeball.**

Answer:

1. As the image has formed behind the retinal so it is the picture of Hypermetropia or far-sightedness defects of the eye.
2. Causes of these defects:
   1. Shortening of the eyeball from front to back.
   2. Too flattening of the lens.
3. Convex lens with appropriate power could rectify these defects.
4. Viscous chambers both side of the lens is the responsible part of the eye to maintain the shape of the lens.

ENDOCRINE SYSTEM.

SECTION-I

Q:Type: [1] Name the followings.

1. The process of maintaining a steady state of functioning with external stress condition.
2. Calcitonin hormone is secretes from.
3. Master gland of the human body.
4. Gull's disease is one type of disorder of this gland.
5. Adrenal medulla secretes this hormone.
6. This hormone is also called the "flight or fight" hormone.
7. Method of forming glucose from non-carbohydrate sources.
8. This types of cell secrete insulin.
9. This hormone converts glycogen to glucose.
10. The removal of the testis is called
11. The plant hormone is gas at ordinary temperature.
12. This hormone stimulates the growth of Graafian follicle in females.
13. Luteinizing hormone in a male body is named this.
14. FSH,ICSH and LH cumulatively called this hormone.
15. Hypo secretion of this hormone caused diabetes insipidus.
16. The endocrine gland is referred to as the gland of an emergency.
17. The structure which holds the master gland.
18. The gland produces testosterone.
19. They are called a chemical messenger.
20. Name the male hormone produced by the interstitial cells.
21. This hormone maintains the colour of the skin.
22. The condition which results in abnormally long bones, long lower jaw bone due to hyper secretion of a pituitary hormone.
23. It is also known as a birth hormone.
24. The term coined by F.W.Went means to grow.

A:Type:[1] Answer

01	Homeostasis.	11	Ethylene.
02	Thyroid.	12	Follicle Stimulating Hormone.
03	Pituitary.	13	ICSH [Interstitial Cell Stimulating Hormone.
04	Thyroid.	14	Gonadotropins.
05	Adrenaline.	15	Vasopressin/ADH.
06	Adrenaline.	16	Adrenal gland.
07	Gluconeogenesis.	17	Infundibulum.
08	Beta cells.	18	Testis.
09	Glucagon.	19	Hormone.
10	Castration.	20	Testosterone.

21	Melanocyte Stimulating hormone.[MSH]	23	Oxytocin.
22	Gigantism.	24	Auxin.

Q:Type:[2] State the exact locations.

1	Alpha cells.	2	Pituitary gland.	3	Adrenal gland.
4	Thyroid gland.	5	Thymus.	6	Testis.

A:Type:[2] Answer

1) **Alpha cells**: Islets of Langerhans in the Pancreas.

2) **Pituitary gland.**: base of the brain.

3) **Adrenal gland**: Top of each kidney.

4) **Thyroid gland**: In front of the neck, below the larynx.

5) **Thymus**: Just behind the breast bone.

6) **Testis**: Outside the lower abdomen in the scrotum.

Q: Type:[3] Find odd term.

1. FSH, ICSH, LH,ADH.
2. Alpha cell, Beta cells, gamma cells, Delta cells.
3. GTH, GH, ACTH, Glucagon.
4. Dwarfism, Goitre, Cretinism, Myxoederma.
5. Pituitary, Thyroid, Sebaceous, Adrenalin.
6. Cushing syndrome, Cons Syndrome, Addison's disease, Gull's disease.
7. Skin, Saliva, Sweat, Tears.

A:Type:[3] Answer

1. FSH, ICSH, LH,**ADH**

Explanation: ADH released from posterior lobe and others from anterior lobe.

2. Alpha cell, Beta cells, **gamma cells**, Delta cells.

Explanation: Nothing called gamma cell in pancreas.

3. GTH, GH, ACTH, **Glucagon.**

Explanation: Except Glucagon all secretes from pituitary.

4. **Dwarfism**, Goitre, Cretinism, Myxoederma

Explanation: Except Dwarfism [related to pituitary] all related to thyroid.

5.   Pituitary, Thyroid, **Sebaceous**, Adrenalin

Explanation: Sebaceous is exocrine gland.

7. Cushing syndrome, Cons Syndrome, Addison's disease, **Gull's disease.**

 Explanation: Gull's disease related to thyroid and other are related to adrenalin.

8. Skin, Saliva, Sweat, Tears.

 Explanation: Except skin, all others are germ-killing secretion of our body.

Q:Type:[4] Match the column.

Sl. No	Column A	Sl. No	Column B
1	Diabetes mellitus.	A	Melanin.
2	Pituitary.	B	Under activity of the thyroid.
3	Black pigment.	C	TRF.
4	Gigantism.	D	Adrenalin.
5	Thymosin.	E	Castration.
6	Gull's disease.	F	Cortisone.
7	Diabetes insipidus.	G	Malfunctioning of the thyroid.
8	Hypo secretion of TSH	H	Hyper secretion of GH.
9	Eunuchs.	I	Master gland.
10	Goitre.	J	Hyper secretion of insulin.
11	Hypoglycemia.	K	Mainly appear in women.
12	Cretinism.	L	Thyrotropin.
13	Secretion of thyroxin.	M	Hypo secretion of ADH.7
14	Adrenalin medulla.	N	Production of antibiotics.
15	Adrenalin cortex.	O	Hypo secretion of insulin.

A:Type:[4] Answer & Explanation.

Sl. No	Column A	Sl. No	Column B
1.	Diabetes mellitus.	O	Hypo secretion of insulin.
Expl.	Hypo secretion of insulin increase glucose in the blood.		
2.	Pituitary.	I	Master gland.
Expl.	The pituitary gland controls almost all the endocrine glands.		
3.	Black pigment.	A	Melanin.
Expl.	MSH control skin colour.		

4.	Gigantism.	H	Hyper secretion of GH.
Expl.	GH is a growth hormone.		
5.	Thymosin.	N	Production of antibiotics.
Expl.	Thymosin improves immunity.		
6.	Gull's disease.	K	Mainly appear in women.
7.	Diabetes insipidus.	M	Hypo secretion of ADH.
Expl.	ADH maintaining electrolytic balance.		
8.	Hypo secretion of TSH.	L	Thyrotropin.
9.	Eunuchs.	E	Castration.
Expl.	Removal of the testis.		
10.	Goitre.	B	Under activity of the thyroid.
11.	Hypoglycemia.	J	Hyper secretion of insulin.
12.	Cretinism.	G	Malfunctioning of thyroid.
13.	Secretion of thyroxin.	C	TRF.
14.	Adrenalin medulla.	D	Adrenalin.
15.	Adrenalin cortex.	F	Cortisone.

Q:Type: [5] Write the special functional activities of the followings.

01	Erythropoietin.	07	Iodized salt.
02	Glucocorticoids.	08	Luteinising hormone.
03	Oxytocin.	09	Thymosin.
04	Thyroxin.	10	Prolactin.
05	MSH(Melanocyte stimulating hormone).	11	ICSH.
06	Vasopressin.	12	Somatotropic.

A:Type:[5] Answer & Explanation.

1) **Erythropoietin:** This hormone is secreted by the kidney and this stimulates red blood cells production.

2) **Glucocorticoids:** It hormone regulate carbohydrates, protein and fat metabolism.

3) **Oxytocin:** This hormone caused contraction of the uterus during childbirth and helps to secrets milk in the female breast during lactation.

4) **Thyroxin:** This hormone promotes tissue metabolism, growth and differentiation.

5) **MSH (Melanocyte stimulating hormone):**This hormone control skin colour.

6) **Vasopressin:** This hormone increase absorption of water from the kidney and contraction of blood vessels to raise blood pressure.

7) **Iodized salt:** The iodine part of this salt helps to control the activity of the thyroid gland.

8) **Luteinising hormone:** This hormone helps to stimulate ovulation, the formation of the corpus luteum.

9) **Thymosin:** This hormone helps to produce antibodies and immune response.

10) **Prolactin:** This hormone stimulates milk production and secretion.

11) **ICSH:** This hormone is responsible for the secretion of testosterone hormone.

12) **Somatotropic:** This hormone regulates protein metabolism and growth.

Q:Type: [6] True or false.

1) Thyroxin inhibits tissue metabolism.
2) The growth of Graafian follicles is controlled by luteinizing hormone.
3) ACTH stimulates secretion from the adrenal cortex.
4) Mineralocorticoids regulate the metabolism of carbohydrates, protein and fats.
5) Heart and kidneys also secrete hormones.
6) Alpha cells of the pancreas secrete insulin.
7) The pituitary gland is both exocrine and endocrine in function.
8) The regulation of the secretion of thyroxin from the thyroid gland is an example of a negative feedback mechanism.
9) Pheromones are used as signals by the members of the same species.
10) Testosterone produces female sexual characteristic.
11) Oxytocin is also known as the Birth hormone.
12) Secretion of milk is controlled by FSH.
13) Islet of Langerhans has three types of cells.
14) Homeostasis is our body is achieved by the endocrine system only.
15) The alpha cells of the pancreas secrete insulin.
16) Hyperactivity of the thyroid results in Goitre.
17) Cushing syndrome is characterized by high blood sugar level.
18) Abscisic acid is a growth-promoting hormone.
19) Progesterone regulates menstruation and prepared the uterus to receive the fertilized egg.
20) The removal of testes is called castration.
21) The liver secretes glucagon to increase the glucose level in the blood.
22) The adrenal medulla produces adrenalin.

23) The Colour of the skin is regulated by Melanocyte stimulating hormone.
24) All hormones are protein.
25) The bending of shoots towards sunlight is positive phototropism.

Q:Type: [6] Answer:

1) **[False]**Thyroxin promotes tissue metabolism.

2) **[False]** Growth of Graafian follicles is controlled by Follicle-stimulating hormone.

3) **[True]**ACTH stimulates secretion from the adrenal cortex.

4) **[False]**Glucocorticoids regulate the metabolism of carbohydrates, protein and fats.

5) **[True]** Heart and kidneys also secrete hormones.

6) **[False]** Beta cells of the pancreas secrete insulin.

7) **[False]**The pancreas gland is both exocrine and endocrine in function.

8) **[True]** The regulation of secretion of thyroxin from the thyroid gland is an example of a negative feedback mechanism.

9) **[True]** Pheromones are used as signals by the members of the same species.

10) **[False]** Oestrogen produces female sexual characteristic.

11) **[True]** Oxytocin is also known as the Birth hormone.

12) **[False]** Secretion of milk is controlled by LH.

13) **[True]** Islet of Langerhans has three types of cells.

14) **[False]**Homeostasis in our body is achieved by the endocrine system and the nervous system.

15) **[False]**The alpha cells of the pancreas secretesglucagon.

16) **[False]**Hypo activity of the thyroid results in Goitre.

17) **[True]** Cushing syndrome is characterized by high blood sugar level.

18) **[False]**Abscisic acid is a growth retarding hormone.

19) **[True]** Progesterone regulates menstruation and prepared the uterus to receive the fertilized egg.

20) **[True]** Removal of testes is called castration.

21) **[False]**Pancreas secrete glucagon to increase glucose Meiosis II is called reduction division.

22) **[True]** Adrenal medulla produces adrenalin.

23) **[True]** Color of the skin is regulated by Melanocyte stimulating hormone Nucleolus produces ribosomes.

24) **[False]** Some hormones are protein.

25) **[True]**Bending of shoots towards sunlight is positive phototropism.

Q:Type: [7]Fill in the blanks.

1) Ductless glands are also called __________ glands.
2) __________ salt is one of the best remedies for controlling goitre.
3) Thyroid gland secretes total ______ hormones.
4) __________ hormone secretes from the lowermost point of our body.
5) Endocrine system signal carrying speed is________.
6) Addison's disease is caused due to deficiency of________ hormones.
7) Production of glucose from non carbohydrates is called ______________.
8) Under secretion of somatotropic hormone leads to __________.
9) Hormone secrets by beta cell of pancreas is ____________.
10) The posterior pituitary is actually an outgrowth of the ______________ of brain.
11) Release of other hormone is controlled by________ hormone.
12) Hormone is transported by __________.
13) Gonadotrophins are a combination of ______ hormones.
14) Hormones generally work on the ________feedback control method.
15) Pancreas produces the __________ hormone.
16) Hypo-secretion of________leads to diabetes insipidus.
17) __________ hormone is also known as flight or fight hormone.
18) Overgrowth of adrenal cortex in mature woman leads to______ _________.
19) Pigment our skin is called_________.
20) Gastrointestinal mucosa is an __________ gland in the stomach.
21) ________ gland is called glands of emergency.
22) The chemical factors responsible for plant growth are called ___________.

A :Type: [7] Answers

01.	Endocrine.	**12.**	Blood.
02.	Iodised.	**13.**	Thre.
03.	Two.	**14.**	Negative.
04.	Testosterone.	**15.**	Insulin.
05.	Slow.	**16.**	ADH
06.	Cortical.	**17.**	Adrenalin.
07.	Gluconeogenesis.	**18.**	Adrenal Virilism.
08.	Dwarfism.	**19.**	Melanin.
09.	Glucagon.	**20.**	Endocrine.
10.	Hypothalamus.	**21.**	Adrenal.
11.	Tropic	**22.**	Phytohormones.

Q:Type: [8]Write One difference of pair (on the given parameter).

SL No.	Components	Parameters
01	Insulin & Glucagon	Function.
02	Prolactin & Oxytocin	Function.
03	Insulin & Glucagon	Source.
04	Pituitary gland &Pineal body.	Function.
05	Glucogenesis & Gluconeogenesis.	Function.
06	Goitre& Cretinism	Cause.
07	Nervous system and Endocrine system	Function.
08	Diabetes insipidus & Diabetes Mellitus	Cause.
09	Endocrine and Endocrine gland	Secreted material.
10	Gigantism & Acromegaly.	Time.
11	Auxin & Cytokinin.	Source.

A :Type: [8] Answers

1) **[Function]**Insulin lowers sugar level and glucagon rise sugar level.

2) **[Function]** Prolactin controls secretion of milk after delivery and enlargement of breasts during pregnancy. Oxytocin cause contraction of the uterus during childbirth and helps to secrete milk in female breasts during lactation.

3) **[Source]**Insulin secretes from β-cells of islets of Langerhans and glucagon secretes from α-cells of it.

4) **[Function]**Pituitary gland control the complete endocrine system and the Pineal body helps to secrete melatonin cyclically at night.

5) **[Function]** Glucogenesis process form glucose from carbohydrates and the Gluconeogenesis process form glucose from non-carbohydrates. lipid and protein.

6) **[Cause]**Under activity of the thyroid results in a swelling called goitre in the throat. Cretinism is a disorder in physical and mental growth due to malfunctioning of the thyroid in infants.

7) **[Function]** Nervous system coordinate between the organs through electric impulse and the endocrine gland coordinate different body activities through a chemical signal.

8) **[Cause]** Diabetic insipidus caused due to deficiency of ADH[Antidiuretic hormone] and diabetes mellitus caused due to deficiency of insulin hormone.

9) **[Secreted material]** Endocrine gland secretes hormones and the exocrine gland secretes enzymes.

10) **[Time]** Gigantism occurs in childhood whereas Acromegaly occurs in adults.

11) **[Source]** Auxin are synthesized primarily in shoots.Cytokinin are synthesized primarily in roots.

Q:Type: [9]Choose the correct answer(MCQ).

1. Which of the following hormone is not comes under Gonadotropins?

a)FSH   **b)**LH   **c)**ICSH   **d)**ACTH.

2. Secretion of thyroxin hormone is regulated by

a)Pituitary gland. **b)**Hypothalamus   **c)**Pineal body. **d)**Both (a) and (b)

3.Hypersecretion of the following gland leads to Gigantism

a)Pituitary gland **b)**Thyroid gland. **c)** Adrenal gland. **d)**Thymus.

4.Color of skin is controlled by

a)TSH. **b)**MSH. **c)**FSH. **d)**ACTH.

5.Hormones are basically

a)Proteins. **b)**Steroids. **c)** Amines. **d)** All of the above.

6.Hormones are transported by

a)RBC **b)**Blood. **c)**Duct **d)**All of the above.

7. Name of Luteinizing hormone in the male body is

a)FSH   **b)**ACTH **c)**ICSH **d)**GHIH

8.Which of the following is a local hormone?

a) STH **b)**LH. **c)**ADH. **d)**Thyroxin.

9.Flight or fight hormones are

a)Adrenalin& nor adrenalin **b)**Insulin &Glucagon **c)**Thyroxin & Calcitonin.

d)Oestrogen & Progesterone

10. Insulin is secreted by

a)Beta cells of the pancreas. **b)**Alpha cells of the pancreas. **c)** Delta cells of the pancreas. **d)**none of the above.

A :Type: [9] Answers

01.	**d.** ACTH.	06.	**b.** blood.
02.	**d.** both (a) & (b)	07.	**c.** ICSH.
03.	**a.** Pituitary gland.	08.	**d.** Thyroxin.
04.	**b.** MSH.	09.	**a.** Adrenalin & nor adrenalin.
05.	**d.** All of the above.	10.	**a.** Beta cells of the pancreas.

Q : [10]Fill the blanks according to relation as indicated in the first case.

1. Bull :castration : : Dolly:________.

2. Pituitary: Master gland: :Adrenal: __________.

3. Hormone: Protein/amine: :Enzyme:________.

4. Thyroid: BMR::Thymus:_________.

5. Adrenalin: Emergency hormone: :Oxytocin: ___________.

6. Enzyme: Exocrine::Hormone: _________.

7. Diabetes mellitus: Insulin:: Diabetes insipidus:_________.

8. Testis: local hormone::Pituitary:_________.

9. Gull's disease: Adult human::Cretinism: _________.

10. Hypothyroidism: Goitre::Hyperthyroidism:____________.

A :Type: [10] Answers

1.Bull :castration : : Dolly: **Cloning**.

Exp: Utilizing the cloning process first cloned lamb Dolly was developed.

2. Pituitary: Master gland: :Adrenal: **supra-renal gland**.

3. Hormone: Protein/amine: :Enzyme: protein.

Exp: All enzymes are protein-based.

4. Thyroid: BMR::Thymus: **Immunity**.

Exp: Thymus secretes Thymosin hormone which stimulates the production of antibiotics and immune response.

5. Adrenalin: Emergency hormone: :Oxytocin: **Birth hormone**.

Exp: Oxytocin hormone cause contraction of the uterus during childbirth.

6. Enzyme: Exocrine::Hormone: **Endocrine**.

Exp: Hormones are produced from the ductless gland and so endocrine.

7. Diabetes mellitus: Insulin:: Diabetes insipidus: **ADH.**

Exp: ADU helps to retain water and maintain electrolytic balance.

8. Testis: local hormone::Pituitary: **topic hormone**.

Exp: Tropic hormones are secreted from one place and act in another place that is far away from that gland.

9. Gull's disease: Adult human::Cretinism: **infants**.

Exp: Cretinism observed in infants due to malfunctioning of thyroid.

10. Hypothyroidism: Goiter::Hyperthyroidism: **grave's disease.**

SECTION-II

Question-1.

1. **What will happen if the Thyroid is removed?**
2. **How blood sugar level is controlled by hormones?**
3. **Why some ladies develop a beard, moustache and masculine voice?**
4. **Why some people face the problem of mouth-drying and heartbeat increase during public speaking?**
5. **Differentiate between hormones and enzymes.**

Answer:

1. Due to the removal of the thyroid, hypothyroidism will lead to cretinism, myxodema and goitre.
2. When glucose content in the blood is increased, insulin initiates the deposition of extra glucose in the liver and muscles as glycogen. When glucose content in the blood decreases, glucagon hormone converts glycogen of the liver to glucose and improve glucose content in the blood. This two hormone maintaining blood sugar level.
3. It is mostly due to the hyper secretion of adrenal cortex hormones or cortical hormone. When sex corticoids are secreted in excess in a female, she develops a beard, moustache and masculine voice. This also called adrenal virilism.
4. When some people stand in front of the public crowd, anxiety results in mouth drying and heartbeat increase which leads to stimulation for the secretion of adrenalin. Adrenalin controls the situation.
5. **Difference:**

Hormones	Enzymes
It can be protein, biogenic, amines or steroids.	All enzymes are proteins.
They are used up during metabolism.	They remain unaffected during the reaction.
Rate of action is slow.	Rate of action is fast.
They are produced in the endocrine glands.	They are produced in exocrine glands.

Question-2.

1) **Why Pituitary gland is known as the "Master gland"?**
2) **What will happen if Hypothalamus does not produce neurosecretions?**
3) **What will happen when the Pituitary does not function properly?**
4) **Briefly explain the reason for the following medical practices:**
a. **Thyroxin may be administered to young children who show symptoms of cretinism.**
b. **Patients suffering from diabetes are treated with insulin.**

Answer:

1. The pituitary gland regulates almost all endocrine glands of our body, so it is called the Master gland.
2. The pituitary gland is controlled by the hypothalamus. If the hypothalamus does not produce neurosecretions then ultimately no message will receive by the pituitary gland from the brain and it will either malfunction or stop working which leads to failure of the endocrine system of the body.
3. If the pituitary gland does not function properly then most of the endocrine gland swill malfunction. This will create some disorder or death of a body.
4. **a.** Cretinism is a disorder of infants due to hyposecretion of thyroxin by the thyroid gland. So medical practitioner administered thyroxin hormone to young children to prevent cretinism.
   b. Patients suffering from diabetes having a problem of hyposecretion of insulin hormone which initiates deposition of extra glucose of blood in the liver and muscles as glycogen. To treat diabetes patients insulin is administered.

Question-3.

Name the hormones which lead to the following conditions?
a. Diabetes Mellitus.
b. Growth of beard in women.
c. Myxodema.
d. Gigantism.
e. Exophthalmic goitre.

Answer:

a. Diabetes Mellitus: Hypo secretion of Insulin hormone.
b. Growth of beard in women: Hyper secretion of Sex corticoids hormone.

c. Myxodema: hyposecretion of Thyroxin.
d. Gigantism: Hyper secretion of Growth hormone or STH.
e. Exophthalmic goitre: Hyper secretion of thyroxin.

Question-4.

1) **In the given figure name the organ system shown in the sketch.**
2) **Write one function of each organ system.**
3) **In what manner do the endocrine glands are different from the other gland?**
4) **What condition in the human body may result due to prolonged deficiency of iodine in the food.**

Answer:

1. Name of the organs:
A: Pituitary gland.
B: Pineal body
C: parathyroid gland
D: Thymus gland.
E: Adrenal gland.
F: hypothalamus.
G: Thyroid gland.
H: Pancreas.
I: Ovaries.
J: testis.

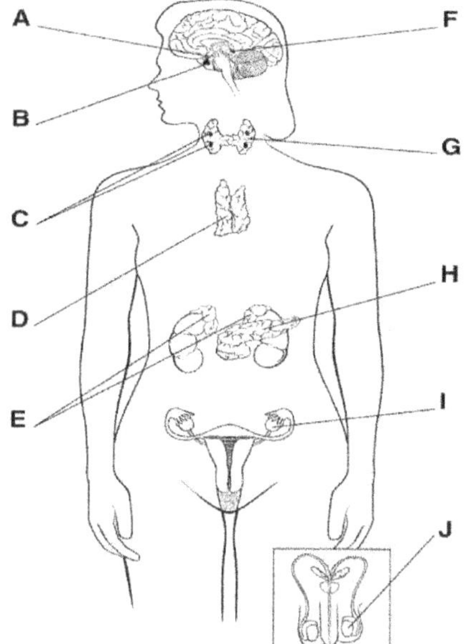

2. Function:
A: *Pituitary gland*: Control all endocrine gland.
B: *Pineal body*: Control melatonin.
C: *parathyroid gland*: Regulates calcium and phosphorus metabolism.
D: *Thymus gland*: Developments of sex glands.
E: *Adrenal gland*: Secretes adrenalin hormone.
F: *hypothalamus*: controlfunctions of pituitary.
G: *Thyroid gland:* secretes thyroxin hormone.
H: *Pancreas:* control blood sugar.
I: *Ovaries:* Egg production and develop secondary sex characteristics.
J: *Testis:* Sperm production and develop secondary sex characteristics.

3. Secretion of endocrine glands is transported through the blood.
4. Prolong iodine deficiency leads to under activity of the thyroid gland and that results in swelling called goitre.

Question-5.

Complete the following table by filling in the blank 1 to 10 with the appropriate terms

GLAND	SECRETION	FUNCTION/EFFECT on BODY
1.	Testosterone.	2.
Adrenal.	3.	4.
5.	6.	Influence of metabolism of cells.
Lachrymal.	7.	8.
9.	Growth Hormone.	10.

Answer:

GLAND	SECRETION	FUNCTION/EFFECT on BODY
1 .**Testis**	Testosterone.	2.**Sperm production and development of masculine features.**
Adrenal.	3.**Adrenalin.**	4.**Act on emergency.**
5.**Thyroid**	6.**Thyroxin.**	Influence of metabolism of cells.
Lachrymal.	7.**Tears.**	8.**Cleaneye.**
9. **Pituitary.**	Growth Hormone.	10. **To develop cell growth.**

Question-6.

Name the hormone responsible for the following functions::

a. **Increase in heartbeat.**
b. **Maintains glucose level in the blood.**
c. **Converting Glycogen to Glucose.**
d. **Regulates basal metabolism.**
e. **Ossification of bones.**
f. **Prepare the body during an emergency.**
g. **Responsible for the normal growth of the whole body.**

Answer:

a. Increase in a heartbeat: **Adrenalin.**
b. Maintains glucose level in the blood: **Insulin.**
c. Converting Glycogen to Glucose: **Glucagon.**
d. Regulates basal metabolism: **Thyroxin.**
e. Ossifiation of bones: **Calcitonin.**
f. Prepare the body during an emergency:**Adrenalin.**
g. Responsible for the normal growth of the whole body: **Growth hormone.**

Question-7.

1) **Name the cells of the Pancreas that produce glucagon and insulin.**
2) **What is the main function of glucagon and insulin?**
3) **Why Pancreas is called an exo-endocrine gland?**
4) **Why is insulin not given orally but injected into the body?**

Answer:

1. Insulin produced from beta cells and glucagon produced from Alpha cells.
2. Glucagon converts glycogen of the liver to glucose and improves blood sugar content. Insulin stimulates cells to take blood for respiration or to store as glycogen to reduce blood sugar.
3. The pancreas gland secretes digestive juices which are the secretions of the exocrine glands and delivered through a duct to the duodenum. This gland also secretes insulin, glucagon etc from the Islets of Langerhans cells. This secretion directly pours into the blood. Therefore pancreas act as an endocrine as well as an exocrine gland and popularly known as the exo-endocrine gland.
4. Insulin is a proteinaceous hormone. If administered orally then it may be broken down in the stomach by the digestive juice during the digestion process. Therefore insulin is injected into the blood directly and not administered orally.

Question-8.

1) **Mention the two difference between endocrine and exocrine glands.**
2) **Why is iodine as a nutrient is important to our body?**
3) **If one adrenal gland is removed and the other one gets enlarged to some extent then how do you explain the change?**

4) **Name the two kinds of diabetes .Mention their symptoms and the causes.**
5) **People living in the low Himalayan hilly regions often suffer from goitre. What could be the possible reason for it?**

Answer:

1. **Difference:**

Endocrine gland	Exocrine gland
It is a ductless gland.	It has ducts.
Secretion transported through the blood.	Secretion transported through a duct.
Secretion secreted at one place and act in another place.	Secretion secreted and act in the same place.
It secretes hormones.	It secretes enzymes.

2. Iodine is an essential element for the development and activity of the thyroid gland.

3. There are two types of diabetes: Diabetes mellitus and Diabetes insipidus.
   Symptom of Diabetes mellitus: High content of glucose in the blood.
   Symptom of Diabetes insipidus: frequent and copious urination and excessive thirst.

   Cause of Diabetes mellitus: hyposecretion of insulin hormone.
   Cause of Diabetes insipidus: hyposecretion of ADH (Antidiuretic hormone].

4. People who live in the high Himalayan region not get sufficient iodine as iodine mainly found in salt from seawater. Insufficient supply of iodine effects on growth of the thyroid gland and its activity. This leads to Goiter.

Question-9.

1) **Compare hormonal response and nervous response with respect t their speed, transmission and the general nature of changes brought about.**
2) **Write in brief about the causes and symptoms of Exophthalmic goiter.**
3) **What is Osteoporosis and what does it cause?**

Answer:

1. **Difference:**

Factor	Hormone	Nerve
Speed	The speed of the signal is slow and the effect is long.	The speed of the signal is rapid but the effect is immediate.
transmission	Hormones are the regulator of chemical signals.	Nerve impulse isanelectrical signal.
Nature of change.	Signal cannot be modified by learning or previous experience.	Signal can be modified by learning or previous experience

2. **Cause:** Over activity of the thyroid gland is the main cause behind Exophthalmic goiter. Symptom: a. Nervousness b. irritability. c. Higher body temperature.
3. Osteoporosis is the disease of bone due to which it become brittle and could fracture due to mild stress or fall of body.
   Bad life style, addiction to smoking, alcohol and lack of Calcitonin effect formation of bone mass.

Question-10.

1) **Write four characteristics of hormones.**
2) **What is the difference between protein hormones and steroid hormones?**
3) **What do you mean by tropic hormones and local hormones?**
4) **Write three basic functions of hormones.**
5) **Briefly explain the feedback control mechanism of the hormone.**

Answer:

1. Characteristics of hormone:
a) Hormones can be amino-acid derivatives, proteins or steroids.
b) Hormones are transported to the target organ by blood.
c) Hormones regulate physiological processes by chemical means.
d) Hormones are produced in very small quantities and they are effective in extremely low concentration.

2. Difference:

Protein Hormone	Steroid hormone
Speed of the signal is slow and effect is long.	Speed of the signal is rapid but effect is immediate.
Hormones are regulator of chemical signals.	Nerve impulse are electrical signal.
Signal cannot be modified by learning or previous experience.	Signal can be modified by learning or previous experience

3. **Tropic hormone:** Tropic hormones are produced from one place and act in another place that is far away from the originating place. Ex; Growth hormone, Thyroid-stimulating Hormone etc.
   Local hormone: These hormones are produced and act at the same place. Example: Oestrogen, Testosterone etc.

4. **Basic functions of hormones:**
a. Hormones control and regulate metabolic activities.
b. Maintain homeostasis.
c. Control and regulates morphogenic activities.
d. transported to the target organ by blood.
e. Hormones regulate physiological processes by chemical means.

g. Hormones are produced in very small quantities and they are effective in extremely low concentration.
5. **Feedback control mechanism:** Feedback control of hormones are mostly negative feedback control. Synthesis of the hormone slows or halt when its level in the blood rises above normal. In positive feedback control, an accumulating hormone increases its production. The regulation of secretion of thyroxin from the thyroid gland and insulin from the pancreas is an example of a negative feedback mechanism.

REPRODUCTIVE SYSTEM.

SECTION-I

Q: Type:[1]Name the followings:

1. When reproduction occurs without the formation of reproductive cells.
2. The kind of development where the young ones do not resemble the adult is called.
3. The dense fibrous coat of testis is called.
4. This cell secretes the male sex hormone testosterone.
5. The thin pouch of skin holding testis is called.
6. This hormone is present in semen.
7. During ejaculation, these muscles control the urinary bladder to prevent the passing of urine.
8. The external female genitalia is called.
9. The homologous part of the oviduct in a male body is.
10. Fusion of male and female gamete produce this.
11. Primary reproductive organ of female.
12. After ovulation, the remaining yellow mass of the follicle is known as.
13. The organelle involved in the formation of the Acrosome of the sperm.
14. This chemical helps in breaking the cell clusters around the mature ovum.
15. Nourishment to sperms provides by these cells.
16. The organ by which the embryo is attached to the wall of the uterus is called.
17. The place where fertilization occurs in the female reproductive system.
18. The mucous membrane lining the uterus.
19. Onset of menstruation in a girl around the age of 13 years is called.
20. Sloughing of the uterine wall during menstrual flow is called.
21. The period of complete intrauterine development of the foetus.
22. Muscular extension of cauda Epididymis.
23. Type of zygote formed after fertilization.
24. Onset of menstruation cycle stopped in a female body.
25. Childbirth in viviparous mammals is called.
26. The pregnancy maintaining hormone is called.
27. Development of an organism from an unfertilized egg is known as.
28. The innermost foetal membrane secretes amniotic fluid.
29. Name the accessory gland in human males whose secretion activates the human sperm.

A:Type:[1]Answer:

1.	Asexual reproduction.	**11.**	Ovaries.	**21.**	Gestation.
2.	Indirect development.	**12.**	Corpus Luteum.	**22.**	Vas deferens.
3.	Tunica albuginea.	**13.**	Golgi apparatus.	**23.**	Diploid cell zygote.
4.	Leydig cells.	**14.**	Sperm lysine.	**24.**	Menopause.
5.	Scrotal sac.	**15.**	Sertoli cells.	**25.**	Parturition.
6.	Prostate glandins.	**16.**	Placenta.	**26.**	Progesterone & Oestrogen.
7.	Sphincter muscles.	**17.**	Fallopian tube.	**27.**	Parthenogenesi
8.	Vulva.	**18.**	Endometrium.	**28.**	Amnion.
9.	Vas deferens.	**19.**	Menarch.	**29.**	Seminal vesicle
10.	Zygote.	**20.**	Menstrual phase.	**30.**	

Q:Type:[2]State the exact locations:

1	**Placenta.**	2	**Birtholin's.**	3	**Graafian follicle.**
4	**Amnion.**	5	**Hymen.**	6	**Prostate gland.**
7	**Fallopian tube.**	8	**Infundibulum.**	9	**Cowper's gland.**

A:Type:[2]Answer:

1) **Placenta**:Muscular wall of the uterus.
2) **Birtholin's**: each side of the vaginal orifice.
3) **Graafian follicle**:Ovary.
4) **Amnion**:Developed around the embryo.
5) **Hymen**: Oat the opening of the vagina.
6) **Prostate gland**:Close to the bladder surrounding the Urethra.

7) **Fallopian tube**: Connected with Uterus.

8) **Infundibulum**: Connected with the ovary.

9) **Cowper's gland**: Opening into the urethra just before enters the penis.

Q:Type:[3]Find odd terms:

1. Estrogen; Progesterone; testosterone; Prolactin.
2. Ovary; Fallopian tube; Ureter; Uterus.
3. Corpus luteum; antrum; follicle; Sertoli cells.
4. Relaxin; Cervix dilates; Amniotic sac ruptures; Childbirth, Follicle.
5. Scrotal sacs; Vasa efferentia; Cowper's glands; Endometrium; Leydig cells.
6. Bartholin's; Cervix ;hymen ;vulva.
7. Ovulation; Capacitation; Menstruation; Luteal phase.
8. Placenta ;Chorion ;Epididymis ; Allantois.
9. The fallopian tube, Vasdeferens, Uterus, Vagina

A:Type:[3]Answer:

1. Estrogen; Progesterone; testosterone; **Prolactin.**
Explanation: First three hormones help to develop gamete but Prolactin helps to rear a child.

2. Ovary; Fallopian tube; **Urete**r; Uterus.
Explanation: Ureter is a part of an excretory system but others are part of the reproductive system.

3. Corpus luteum; antrum; follicle; **Sertoli cells.**
Explanation: Sertoli cells are part of the Male reproductive system which helps to nourish sperm.

4. Relaxing; Cervix dilates; Amniotic sac ruptures; Childbirth,**Follicle.**
Explanation: All are related to the uterus and the follicle is related to the ovary.

5. Scrotal sacs;Vasa efferentia; Cowper's glands; **Endometrium**; Leydig cells.
Explanation: Endometrium is related to the uterus but all others are related to the male reproductive system.

6. Bartholin's ;**Cervix**; hymen ;vulva.
Explanation: Cervix is a part of the Uterus but all others are part of the vagina.

7. Ovulation; **Capacitation**; Menstruation;Luteal phase.

Explanation: Capacitation is related to changes occurring in sperms but all others are related to ova.

8. Placenta ;Chorion ;**Epididymis**; Allantois.

Explanation: Epididymis is related to male testes but the remaining are related to the placenta.

9. Fallopian tube, **Vasdeferens**, Uterus, Vagina

Explanation: Other than Vasdeferens all are parts of the female reproductive system.

Q:Type:[4] match the column.

Sl. No	Column A	Sl. No	Column B
1	Uterus.	A	28 days.
2	External female genital.	B	Sperm.
3	Gastrulation.	C	Produced from one egg.
4	Testes.	D	14 days.
5	Ampulla.	E	Young one resembles adults.
6	Corpus luteum.	F	Infundibulum.
7	Amnion.	G	Formation of germ layers.
8	Graafian follicle.	H	Vulva.
9	Direct development.	I	Implantation.
10	Luteal phase.	J	Equivalence of penis.
11	Cowper's gland.	K	Progesterone.
12	Acrosome.	L	Scrotal sac.
13	Menstrual cycle.	M	A sac protecting the embryo.
14	Siamese twins.	N	Maturing egg.
15	Clitoris.	O	Secretion of lubricant during copulation.

A:Type:[4]Answer & Explanation:

Sl. No	Column A	Sl. No	Column B
1.	Uterus.	I	Implantation.
Expl.	Implantation is the attachment of the blastocyst to the uterine wall of the Uterus.		
2.	External female genital.	H	Vulva

Sl. No	Column A	Sl. No	Column B
Expl.	External female genitalia is called Vulva.		
3.	Gastrulation.	G	Formation of germ layers
Expl.	It is the movement of cells to form germ layers.		
4.	Testes.	L	Scrotal sac
Expl.	Testes are suspended in the scrotal sac.		
5.	Ampulla.	F	Infundibulum.
Expl.	Infundibulum is the part of the fallopian tube before Ampulla towards the ovary.		
6.	Corpus luteum.	K	Progesterone.
Expl.	Progesterone is producing by the Corpus luteum.		
7.	Amnion.	M	A sac protecting the embryo.
Expl.	Amnion is filled with amniotic fluid, provide cushion for the embryo and protect it.		
8.	Graafian follicle.	N	Maturing egg.
Expl.	Maturing egg is present inside the Graafian follicle.		
9.	Direct development	E	Young one resembles adults.
Expl.	Development where a young one resembles adults is called direct development.		
10.	Luteal phase.	D	14 days.
Expl.	The luteal phase required 14 days to thickens the uterus lining.		
11.	Cowper's gland.	O	Secretion of lubricant during copulation.
Expl.	Cowper's gland opening into the urethra to secret lubricating sap.		
12.	Acrosome.	B	Sperm.
Expl.	Acrosome release lysine to break cell clusters around the mature ovum.		
13.	Menstrual cycle.	A	28 days.
Expl.	The menstrual cycle generally stayed 28-31 days.		
14.	Siamese twins.	C	Produced from one egg.
Expl.	Siamese twins are produced from one egg and inseparable.		
15.	Clitoris.	J	Equivalence of penis.
Expl.	The clitoris is a small erectile tissue like a male penis.		

Q:Type: [5] Write the special functional activities of the followings.

1	Infundibulu m.	2	Placenta (as an endocrine organ).	3	Tunica albuginea.
4	Bartholin's.	5	Nurse cells.	6	Acrosome in sperm.
7	Corpus luteum.	8	Amnion.	9	Sphincter muscles.
10	Penis.	11	Secretory phase.	12	Leydig cells.

A:Type:[5] Answer:

1) **Infundibulum:** Receives eggs when released.

2) **Placenta (as an endocrine organ):** Secretes Oestrogen and Progesterone during the last six month of pregnancy.

3) **Tunica albuginea:** Enclose testes in a dense fibrous coat.

4) **Bartholin's:** Secrete lubricant during copulation.

5) **Nurse cells:** Also known as Sertoli from which sperm gets nutrients.

6) **Acrosome in sperm:** Helps the sperm to penetrate the egg cells by secreting sperm Lysin enzyme.

7) **Corpus luteum:** When pregnancy occurred the corpus luteum persists to maintain pregnancy.

8) **Amnion:** This fluid act as a cushion for the embryo and protects it from jerks.

9) **Sphincter muscles:** During ejaculation, the sphincter muscles at the base of the urinary bladder are tightened to ensure the only semen is ejaculated.

10) **Penis:** Its act as a copulatory organ used for discharging semen into the female vagina.

11) **Secretory phase:** secretes nutrients in preparation for implantation.

12) **Leydig cells:** It secretes sex hormone Testosterone into the blood.

Q:Type: [6] True or false:

1) Reproduction is only a biological necessity of human beings.
2) Spermatogenesis takes place in semniferous tubules.
3) Copulation is the process of fusing male and female gamete.
4) Testes temperature is equal to human body temperature.

5) Vasa efferentia conduct the spermatids into the Epididymis.
6) The endometrium is rich in tubular glands.
7) The fallopian tube is differentiated into five parts.
8) Ampulla receives eggs from the ovary.
9) Corpus luteum starts producing estrogen onset of pregnancy.
10) Semen is acidic due to presence of ascorbic acid.
11) Semen contains prostate glandins hormone.
12) Fructose provides energy to the spermatozoa for swimming.
13) Cowper's gland pours an alkaline secretion into the semen.
14) Cyclic changes occur in the structure of the Uterus.
15) The onset of menstruation in a young female body is called menopause.
16) Gestation period of a human female is about 280 days.
17) Siamese twins could be formed from one egg fertilized by two sperm.
18) The clitoris of a female is an equivalent part of a male penis.
19) Leydig cells secret the male sex hormone testosterone.
20) The yolk sac functions as a site of blood cell formation until 3rd week.
21) Amniotic fluid acts as a shock absorber.

A:Type:[6] Answer:

1) **[False]**Reproduction is also necessary for the survival and continuation of the species.
2) **[True]** Spermatogenesis takes place in seminiferous tubules.
3) **[False]**Fertilisation is the process of fusing male and female gamete.
4) **[False]**Testes temperature 2°C lower than human body temperature.
5) **[True]** Vasa efferentia conduct the spermatids into the Epididymis.
6) **[True]** Endometrium is rich in tubular glands.
7) **[False]**Fallopian tube is differentiated into four parts.
8) **[False]** Ostium receives eggs from the ovary.
9) **[False]**Corpus luteum starts producing Progesterone onset of pregnancy.
10) **[False]**Semen is alkaline.
11) **[True]** Semen contains prostate glandins hormone.
12) **[True]**Fructose provides energy to the spermatozoa for swimming.
13) **[False]**Cowper's gland produces lubricating sap during intercourse.
14) **[True]**Cyclic changes occur in the structure of the Uterus.
15) **[False]**The onset of menstruation in a young female body is called Menarch.
16) **[True]**Gestation period of a human female is about 280 days.
17) **[False]**Siamese twins could be formed when conjugate twins produced from a single egg & failed to separate.
18) **[True]**Clitoris of a female is an equivalent part of a male penis.
19) **[True]**Leydig cells secret the male sex hormone testosterone.

20) **[False]**Yolk sac function as a site of blood cell formation until 6th week.
21) **[True]** Amniotic fluid acts as a shock absorber.

Q:Type: [7] Fill in the blanks.:

1) Mesovarium helps to fixed __________ to the abdominal wall.
2) Cervix opens into the _________.
3) After 6th week ____________ function as the site of blood cell formation for embryo.
4) ___________ acts as an excretory organ for embryo.
5) High blood pressure of mother could rupture ____________ of embryo.
6) The villi which absorb nutrients and grow into the surrounding uterine tissue are developed from___________.
7) For cattle breed, _______ insemination is generally used.
8) The development of an organism from an unfertilized egg is called ___________.
9) Longest Gestation period observed with _____________ elephant.
10) Sperm ability to fertilize the ovum is called _________.
11) _________ helps in breaking the cell clusters around the mature ovum by sperm.
12) Sertoli cells give nourishment to __________.
13) Opening of the vagina is closed by_________.
14) __________ provide energy to the spermatozoa for swimming.
15) Ampulla is a part of ____________ .
16) _____________ ____________ pours an alkaline secretion into the semen.
17) Sperm may swim inside the uterus at a speed of _______ m/min.
18) Male sex hormones secrete by ________ cells.
19) After the rupture of Graafian follicle, ovum released on ________ day.
20) Cells of follicle produce __________ .
21) The duct which leads from the Epididymis to the urethra is the ___________.
22) The embryo inside the uterus is protected from mechanical injury by the _________ fluid.

A:Type:[7] Answer:

01	Ovary.	09	Asiatic.	17	1-54
02	Vagina.	10	Capacitation.	18	Leydig
03	Liver.	11	Lysin.	19	14th
04	Placenta.	12	Sperms.	20	Oestrogen.
05	Placenta.	13	Hymen.	21	Vasdeferens.

06	Chorion.	14	Fructose.	22	Amniotic.
07	Artificial.	15	Oviduct.		
08	Parthenogenesis.	16	Prostate gland.		

Q: Type: [8]Write One difference of pair (on the given parameter).

SL No	Components	Parameters
01	Identical & Fraternal twins.	**Process.**
02	Luteal phase & Follicular phase.	**Function.**
03	Lysin & Amniotic fluid.	**Function.**
04	Cowper's gland & Bartholin's gland.	**Location.**
05	Spermatogenesis & Parthenogenesis	**Process.**
06	Scrotum & Fundus	**Location.**
07	Urethra & Uterus.	**Purpose.**
08	Infundibulum & Isthmus	**Structure.**
09	Myometrium & Vagina	**Appearance.**
10	Siamese twins & Identical twins	**Process.**
11.	Corpus callosum & corpus luteum.	**Structure.**

A:Type:[8] Answer:

1) **[Process]**When two eggs one from each ovary released simultaneously and both are fertilized then Fraternal twins occurs but Siamese twins produced when twins produced from the same egg failed to separate.

2) **[Function]** During the Luteal phase emptied follicle turns into the corpus luteum which produces progesterone that influences the thickening of the Uterus and during the Follicular phase follicle matures and oestrogen secretes.

3) **[Function]**Lysin help in breaking the cell clusters around the mature ovum and Amniotic fluid act as a cushion for the embryo to protect it from jerks.

4) **[Location]**Cowper's glands located into the urethra just before it enters the penis and Bartholin's presence on each side of the vaginal orifice.

5) **[Process]** Spermatogenesis is the process of transformation if spermatgonia into spermatozoa and parthenogenesis are the development of the organism from an unfertilized egg.

6) **[Location]**Scrotum present outside the abdomen and behind the penis whereas Fundus is the dome-shaped expanded part of the fallopian tube.

7) **[Purpose]** Urethra use to urinate and transferring semen in the vagina for the male body but in the female body, it only helps to urinate whereas the uterus receives ovum, from the placenta and finally after complete development of the foetus it expels the young one at birth.

8) **[Structure]** Infundibulum hasa broad funnel-shaped structure and Isthmus is a narrow, thick-walled straight part that follows Ampulla.

9) **[Structure]** Myometrium have smooth muscle and the vagina have transverse folds.

10) **[Process]** Siamese twins and identical twins both are produced from the same egg but Siamese twins failed to separate.

11) **[Structure]** Corpus callosum is a sheet of fibers connecting the two cerebral hemispheres whereas the corpus luteum is a yellow mass formed after the release of matured ovum during ovulation.

Q: Type: [9] Choose the correct answer.

1.Sperm mature in the

a)Testes **b)** Epididymis. **c)**Vas deference. **d)**Cowper's gland

2. Parturition is the process of

a) Giving childbirth by viviparous mammals. **b)** movement of cells to form germ cells. **c)** Blood discharge due to breakdown of the uterus lining.
d) Development of an organism from an unfertilized egg.

3. Gestation period is the

a)Onset of the menstrual cycle.**b)** Period between Ovulation and implantation.**c)**The period for which a female remains sexually active. **d)** Period during which the foetus remains in the uterus.

4. Acrosome helps the sperm to

a) Locate the ovum. **b)** Swim to the ovum.**c)** Penetrate the ovum**d)**All of the above.

5.Cowper's gland secretes a substance to

a)Provide nourishment to sperms.**b)** Serve as a lubricant**c)** Help the sperm in penetrating the ovum. **d)**Help sperms to swim inside the uterus.

6. Menarch start around the age of

a)10**b)**12**c)** 13**d)** 18

7. The onset of menstruation in the female is named as

a)Menopause **b)**Menarche **c)**Ovulation **d)** parthenogenesis.

8. Follicular phase also known as

a) Ovulatory phase. **b)** Luteal phase. **c)** Menstruation. **d)** Proliferative phase.

9. Implantation is

a) Attachment of the blastocyst to the uterine wall **b)** Release of an ovum from the follicle **c)** Development of an embryo without fertilization. **d)** Formation of ova from germ cells.

10. Placenta acts as a

a) Nutritive organ to feed the foetus.**b)** Respiratory organ. **c)** Excretory organ. **d)**All of the above.

A:Type:[9] Answer:

01	**b.** Epididymis.	06	**c.** 13.
02	**a.**Giving childbirth by viviparous mammals.	07	**b.** Menarche.
03	**d.** Period during which foetus remains in the uterus.	08	**d.** Proliferative phase.
04	**c.** Penetrate the ovum.	09	**a.** Attachment of the blastocyst to the uterine wall.
05	**b.** Serve as a lubricant.	10	**d.** All of the above.

Q:Type: [10]Fill the blanks according to relation as indicated in the first case

1.Luteal phase : 14 days : : Ovulatory phase :______.
2.Lysin :Acrosome: : testosterone: ________.
3.Areola: Mammary gland: : Clitoris:______.
4.Ovaries: Testes:: Scrotum:________.
5.Menstrual cycle: 28-29 days: : Gestation period: _________.
6. Penis :Cowper's glands::Vagina: ________.
7.Oviduct: 10-12 cm::Ovary :________.
8.Umbilical cord: Blood vessels: Vasa efferentia:________.
9.Identical twins: Single ovum:: Fraternal twins: ________.
10. Fundus: Dome shape:: Infundibulum:___________.

A:Type:[10] Answer & Explanation:

1. Luteal phase : 14 days : : Ovulatory phase :**1**

Exp: Ovulatory phase of a female menstrual cycle is 1 day.

2. Lysin: Acrosome: : testosterone: **Leydig cells**

Exp: Leydig cells release testosterone into the blood.

3. Areola: Mammary gland: : Clitoris: **Vulva.**

Exp: in front of the urethral opening of the Vulva a small erectile tissue is present in a female body is called Clitoris.

4. Testes: Ovaries:: Scrotum: **Labia majora**

Exp: Ovaries is homologous to the male reproductive system Testes and similarly Labia majora is homologous to the male reproductive system Scrotum.

5. Menstrual cycle: 28-29 days: : Gestation period: **280 days.**

Exp: The gestation period of a human being is 280 days and the general menstrual cycle is 28-29 days.

6. Penis: Cowper's glands::Vagina: **Bartholin's gland**

Exp: Cowper's gland and Bartholin's glands help to lubricate the penis and vagina respectively.

7. Oviduct: 10-12 cm:: Ovary:3**-4 cm.**
Exp: Size of the ovary is 3-4 cm.

8. Umbilical cord: Blood vessels: Vasa efferentia:**spermatids**

Exp: Spermatids flows through Vas Efferentia.

9. Identical twins: Single ovum:: Fraternal twins:**Double ovum.**

Exp: Fraternal twins produce when two Ovum of Uterus are fertilized simultaneously.

10. Fundus: Dome shape:: Infundibulum: **Funnel shape.**

Exp: Infundibulum is a funnel-shaped part of the oviduct to collect Ovum.

SECTION-II

Question-1:

1. **Ova is not motile then how Zygote propelled towards the uterus?**
2. **Write these phases of the menstrual cycle in the proper sequence:**

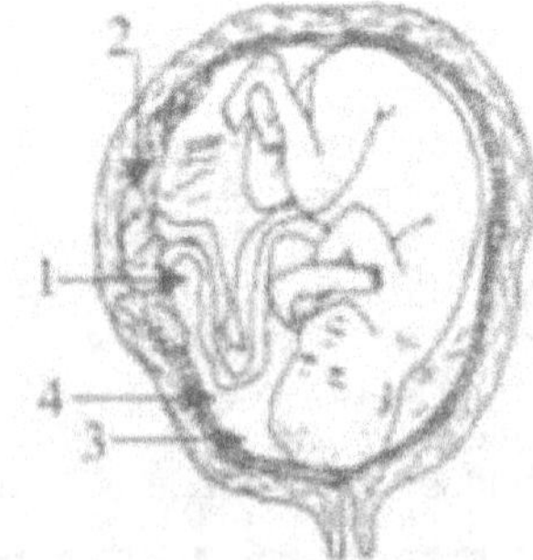

Luteal phase, Menstrual phase Follicular phase, Ovulatory phase.

3. **The given figure represents the human foetus in the uterus.**

a) **Level the parts 1 to 4.**
b) **State the functions of part 2 and 3.**
c) **Explain briefly the process of respiration of the embryo.**

Answer:

1. The tiny hair-like cilia lining of the fallopian tube propelled the fertilised ovum.

2. Menstrual phase →Follicular phase → Ovulatory phase →Luteal phase.

3. **a.** 1: Umbilical cord. 2: Chorion 3: Amnion 4: Amniotic fluid.

b. **Chorion**: It develops will which grows into the surrounding uterine tissue from which they absorb nutrients.
Amnion: It holds the amniotic fluid which acts as a cushion for the embryo and protects it from jerks.

c. Respiration of an embryo: There are two parts of the umbilical cord.Umbilical artery and Umbilical vein. CO_2 and other waste products from embryo transfer to the placenta through the Umbilical vein.This wasted and CO_2 then goes to mother body through the Uterine vein. From mother body O_2 and food, nutrients come to placenta through Uterine artery. Afterwards,the placenta delivers it to the embryo through the umbilical artery. The placenta acts as an interconnecting media between the vein and artery.

Question-2:

Give the biological/technical terms for the followings

1) A structure that connects the placenta with the foetus.
2) The onset of menstruation in a young girl.
3) The process of giving birth to a baby.
4) Cessation of menstruation in females.
5) Membrane that protects the foetus and secretes a

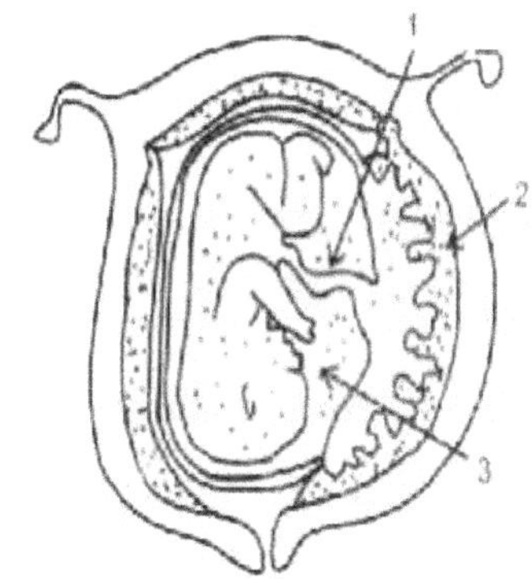

protective fluid.

Answer:

1) Umbilical cord.
2) Menarch.
3) Parturition.
4) Menopause.
5) Embryonic membranes.

Question-3:

Given below is the diagram of a developing human foetus in the womb. Study the same and answer

1) **Name the part labelled 1.**
2) **Mention any two functions of the part labelled 2.**
3) **Explain the role played by the part labelled 3.**
4) **What is the normal gestation period (in days) of the developing foetus?**
5) **What is the role of the umbilical cord in the development of the foetus?**

Answer:

1. Umbilical cord.
2. Chorion:
   1. Develop villi.
   2. Absorb nutrients.
3. Amniotic fluid: **a**. Act as a cushion for the embryo and protects it from jerks. **b**. Prevents sticking of the foetus to the amnion.
4. 280 days.
5. Umbilical cord: It is also called a supply line of the baby which carries the blood of the baby back and forth between the baby and placenta. It delivers nutrients and oxygen to the baby and removes waste and CO_2 from the baby.

Question-4:

The figure shows the male urinogenital system in mammals.Observe the diagram and answer the following.

a. **Level the parts 1 to 5. Write their function.**
b. **Where are the seminiferous tubules located?**
c. **In which tissue does the sperm mature?**

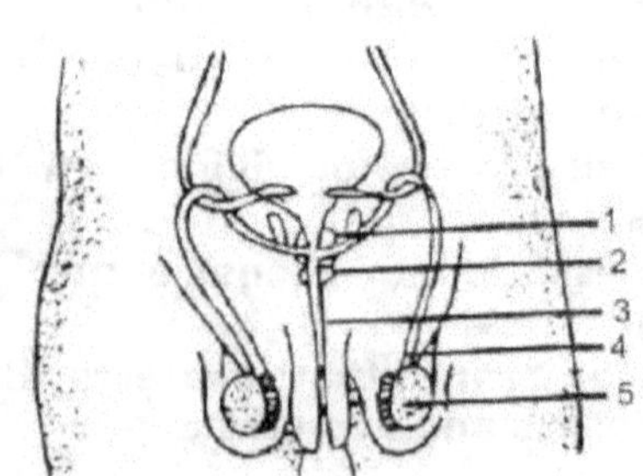

d. How does the sperm be different from an ovum?

Answer:

a) **Labelare:**

1:Prostate gland: Prostate gland pours an alkaline secretion into the semen which neutralisedthe acid in women vagina.

2:Coupers gland: secretes lubricant during copulation.

3:Urethra:Its acts as a passage for transferring sperm from male to female vagina during intercourse.

4:Sperm duct: It transfers sperms from the epididymis to the urethra.

5:Testis: It produces semen.

b) Seminiferous tubules are located inside the testis.

c) Leydig cells or interstitial cells.

d) Sperm is motile and Ovum is stationary.

Question-5:

In the given figure below represents a technique

a. Name the process.
b. Name the fluid being taken out through the syringe.
c. How is this process helpful.
d. How is it misused?
e. Level the parts 1 to 4.

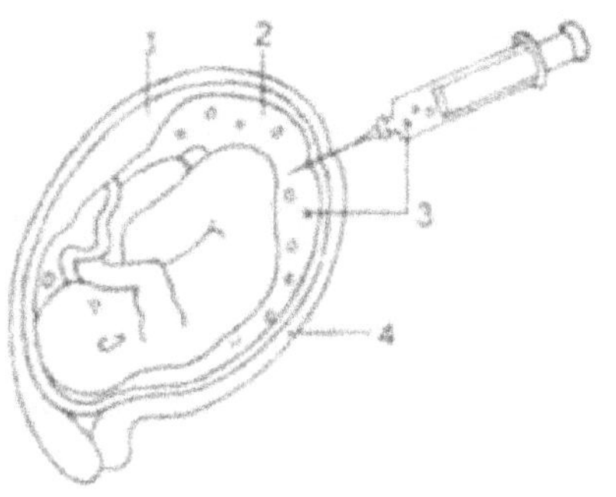

Answer:

a) Amniocentesis.
b) Amniotic fluid.
c) This process helps to analyse the genetic disorder of the foetus.
d) It is misused to establish the sex of a foetus.
e) Lebel: 1. Placenta. 2.Amniotic sac. 3. Amniotic fluid. 4.Uterus.

Question-6:

Given below is a diagram which represents the human male reproductive system and its various parts.

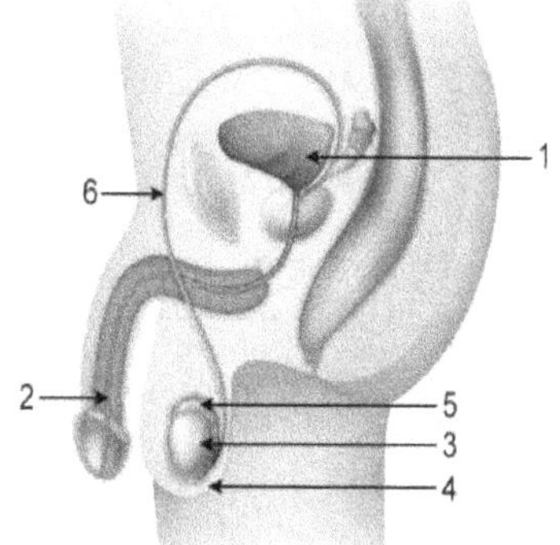

a. **Name the parts labelled 1-6.**
b. **Mention one functional difference of parts labelled 3 & 4.**
c. **Name the three accessory glands of the human male reproductive system.**

Answer:

a. **Label: 1:** Urenary bladder. **2.** Urethra. 3. Testis. 4. Scrotum. 5.Epididymis. 6. Vas deference.
b. **3.** testis: to produce sperms.
4. Scrotum: Protectioonof testis and to maintain suitable temperature to produce sperms.

c. Three accessory glands of the human male reproductive systems are Seminal vesicles, Prostate glands and Cowper's gland.

Question-7:

The diagram given alongside is that of a developing human foetus in the uterus. Study the same and answer the questions below.

a. **Name the parts labelled 1-5.**
b. **What term is given to the period of development of the foetus in the womb.**
c. **How many days does the foetus normally take to fully develop?**
d. **Mention two functions of the part labelled 2 other than its endocrine function.**
e. **Name the hormone produced by the part labelled 2.**

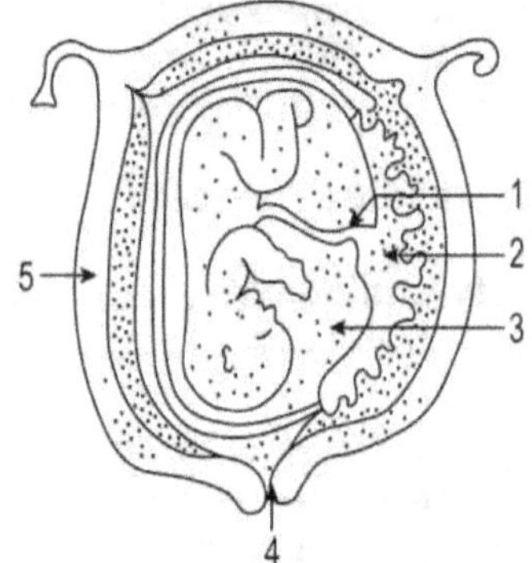

Answer:

a. **Label: 1.**Umbilical cord. **2.** Placenta. **3.** Amniotic fluid. **4.** Mouth of uterus. **5.** Uterus wall.
b. Gestation period.
c. In human gestation period is about 280 days.
d. Placenta acts as a digestive organ as its digest the complex protein before allowing them to pass to the foetus.
e. Part labelled as 2 secretes Oestrogen and progestrone.

Question-8:

Define the followings:

1) Artificial insemination.

2) **Capacitation.**
3) **Placenta.**
4) **Ovulation.**
5) **Corpus luteum.**

Answer:

1. **Artificial insemination:** By artificial means when sperms are transferred to female body and egg fertilized is called artificial insemination. It is done in three stages. Mainly carried out for cattle breed. First good quality semen of good breeds are collected and then stored carefully. During ovulation those semen transfer into the vagina of the female.

2. **Capacitation:** The changes occurring in mammalian sperm that enables it to fertilize the ovum is known as Capacitation.

3. **Placenta:** The organ by which the embryo is attached to the wall of the uterus is called placenta.

4. **Ovulation:** Ovulation is a process of releasing egg from ovary and send it to fallopian tube for fertilization.

5. **Corpus luteum:** After ovulation the remaining yellow mass of follicle is known as corpus luteum. Oestrogen is secreted by this.

Question-9:

Given below is a diagram of the lateral section of the testis of man. Study the diagram and answer the questions given below.

Label the parts 1-4.

1) **State the functions of the parts labeled 1 and 3.**
2) **What is the significance of the testes being located in the scrotal sac outside the abdomen?**
3) **What is the role played by the inguinal canal?**
4) **What is semen?**

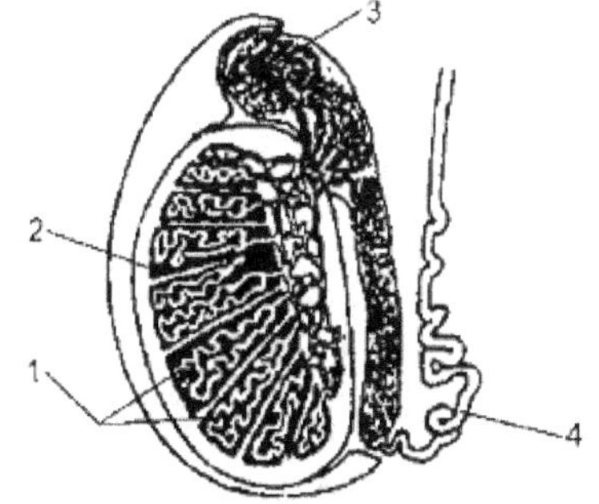

Answer:

1. **Labels are** 1. Semniferous tubules. 2. Segment or lobule 3. Epididymis. 4. Vas deferens.

2. **1.Seminiferous tubule:** By the process of spermatogenesis sperms are produced here.

3. **Epididymis:** It stores sperms for some time for maturation and make them become functional spermatozoa.

4. Production of spermatozoa required a temperature that is lower than the normal body temperature. Testis is situated inside a scrotal sac and sac outside surface area is more due to its specific surface structure.This is located outside the body so that air could esily cool the testis and maintain 2-3 deg c less temperature than body.

5. It allows the descent of testis along with their ducts , blood vessels and nerves.

6. Semen: it is the mixture of sperm, secretion of seminal vesicles, cowper's gland and prostate glands.

Question-10:

a. **Choose the odd one in each of the following with justification:**

1) **Oestrogen; Progesterone; Testosterone; Prolactin.**

2) **Ovary; Fallopian tube; Ureter; Uterus.**

3) **Relaxin; Cervix dilates; Amniotic sac ruptures; Childbirth; Follicle.**

4) **Corpus luteum; antrum; follicle; sertoli cells.**

b. **Briefly explain structure of sperm.**

Answer:

1) **Oestrogen; Progesterone; Testosterone; Prolactin.**

Odd: testosterone. Its helps to produce sperm in male body and all others are mainly found in female body.

2) **Ovary ; Fallopian tube; Ureter ; Uterus.**

Odd: Ureter is a part of excretory system of male. All others are parts of female reproductive system.

3) **Relaxin ; Cervix dilates ; Amniotic sac ruptures; Childbirth ; Follicle.**

Odd: All are related to child birth process except follicle which is related to ovulation.

4) **Corpus luteum ; antrum ;follicle ; Sertoli cells.**

Odd: Sertoli cells. Its related to nourishment of sperms and all others are to maturation of ova.

c. **Structure of sperm**: A sperm is consists of three parts and they are head, middle piece and tail. The head contains haploid chromosomal nucleus and a modified Golgi body and Acrosome. The Acrosome helps sperm to penetrate egg cells by secretion of Lysin enzyme. The middle piece contains mitochondria to provide energy to sperm. The tail helps to swim inside uterus and fallopian tube to reach at egg.

Question-11:

1. **Enumerate the steps involved during fertilization of an ovum by a sperm.**

2. Although the embryo depends on the mother blood for its nutrition and supply of Oxygen, its circulatory system is never directly connected with the maternal blood vessels. What will be the effect on the embryo if its circulatory system is directly connected with the maternal blood vessels.

3. What are secondary sexual characters?

4. What are accessory glands in reproductive system?

Answer:

1. **Step-1:** After copulation and coitus semens are ejaculated by the penis inside the vaina at the mouth of the uterus.

   Step 2: Spermas are swim towards the fallopian tube and reach at egg that is waiting for fertilisation after ovulation.

   Step 3: Sperms are trying to penetrate egg cell outer membrane with the help of acrosome by the help of lysin enzyme.

   Step 4: Once any one spem succeed to penetrate the egg cell , the egg membrane gradually dissolves and sperm nucleus and cytoplasm get entry.

   Step 5: Following the chemical signal evoked by the egg surface incapacitationg other sperms in the vacinity of egg. Now fertilized egg implant shortly in the uterus.

2. **If the circulatory system is directly connected with mother blood then following problem will occur:**
   The placenta acts as an exchange surface between the mother and the fetus. Nutrients and oxygen are passed over by diffusion process. This also used to throw away waste from fetus through mother body. If the mother and fetus are of different blood group and if the mother's and fetus's blood mixed, it could be deadly for both of them and could die.

3. **The secondary sexual characteristics are:**
   1. Change in voice.
   2. Appearance of pubic hair.
   3. Appearance of beard.
   4. Development of breast.

4. **Accessory glands are those glands which are indirectly helps in sexual reproduction in human body. The glands are**
   1. Cowper's gland.   2. Bartholin's.   3. Mamary glands.
   4. Prostate glands.   5. Seminal vesicles.

POPULATION & RELATED PROBLEMS IN INDIA.

SECTION-I

Q:Type: [1] Name the followings.

1. Number of individuals per unit area is called.
2. The process by which fallopian tubes are ligated.
3. By this process, Vas deference is ligated and a small piece between the two ligatures is removed.
4. Average number of children per unit time.
5. Prenatal diagnosis of a foetus is termed as this.
6. The number of death per 1000 individuals in the population per year.
7. The factors which check population growth are called.
8. About 56% of the world population lives on this continent.
9. The statistical study of the human population of a region.
10. The physiological capacity to produce offspring is known as.

A:Type:[1] Answer:

01.	Population density.	6.	Death rate.
02.	Tubectomy.	7.	Environmental resistance.
03.	Vasectomy.	8.	Asia.
04.	Birth rate.	9.	Demography.
05.	Amniocentesis.	10.	Biotic potential.

Q:Type: [2] Find odd one:

1. Copper-T; Diaphragm; Femidom; Condom.

2. Test tube babies; Surrogate mother;tubectomy; Artificial insemination.

3. Natality; Cervix; Mortality; Biotic potential.

4. IUCD; Vasectomy; test-tube babies; tubectomy.

5. ASHA workers; NGOs; Mary stops; Astha.

A:Type:[2] Answer:

1. Condom.

Explanation: All other female contraceptives.

2. Tubectomy.

Explanation: tubectomy is related to birth control.

3. Cervix.

Explanation: cervix related to female reproductive organ and others are related to demographic science.

4. Vasectomy.

Explanation: Vasectomy is related to the birth control of male.

5. Astha.

Explanation: Astha is an NGO to educate people regarding population control.

Q:Type: [3] match the column:

Sl No.	Column A	Sl no.	Column B
01.	Census.	A	Copper-T.
02.	Mini-pill.	B	Capacity to produce offspring.
03.	Natality.	C	Prenatal diagnosis of foetus.
04.	IUCD.	D	Asia.
05.	Tubectomy.	E	Arithmetic progression.
06.	Amniocentesis.	F	Vagina.
07.	Combined pill.	G	Geometric progression.
08.	Biotic potential.	H	Laparoscope.
09.	Food production.	I	Total count of individuals in an area.
10.	Diaphragm.	J	Oestrogen & progesterone.
11.	Femidom.	K	Progesterone.
12.	Most populated continent.	L	Kerala.
13.	Most populated state(India).	M	Cervix.

A:Type:[3] Answer:

Sl. No	Column A	Sl. No	Column B
1.	Census.	I	Total count of individuals in an area.
Expl.	Census is the method to count individuals in an area.		
2.	Mini-pill.	K	Progesterone.
Expl.	Mini-pill only contains one hormone.		
3.	Natality.	G	Geometric progression.
Expl.	Natality is Birth rate.		
4.	IUCD.	A	Copper-T.

Sl. No	Column A	Sl. No	Column B
5.	Tubectomy.	H	Laparoscope.
Expl.	Tubectomy is performed with a laparoscope.		
6.	Amniocentesis.	C	Prenatal diagnosis of foetus.
Expl.	Process of withdrawing fluid from the amniotic sac.		
7.	Combined pill.	J	Oestrogen & progesterone.
Expl.	A combination pill is a combination of two hormones.		
8.	Biotic potential.	B	Capacity to produce offspring.
Expl.	The biotic potential is the physiological capacity to produce offspring.		
9.	Food production.	E	Arithmetic progression.
10.	Diaphragm.	M	Cervix.
Expl.	Diaphragm placed on the cervix.		
11.	Femidom.	F	Vagina.
Expl.	Femidom is a female condom & placed inside the vagina.		
12.	Most populated continent.	D	Asia.
13	Most populated state(India)	L	Kerala.

Q:Type: [4] True or false.

1) Mortality is the number of deaths per thousand of the population per decade.
2) Inverted red triangle is the popular sign of Tubectomy.
3) Overpopulation does not affect resources.
4) WHO full name is World Hospital Organization.
5) Amniocentesis is the technique to know congenital defects of the foetus.
6) The cutting of the fallopian tube in the female is called vasectomy.
7) Carrying capacity is the minimum number of individuals which an environment can support.
8) S- shape growth curve is obtained when initial population growth is slow.
9) Tubectomy is the surgical method of sterilization.
10) Kerala is the most thickly populated state.

A:Type:[4] Answer:

1) **[False]**Mortality is the number of deaths per thousand of the population per year.

2) **[True]**Inverted red triangle is the popular sign of Tubectomy.

3) **[False]**Overpopulation has an adverse effect on resources.

4) **[False]**WHO full name is the World Health Organization.

5) **[True]**Amniocentesis is the technique to know congenital defects of the foetus.

6) **[False]**The cutting of the fallopian tube in the female is called tubectomy.

7) **[False]**Carrying capacity is the maximum number of individuals which an environment can support.

8) **[True]**S- shape growth curve is obtained when initial population growth is slow.

9) **[True]**Tubectomy is thesurgical method of sterilization.

10) **[True]**Kerala is the most thickly populated state.

Q:Type: [5]Fill in the blanks.

1) The scientific study of population is called __________.

2) __________ is the technique used to know congenital defects of foetus.

3) The birth rate is the number of __________ per thousand of the population per year.

4) A popular symbol of family planning is ________ triangle.

5) Between man and Woman , ____________ is biologically superior.

6) __________ density is the number of individuals per unit area.

7) A population that doubles in size in a constant time period show ________ growth.

8) ____________ is the cutting of spermatic ducts in males.

9) Population increases in ________ ratio while food production increases in arithmetic ratio.

10) The combined pill contains ____________ and progesterone.

A: Type: [5] Answers.

01.	Demography.	6.	Population.
02.	Amniocentesis.	7.	Exponential.
03.	Birth.	8.	Vasectomy.
04.	Inverted red triangle.	9.	Geometric.
05.	Women	10.	Oestrogen.

Q:Type: [6]Write One difference of pair (on the given parameter).

SL No.	Components	Parameters
01	Condom & femidom.	Use.
02	Mini pills & Combined pills.	Function.
03	Mini pills & Combined pills.	Compositio n.
04	Tubectomy & Vasectomy.	Method.
05	Amniocentesis & oral rehydration therapy.	Process.

A: Type: [6] Answers.

1) **[Use]**Condom used on the penis and femidom used inside the vagina.

2) **[Function]** Mini-pills cause changes inside the uterus and combined pills prevents ovulation.

3) **[Composition]**Mini-pills consist of only one hormone i.e. synthetic progesterone whereas combined pills are a combination of synthetic progesterone and Oestrogen hormone.

4) **[Method]**Tubectomy ligated oviducts and vasectomy ligated sperm duct.

5) **[Process]** Amniocentesis is a prenatal diagnosis of the foetus by using amniotic fluid. Oral rehydration therapy is used to rehydrate the child body.

Q: Type: [7]Choose the correct answer(MCQ).

1.The growth of the human population is indicated by

a)S-shaped growth curve. **b)** J-shaped growth curve. **c)**aparabola. **d)**k-shape curve.

2. Modern man appeared __________ ago

a)15,000 years**b)**20,000 years**c)**25,000years**d)**50,000 years.

3. Congenital defects of the baby can be checked by

a) X-rays. **b)**Gamma rays. **c)** Alpha rays. **d)**Beta rays.

4. Population explosion has led to

a) Environmental pollution. **b)** Deforestation**c)** shortage of natural resources. **d)** Better medical facilities for people.

5. Cutting and ligating vas deferens is called

a) Amniocentesis**b)**vasectomy**c)**tubectomy **d)** IUCD

6. Due to scientific and technological advancement food production has

a) Increased. **b)** Decreased. **c)** Unaffected. **d)** Noneof the above.

7. Following is the popular sign of family planning centers.

a) Inverted green triangle. **b)** Erectedred triangle. **c)**inverted red triangle**d)**downward red arrow.

8. Which of the following is not a method of birth control?

a)amniocentesis**b)**vasectomy**c)**tubectomy**d)**contraceptive pills.

9. Ovulation is prevented by

a)IUD**b)**Diaphragm**c)**pills. **d)**rhythm method.

10. Maximum number of individuals an environment can support is called

a)Bioticpotential**b)**Mortality**c)** carrying capacity**d)**Natality.

A: Type: [7] Answers.

01.	J-shaped growth curve.	6.	Increase.
02.	25,000 years.	7.	Inverted red triangle.
03.	Beta rays.	8.	Amniocentesis.
04.	shortage of natural resources.	9.	Pills.
05.	Vasectomy.	10.	Carrying capacity.

SECTION-II

Question-1:

Define the followings:
1. Death rate.
2. Natality.
3. Census.
4. Population density.
5. Amniocentesis.

Answer:

1) **Death rate:** Number of deaths per 1000 individuals in the population per year.

2) **Natality:**[Birth rate] The number of births per 1000 individuals in the population per year or an average number of children born per unit time.

3) **Census:**The physical counting of individuals at present in a given area at a given time is known as Census.

4) **Population density:**It is the number of individuals per square kilometre at any given time.

5) **Amniocentesis:** It is a prenatal diagnosis process of the foetus to know genetic defects if any with the foetus.

Question-2:

1) **Differentiate between J-shaped and S-shaped curve.**
2) **Our resource cannot keep pace with the rising population. Give three examples in support of this statement.**
3) **Suggest any three steps which may be taken towards controlling the rapid rise in the human population in India.**

Answer:

1) **Difference:**

Sl No.	J-shaped curve.	S-shaped curve.
01.	When the population size is growing exponentially.	When initial population growth is slow and later increasing and then again become steady.
02.	Applicable tothesmall population.	Applicable toa huge population.
03.	Population stability is very low.	The growth curve represents the maximum size of the population that can be held by the environment.

2) **Supporting statement:**
   a. There will be an acute shortage of space, food, clothing, drinking water and all-natural resources with increased population.
   b. It will be difficult to maintain sanitation in the congested area and so new slum will develop. This becomes a thread to an epidemic.
   c. Proper medical aid will not be available to a great majority of people.

3) **Suggestions:**
   a. The age of marriage should be raised.

b. Family planning education should be imparted to the education system.
c. The consequences of population explosion should be conveyed to the people through the mass media.

Question-3:

1) Mention three reasons for the sharp rise in the human population in the world.
2) Mention any three functions of the Red cross.
3) Mention three reason why the growth of population has not been appreciably checked in India?

Answer:

1. Three reasons:
a). lack of education in underdeveloped and developing countries.
b).Religious customs and old beliefs.
c). Improvement in medical science and development of vaccines.

2. Three functions:
a). Provides relief and helps the victim of calamity such as flood, tsunami, famine etc.
b). Gives first aid to all the wounded soldiers during the war.
c). It looks after the mother and child welfare scheme.

3. Three reasons:
a). lack of education: As large in population belongs to the rural community. they are mostly illiterate. they are unaware of the consequence of a large family.
b). High mortality rate: Higher infant mortality rate found in village areas in India due to lack of education and medical service availability. People from the economically weaker sections think it safer to produce more children so that at least some may survive.
c). lack of recreation: Poor standard of living and poverty do not provide any recreation other than sex.

Question-4:

1. What is the age limit for marriage by law for boys and girls in India?
2. Name the two surgical techniques (One each for human male and female) which can be used to prevent pregnancy.
3. What is the symbol of family planning and family welfare in India?
4. Mention two reason for the high birth rate in India.

Answer:

1. Marriage age for Girl: 18 years and for Boy: 21 years.
2. Male: Vasectomy. Female: Tubectomy.
3. Inverted red triangle.
4. a). lack of education: As large in population belongs to the rural community. they are mostly illiterate. they are unaware of the consequence of a large family.

b). High mortality rate: Higher infant mortality rate found in village areas in India due to lack of education and medical service availability. People from the economically weaker sections think it safer to produce more children so that at least some may survive.

Question-5:

1. The diagram below represents a surgical sterilisation method in males. Study the same and answer the questions that follow

a) Name the part marked A,B,C,D and E
b) Give the name of the surgical method represented in the diagram.
c) Which part is ligated or cut?
d) Name the corresponding surgical method conducted on females.

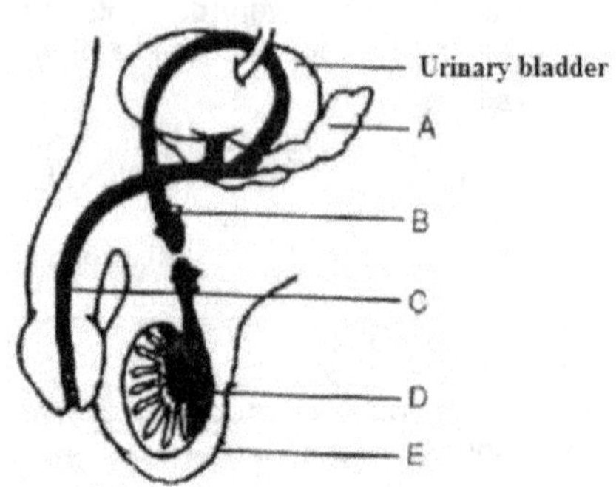

e) Name the part which is ligated in females.Why?

Answer:
a) **A:** Seminal Vesicle.
   B: Vas deferens.
   C: Urethra.
   D: Testes.
   E: Scrotum.

b) Vasectomy.
c) Vas deferens.
d) Tubectomy.
e) Fallopian tubes are ligated. Fallopian tubes are the site of fertilization and due to ligated joint sperm could not reach to ovum and fertilization could not take place.

Question-6:

1. The figure given alongside is a technique.Answer the questions that follow:

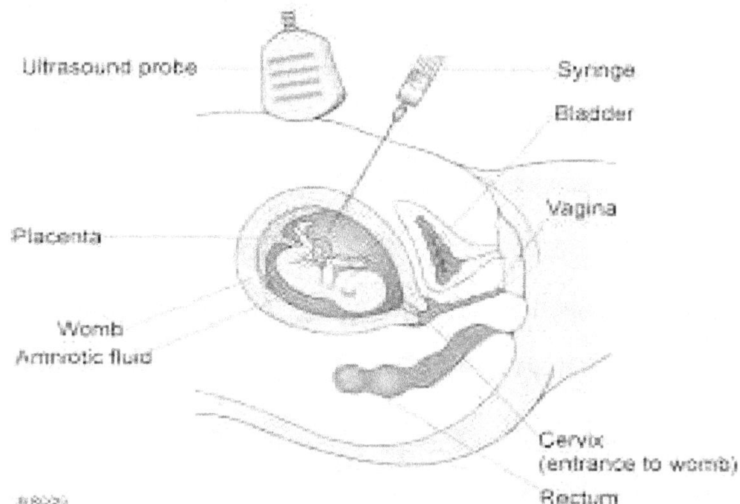

a) Name the process/technique shown.
b) What is the purpose of the technique?
c) Name the organs numbered 1 to 4.
d) What are the demerits of this test method?

Answer:

a. The process is called Amniocentesis.
b. This method is used to found any congenital defects of the foetus.
c. 1.Cervix. 2. Bladder. 3. Anus. 4. Placenta.
d. This method could be misused to establish the sex of the foetus.

AIDS TO HEALTH.

SECTION-I

Q:Type: [1] Name the followings.

1. World health day is celebrated on this day.
2. The blood cells act as an internal defence of our body.
3. The method of squeezing out WBCs from blood capillaries is called.
4. Commercial production of penicillin has been done from this.
5. The mild chemical applied to the skin to kill germs.
6. The tear gland contains this enzyme to prevent eye infection.
7. A state of complete physical, mental and social well being is called.
8. The stomach kills germs by secreting this acid.
9. Foreign invaders inside our body are also called this.
10. The full form of HIV is.
11. One combined vaccine is given to babies which helps to build immunity against three common diseases.
12. The process by which white blood cells engulf harmful microbes.
13. At birth, this vaccination is carried out.
14. Extracts of toxins secreted by bacteria.
15. Antibodies produced in other organism are injected into a person to counteract antigen is called.
16. This vaccine is administered orally before 5th birthday of children in India.
17. Vaccines when administered by injection is known as.
18. The readymade antibodies of mother reach the developing foetus.
19. The full name of BCG is.
20. The serum containing antibodies against a particular antigen is called.
21. What type of health aid Carbolic acid is?
22. The first antibiotic name is.
23. The scientific name of Penicillin producing source fungus is.
24. The scientist who discovered vaccination.
25. The immunity developed after vaccination.

A:Type:[1] Answer:

1.	7th April.	7.	Health.
2.	WBC[White Blood Corpuscles]	8.	Hydrochloric acid.
3.	Diapedesis.	9.	Antigen.
4.	P. Chrysogenum.	10.	Human Immunodeficiency Virus.
5.	Antiseptic.	11.	DPT vaccine.
6.	Lysozyme.	12.	Phagocytosis.

13.	BCG [Bacillus of Calmette & Guerin]	20.	Antiserum.
14.	Toxoids.	21.	Antiseptic.
15.	Passive immunity.	22.	Penicillin.
16.	Polio vaccine.	23.	*Penicillium notatum.*
17.	Inoculation.	24.	Edward Jenner.
18.	Placenta.		Artificial passive acquired immunity.
19.	Bacillus of Calmette & Guerin.	25.	

Q:Type: [2] State the exact use of the following.

1	Antiseptic	2	P.chrysogenum.	3	Serum.
4	Toxoids.	5	Disinfectants.	6	Streptomycin.

A:Type:[2] Answer:

1) **Antiseptic**:Applied locally on the skin and which used to destroy bacteria e.g. Lysol, Benzoic acid etc.

2) **P.chrysogenum**: Commercial production of penicillin largely done form P. chrysogenum.

3) **Serum**:Used to develop passive immunity by using antibodies produces in the body of other person or animals.

4) **toxoids**:Used against diphtheria and tetanus.

5) **Disinfectants**:Used to destroy microbes on the floor, surgical instruments, hospitals and toilets.

6) **Streptomycin**:It is widely used as an antibiotic.

Q: Type: [3] match the column.

Sl. No	Column A	Sl. No	Column B
1	Natural passive acquired immunity.	A	Lysol.
2	BCG.	B	Poliomyelitis.
3	First antibiotic.	C	Active immunity.
4	Covaxin.	D	Vaccine.
5	Serum.	E	Gonorrhoea.
6	Disinfectant.	F	Combined vaccines.

Sl. No	Column A	Sl. No	Column B
7	Antibiotic.	G	Formalin.
8	Edward Jenner.	H	Alexander Fleming.
9	Vaccine.	I	Typhoid.
10	Penicillin.	J	Inoculation.
11	DPT.	K	Passive immunity.
12	Toxoids	L	Strong chemicals used to destroy microbes on the floor.
13	Salk's Vaccine.	M	Mothers antibodies to the foetus.
14	Antiseptic.	N	Introduced at birth.
15	TAB vaccine.	O	Selman Waksman.

A:Type:[3] Answer:

Sl. No	Column A	Sl. No	Column B
1.	Natural passive acquired immunity.	M	Mothers antibodies to the foetus.
Expl.	Antibodies of mother reach the developing foetus through the placenta.		
2.	BCG.	N	Introduced at birth.
Expl.	BCG was given within 7 days after the birth of the child.		
3.	First antibiotic.	H	Alexander Fleming.
Expl.	Alexander Fleming was the inventor of the first antibiotic.		
4.	Covaxin.	J	Inoculation.
Expl.	Covaxin administered through injection.		
5.	Serum.	K	Passive immunity.
Expl.	Serum introduced passive immunity.		
6.	Disinfectant.	L	Strong chemicals used to destroy microbes on the floor.
7.	Antibiotic.	O	Selman Waksman.
Expl.	Selman Waksman first coined this term "Antibiotic".		
8.	Edward Jenner.	D	Vaccine.
Expl.	Edward Jenner first coined this term "vaccine".		
9.	Vaccine.	C	Active immunity.
Expl.	Serum introduced active immunity.		
10.	Penicillin.	E	Gonorrhoea.
Expl.	Penicillin used to treat Gonorrhoea.		
11.	DPT.	F	Combined vaccines.
Expl.	DPT is a combined vaccine for Diphtheria, Pertussis and tetanus		

Sl. No	Column A	Sl. No	Column B
12.	Toxoids	G	Formalin.
13.	Salk's Vaccine.	B	Poliomyelitis.
14.	Antiseptic.	A	Lysol.
15.	TAB vaccine.	I	Typhoid.

Q:Type: [4] True or false. If false the rewrite the correct statement.

1) Alexander Fleming discovered Sulphonamide.
2) Overdose of the medicine may cause anaemia.
3) Certain antibodies are used as food preservatives.
4) Streptomycin is an example of Toxoid.
5) Serum containing antibodies is called Antiserum.
6) In toxoids, formalin is used to make them harmless.
7) The process of producing a state of immunity in a subject is called vaccination.
8) Antibodies are produced by plasma cells derived from lymphocytes.
9) Penicillin obtained from a fungus is an example of an antibody.
10) Penicillin was named in 1929.
11) Edward Jenner discovered the vaccine for cowpox.
12) Chemical applied to spots and places to kill harmful microorganisms are called disinfectants.

A:Type:[4] Answer:

1) **[False]**Alexander Fleming discovered Penicillin.
2) **[True]**Overdose of the medicine may cause anaemia.
3) **[False]**Certain antibiotics are used as food preservatives.
4) **[False]**Streptomycin is an example of an antibiotic.
5) **[True]**Serum containing antibodies is called Antiserum.
6) **[True]**In toxoids formalin are used to make them harmless.
7) **[False]**The process of producing a state of immunity in a subject is called immunization.
8) **[True]**Antibodies are produced by plasma cells derived from lymphocytes.
9) **[False]** Penicillin obtained from a fungus is an example of an antibiotic.
10) **[True]**Penicillin was named in 1929.
11) **[False]**Edward Jenner discovered the vaccine for smallpox.
12) **[True]**Chemical applied to spots and places to kill harmful microorganisms are called disinfectants.

Q:Type: [5] Fill in the blanks.

1) April 7, is celebrated as world _______ day.
2) Liver cells secrets __________.
3) Serum gives ____________ immunity.

4) Snake bite patient is treated by _________.
5) Antitoxins are _____________.
6) Dettol is a/an __________.
7) Inside ear _______ contains an effective antibacterial component.
8) Serum is collected in ____________ bottles.
9) DPT contains vaccine for Diphtheria, Tetanus and ____________.
10) The vaccine is a preparation consisting of _________ microbes which help to build immunity in the human body.
11) Tear contain _____________ which prevents eye infection.
12) The foreign invaders are called __________.
13) Contaminated needle could be a cause of ___________.
14) Antiseptics are chemical substances applied to the __________ to destroy or prevent the growth and multiplication of harmful microbes.

A:Type:[5] Answer:

1.	Health.	8.	Sterilized.
2.	Bile.	9.	Pertussis.
3.	Passive.	10.	Dead.
4.	Antitoxin.	11.	Lysozyme.
5.	Antibiotics.	12.	Antigen.
6.	Antiseptic.	13.	AIDS.
7.	Wax.	14.	Skin.

Q:Type: [6] Write One difference of pair (on the given parameter).

SL No.	Components	Parameters
01	Antiseptic & Disinfectant.	Working method.
02	Antigen & Antitoxins.	Function.
03	Vaccination & Immunization.	Process.
04	Vaccine & Antiserum.	Function.
05	Antiserum & Toxoids.	Purpose.
06	Antibiotic & Pro-biotic.	Production.
07	Innate & acquired immunity.	Method.
08	Active & passive immunity.	Method.
09	Active & passive immunity.	Time.
10	BCG & DPT	Contains.

A:Type:[6] Answer:

1) **[Working method]**Antiseptic destroy bacteria on skin & disinfectants used to destroy microbes on the floor or used surfaces.

2) **[Function]** Antigen are acted as foreign substances and therefore elicits an immune response and that produces antibodies. Antitoxins are antibodies that neutralize toxins produced in the body.

3) **[Process]**vaccination [oral or inject able] is a part of Immunization and it is an artificial method whereas any method either natural or artificial which leads to improving immunity is called immunization.

4) **[Function]**vaccine is the process of injecting germ culture in the body to develop antibodies in the injected body. Antiserum contains antibodies which were developed in other body and used to work in another body.

5) **[Purpose]** Antiserum contains antibodies which were developed in other body and used to work in another body. Toxoids are used against some specific diseases where extracts of toxins secreted by bacteria used to produce antibodies in the affected body.

6) **[Production]**Antibiotics are produced by the body due to the presence of antigen and pro-biotics are made of good bacteria.

7) **[Method]** innate immunity developed due to the genetic make-up of an individual. Acquired immunity developed during the life time of an individual.

8) **[Hazards]** Inactive immunity antibodies are produced in the same body whereas in passive immunity antibodies are produced in other bodies before injecting into the affected body.

9) **[Time]** Active immunity required a long time compared to passive immunity as antibodies are already available to act in passive immunity.

10) **[Contains]** BCG contains a vaccine for one disease and that is tuberculosis. DPT contains a vaccine for three diseases and they are Diphtheria, Pertussis & tetanus.

Q:Type: [7]Choose the correct answer(MCQ).

1. DPT stands for

a) Diphtheria, Polio &Tetanus.**b)** Dysentery, Pertussis &Tuberculosis.
c) Diphtheria, Pertussis&Tetanus.**d)**Diphtheria, Parkinson & Tetanus.

2. Artificial introduction of germs into the body for developing resistance to a particular disease is called

a) Parturition **b)** Vaccination. **c)** Inoculation.**d)** Immunization.

3. Antiserum contains

a)Antibodies. **b)** Platelets. **c)** WBCs. **d)** Antigen.

4. Which of the following diseases are infectious?

a)Degenerativediseases.**b)** Allergies.**c)**Communicable diseases
d)Deficiency diseases.

5. Polio vaccine is administered

a) Orally. **b)** Byinjection. **c)**By inhaling spray. **d)** Through tablets.

6.First vaccine was developed to protect from

a)Pertussis**b)** Chickenpox.**c)** Cow pox.**d)**Small pox.

7. Salk's vaccine is used to build immunity against

a)Tuberculosis. **b)**Malaria. **c)** Poliomyelitis. **d)**Diphtheria.

8.Poisonous toxins secreted by bacteria are made harmless by the addition of

b) Alcohol. **b)**Formalin**c)**Acetone. **d)** Antibodies.

9.BCG vaccine provides immunity against

a) Tetanus. **b)**AIDS**c)**Cholera. **d)**Tuberculosis.

10. Antiserum is produced by

b) Artificial insemination. **b)** Injecting toxin into the body of the animal.
c) Centrifuging blood of the animal. **d)** All of the above.

A:Type:[7] Answer:

0 1.	c. Diphtheria, Pertussis&Tetanus.	**06.**	b. Chicken pox.
02.	b. Vaccination	**07.**	c. Poliomyelitis.
03.	a. Antibodies.	**08.**	b. Formalin.
04.	c. Communicable diseases.	**09.**	d. Tuberculosis.
05.	a. Orally.	**10.**	b. Injecting toxin in the body of the animal.

SECTION-II

Question-1

Define the following
1. Vaccine.
2. Antiserum.
3. Antiseptic.
4. Natural immunity.
5. Antibiotic.

Answer:

1) **Vaccine:** **the** vaccine is the process of injecting germ culture intothebody to develop antibodies in the injected body.

2) **Antiserum:** Antiserum contains antibodies which were developed in other body and used to work in another body.

3) **Antiseptic:** These are the chemicals applied locally on the skin to destroy bacteria. Example: Savnol, Dettol.

4) **Natural immunity:**Natural immunity is the immunity developed in the body utilizing natural ways such as from mother to child or by natural infection or antigen.

5) **Antibiotic:**Antibiotics are the chemical substances produces by a microorganism, which inhibits or kills another organism.

Question-2

Choose the odd one out from each of the following sets, giving the reason for your choice.
1) AIDS, Smallpox, Diphtheria, Measles.
2) Carbolic acid, Mercurochrome, Phenol, Benzoic acid.
3) Antitoxin, Antibody, Antigen, Pathogen.
4) Diphtheria, Polio, Tetanus, Typhoid.
5) Penicillin, Streptomycin, Ampicillin, Urea stebamine.

Answer:

1) **AIDS**: till date, no vaccine developed for AIDS but all other given disease have a vaccine.
2) **Phenol:** It is not used as an antiseptic.
3) **Antibody:** This substance is produced due to the presence of the other three given substances.
4) **Typhoid**: It is caused by bacteria and other given disease are viral diseases.
5) **Urea steabamine**: it is not an antibiotic.

Question-3

What is antiserum? How serum is obtained? What type of immunity could build up with serum?

Answer:

Antiserum: The serum containing antibodies against a particular antigen is called Antiserum.

Serum obtaining procedure:
a. Microbes are cultured.
b. Toxin is separated.
c. Toxin is injected into the body of an animal in a mild dose.
d. After recovery of the animal, it is given a slightly stronger dose. This process is repeated still animal can fight but not die.
e. Blood is drawn from the neck of an animal and then coagulates.
f. Serum separated.
g. Serum is collected in a sterilized bottle.

Serum builds passive immunity inour body.

Question-4

What is the sulphonamide family of drugs? Give example. Name the disease it can control.Why its importance is reduced at present time?

Answer:

Sulphonamideis synthetic drugs used to prevent and cure diseases and disorders.

Ampicillin is an example of a Sulphonamide family drug.

Pneumonia, Urinary and bowel infection diseases are cured by the Sulphonamide family drug.

Due to the development of strains of bacteria resistant to Sulphonamide these synthetic drugs reduce importance.

Question-4

a. **What do you know about paramedics?**
b. **Mention any three main functions of WHO.**
c. **Name the three germ-killing secretions of our body.**
d. **Name any two vaccines and mention the diseases from which they give immunity.**

Answer:

a) **Paramedics:** a person trained to give emergency medical care to people who are injured or ill, typically in a setting outside a hospital is the function of paramedics.

b) Three function of WHO:

a. Combating diseases especially communicable diseases and mental illness.
b. Issue endemic warning.
c. Lay pharmaceutical standards for important drugs, to ensure correctness and size of the dose.

c) Three germ-killing secretions:

1. Tears.
2. Saliva.
3. Sweat.

d) Two vaccines and disease :

1. Covaxin: Covid-19 or Corona disease.
2. Smallpox vaccine: smallpox.

HEALTH ORGANISATIONS.

SECTION-I

Q:Type: [1]Name the followings:

1. Headquarter of WHO is located in.
2. Disorder due to fault in the chromosome.
3. Persons from this organization can go anywhere during war or peace or in disaster-prone areas.
4. WHO has this number of states members.
5. An organization that looks after maternal and child welfare centres.
6. Lack of calcium and vitamin D is the cause of this disease.
7. Haemophilia is an example of this type of disease.
8. Scurvy is a disease due to a deficiency of this vitamin.
9. Diseases that are transmitted from parents to offspring.
10. A common mental disorder disease in India is this.
11. This disease is caused due to uncontrolled growth of tissues in any part of the body.
12. Diseases /disorders caused due to hypersensitivity of the body to foreign materials.

A:Type: [1] Answer:

1.	Geneva.	7.	Hereditary disease.
2.	Congenital disease.	8.	Vitamin-C.
3.	Red cross.	9.	Hereditary.
4.	199.	10.	Epilepsy.
5.	UNICEF.	11.	Cancer.
6.	Rickets.	12.	Allergies.

Q:Type: [2] State the exact functions:

1	WHO	2	Red cross	3	UNICEF.
4	NACO.	5	NFCP.	6	NMEP.

A:Type: [2] Answer:

1) **WHO**: Combating diseases, especially communicable diseases and mental illness.

2) **Red cross**: To provide relief to the victim of calamity and first aid to wounded soldiers during the war.

3) **UNICEF**:Fighting silent emergencies-a combination of diseases including malnutrition and poverty.

4) **NACO**:To implement and closely monitor the various components of the national AIDS control programme.

5) **NFCP**:To control filarial disease in the country.

6) **NMEP**:To do work for the eradication of Malaria.

Q:Type: [3] Match the column.

Sl. No	Column A	Sl. No	Column B
1	Mongolism.	A	Geneva.
2	Cancer.	B	National organizations.
3	WHO.	C	Malaria.
4	NGO	D	1992.
5	Ades.	E	Congenital disorders.
6	Anopheles.	F	Uncontrolled growth.
7	The spray of DDT.	G	Dengue.
8	NACO.	H	UNICEF.
9	Hay fever.	I	NMEP.
10	Expanded program on immunization.	J	Allergies.

A:Type: [3] Answer & explanation:

Sl. No	Column A	Sl. No	Column B
1.	Mongolism.	E	Congenital disorders.
Expl.	Mongolism is caused due to a fault in the chromosome.		
2.	Cancer.	F	Uncontrolled growth.
3.	WHO.	A	Geneva.
Expl.	Headquarter of WHO is located in Geneva.		
4.	NGO.	B	National Organizations.
Expl.	NGO means None Governmental Organization.		
5.	Ades.	G	Dengue.
Expl.	Ades Egypt mosquitoes are the vector of dengue.		
6.	Anopheles.	C	Malaria.
Expl.	Anopheles mosquitoes are the vector of malaria.		

Sl. No	Column A	Sl. No	Column B	
7.	The spray of DDT.	I	NMEP.	
Expl.	During the NEMA programme, DDT sprayed twice a year in the endemic area to control malaria.			
8.	NACO.	D	1992.	
Expl.	NACO established in 1992 to control AIDS.			
9.	Hay fever.	J	Allergies.	
10.	Expanded programme on immunization.	H	UNICEF.	
Expl.	EPI programme is supported by UNICEF.			

Q:Type [4] True or false. If false then rewrite the correct statement.

1) The Red Cross symbol can be seen on the Doctors car.
2) World Health Day is celebrated on 17th April.
3) NICD in Luck now is seriously engaged in researchingtheinfectious disease.
4) UNICEF full form is the United Nations International Children's Emergency Forum.
5) Background of the red cross symbol should be White.
6) First launched health programme in India was against Filaria.
7) EPI full form is Extended Programme on Immunization.
8) IDD programme is related to Goiter disease control.
9) Headquarter of WHO is located in New York.
10) The oldest health organization is the Red Cross.

A:Type: [1] Answer & explanation:

1) **[True]** The Red cross symbol can be seen on the Doctors car.
2) **[False]**World Health Day is celebrated on 7th April.
3) **[True]**NICD in Luck now is seriously engaged in researchingtheinfectious disease.
4) **[False]** UNICEF full form is the United Nations International Children's, Emergency Fund.
5) **[True]** Background of the red cross symbol should be White.
6) **[False]** First launched health programme in India was against malaria.
7) **[True]** EPI full form is Extended Programme on Immunization
8) **[True]**IDD programme is related to Goiter disease control.
9) **[False]** Headquarter of WHO is located in Geneva.
10) **[True]** Oldest health organization is the red cross.

Q: Type: [5]Fill in the blanks:

1) The emblem of the Red cross is __________.
2) Typhoid is one kind of ________ borne disease.

3) Haemophilia and colour blindness are examples of _________ disease.
4) German measles is one kinds of _________ disease.
5) Pulse polio was launched in the country in _________.

6) The strategy for Kala-Azar control broadly includes _______ major activities.
7) Rickets are the result of deficiency in _________ & _________.
8) Accelerated Rural Water supply programme is a supplement to the national _______ supply & _________ programme.
9) Govt. of India constituted a task force on AIDS control in _______.
10) Pellagra is a _____________ deficiency disease.
11) WHO was founded in __________.
12) Parkinson's disease is one kind of _________ disease.
13) UNICEF is an agency under __________.

A:Type: [1] Answer & explanation:

1.	Plus sign.	8.	Water, Sanitation.
2.	Water.	9.	1985.
3.	Hereditary.	10.	Vitamin B.
4.	Congenital.	11.	1948.
5.	1995.	12.	Degenerative.
6.	3	13.	United nation.
7.	Vit. C, Calcium.		

Q:Type: [5] Write one difference.

SL No.	Components	Parameters
01	Congenital & communicable disease.	**Cause.**
02	Degenerative & Deficiency disease.	**Cause.**
03	WHO & UNICEF	**Function.**
04	WHO & Red cross.	**Function.**
05	DPT & BCG	**Purpose.**
06	Congenital disorder & Acquired disease.	**Cause.**
07	NFCP & NMEP	**Purpose.**
08	Cancer & Allergies.	**Cause.**

A:Type: [1] Answer:

1) **[Cause]** Congenial disease is caused due to fault in the chromosome structure or damage inflicted in the developing embryo.

   Communicable diseases caused due to the entry of disease causing germs called pathogen into the body.

2) **[Cause]** Degenerative diseases are due to degeneration of tissues in old age which are unable to repair due to a decline in the ability of the body. Deficiency disease caused due to deficiency in certain nutrients.

3) **[Function]WHO:** Combating diseases, especially communicable diseases and mental illness. **UNICEF:** Fighting silent emergencies-a combination of diseases including malnutrition and poverty.

4) **[Function]WHO:** Combating diseases, especially communicable diseases and mental illness. **Red Cross:** To provide relief to the victim of calamity and first aid to wounded soldiers during the war.

5) **[Purpose]** DPT is a vaccine used to immune the body against Diphtheria, Pertussis and Tetanus. BCG is a vaccine against Tuberculosis.

6) **[Cause]**Congenial disease is caused due to fault in the chromosome structure or damage inflicted in the developing embryo. Acquired diseases develop in an individual after birth.

7) **[Purpose] NFCP** has been in operation to control Filaria disease. **NMEP** was launched to eradicated malaria.

8) **[Cause]** Though there is no basic cause behind Cancer, it is the uncontrolled growth of cells. Allergies are caused due to hypersensitivity of the body to certain foreign substances.

Q:Type: [7]Choose the correct answer(MCQ).

1. NMEP stands for

b) National Moral Education policy.   **b)** National Mental Education Policy.   **c)** National Malaria Eradication Programme.   **d)** National Malaria Education Programme.

2. NFCP stands for

a) National Filaria Control Programme. **b)**National Food Control Programme. **c)**national Flood Control Programme. **d)** National Female Care programme.

3. Filaria disease is caused by

a)Antibodies. **b)**Virus **c)** Parasites. **d)**bacterium.

4. This halogen should present in common salt to control Goiter

a)Fluorine.   **b)** Chlorine. **c)**Bromine **d)**Iodine.

5. Goiter is a

b) Congenital disease. **b)** Deficiency disease. **c)** Viral disease. **d)**Hereditary disease.

6.Which of the following is a voluntary health organization?

a)WHO   **b)** UNO. **c)** UNICEF. **d)** Red cross.

7.Which one for the following is the oldest organization?

a)WHO   **b)** UNO. **c)** UNICEF.   **d)** Red cross.

8. Five years AIDS control programme was launched in India in

a) 1985   **b)**1987   **c)**1995   **d)**1992

9.In India Eighth five years plan emphasis the prevention of

a) Tetanus.   **b)**AIDS   **c)** Cancer.   **d)** Tuberculosis.

10.   Member countries of WHO is

a) 199.   **b)**189.   **c)** 179   **d)** 159.

A:Type: [1] Answer:

1.	c.National malaria Eradictionprogramme.	**6.**	d.Red Cross.
2.	a.National Filaria control programme.	**7.**	d.Red Cross.
3.	c.Parasites.	**8.**	d.1992.
4.	d.Iodine.	**9.**	c.Cancer.
5.	b.Deficiency disease.	**10.**	a.199.

SECTION-II

Question-1.

Define the following
1. Congenital disease.
2. Acquired disease.
3. Communicable disease.
4. EPI.
5. Degenerative disease.

Answer:

1) **Congenital disease:** Diseases that are caused due to fault in chromosome structure or damage inflicted to the developing embryo is called congenital disease. Club foot, mongolism are an example of such disease.

2) **Acquired disease:** Diseases which are developed in an individual after birth are called acquired disease.There are two kinds of such diseases:Communicable diseases [malaria,Filaria] and Non-communicable disease[Hay fever,cancer].

3) **Communicable disease:** Diseases which are caused due to entry of pathogens into the body and are easily transmitted from person to person by direct or indirect contact or through vector are called communicable disease. Example": Malaria, Covid, Influenza etc.

4) **EPI:** WHO has launched Expanded Programme on Immunization [EPI] against six most common preventable childhood diseases, Viz. Diptheria, Pertusis, Tetanus, Polio,Tuberculosis and measles.

5) **Degenerative disease:** These diseases are due to degeneration of tissues in old age, that is diseases caused due to a decline in the ability of the body to repair its tissues.it's lead to malfunctioning of the heart, lungs and CNS e.g. Parkinson, cataract etc.

Question-2.

Expands the following:

1) AIDS,
2) UNICEF.
3) WHO.
4) NFCP.
5) IDDP.
6) NMEP.
7) EPI

Answer:

1) **AIDS**: Acquired Immuno Deficiency Syndrome.
2) **UNICEF**: United Nations International Children's Emergency Fund.
3) **WHO**: World Health Organisation.
4) **NFCP**: National Filaria Control Programme.
5) **IDDP**: Iodine Deficiency Disorders programme.
6) **NMEP**: national malaria Eradication Programme.
7) **EPI:** Expanded Programme on Immunisation.

Question-3.

1. **List three functions of the Red cross.**
2. **What is the common health problem in India?**
3. **Write a short note on the red cross.**
4. **What is the purpose of UNICEF?**

Answer:

1) **Three functions of the red Cross:**
   a. To provide relief and help the victims of natural calamities.
   b. To give first aid to all the wounded soldiers during the war.

c. To extend all possible first aid in case of an accident.

2) **Common health problem in India:** malaria, Typhoid, Filaria, AIDS and Dengue.

3) **Red Cross:** It is the world oldest voluntary Organisation founded in 1864.it is an international agency and having a symbol + in redcolour.Red Cross personnel can go anywhere during war or peace or in a disaster-prone area.

The basic functions of the Red Cross are as follows:
a. To provide relief and help the victims of natural calamities.
b. To give first aid to all the wounded soldiers during the war.
c. To extend all possible first aid in case of an accident.
d. To look after mother & Child welfare scheme.
e. To train personnel in first aid and related skills.

4) **UNICEF:** It is the agency of the UN which look after the welfare of children all over the world.The UNICEF concentrates its efforts on fighting silent emergencies-a combination of diseases including malnutrition and poverty that kills children.It works to encourage peace and an understanding of developmental issues among children of the world. The main two functions of UNICEF are Elimination of neonatal tetanus and elimination of Polio and vitamin A deficiency.

Question-4.

1. Write three functions of WHO.
2. Explain briefly the Universal immunisation programme.

Answer:

1) **Three functions of WHO:**
   d. Combating diseases especially communicable diseases and mental illness.
   e. Issue endemic warning.
   f. Lay pharmaceutical standards for important drugs, to ensure correctness and size of the dose.

2) After experiencing the smallpox eradication programme world realised that immunisation is the most powerful and cost-effective weapon against vaccine-preventable diseases. In 1974, WHO has launched Expanded Programme on immunisation [EPI] against six diseases namely Diptheria, Tetanus,Pertussis, Polio, Tuberculosis, measles.

POLLUTION & ITS SOURCES.

SECTION-I

Q:Type:[1] Name the followings:

1. An undesirable change in the physical, chemical or biological characteristics in the environment which is hazardous to the living organisms is called.
2. Write one inorganic chemical agent responsible for water pollution.
3. Domestic sewage and wastewater comprise this much percentage of water.
4. Accumulation of nutrients through natural succession is called.
5. Percentage of Oxygen in the air by volume.
6. Compounds responsible for Ozone layer depletion.
7. A process of burning waste is called.
8. Wrong sound in the wrong place at the wrong time is called.
9. Noise is measured on the scale of this.
10. Problem related to whistling and buzzing in the ears is called.
11. Incineration is the process of burning these types of waste.
12. Any substance which causes pollution.
13. A major source of fluorine to man.
14. The type of pollution which causes an increase in the number of cancer.
15. Name one greenhouse gas.

A:Type:[1] Answer:

1.	Pollution.	9.	Decibel.
2.	Nitrate salt.	10.	Auditory fatigue.
3.	99.9%	11.	Solid waste.
4.	Biomagnifications.	12.	Pollutant.
5.	20.95	13.	Drinking water.
6.	Chlorofluorocarbon.	14.	Radiation.
7.	Incineration.	15.	Methane.
8.	Noise.		

Q: Type: [2] match the column.

Sl. No	Column A	Sl. No	Column B
1	Pollution of water	A	Typhoid.
2	Lead.	B	DDT.
3	Polluted water.	C	Pond.
4	Incineration.	D	NO_2.
5	Noise.	E	Brain damage.

6	Pesticides.	F	MIC.
7	Eutrophication.	G	CFCs.
8	Acid rain.	H	BOD.
9	Bhopal.	I	Decibel.
10	Ozone depletion.	J	Burning of solid waste.

A:Type:[2] Answer:

Sl. No	Column A	Sl. No	Column B
1.	Pollution of water.	H	BOD
Expl.	BOD i.e. Biological Oxygen Demand decrease due to pollution of water as pollutants reduced oxygen content in water.		
2.	Lead.	E	Brain damage.
3.	Polluted water.	A	Typhoid.
Expl.	Contaminated water is the cause of Typhoid disease.		
4.	Incineration.	J	Burning of solids.
Expl.	The burning of solid waste is called incineration.		
5.	Noise.	I	Decibel.
Expl.	Decibel unit used to measure sound pollution.		
6.	Pesticides.	B	DDT
Expl.	DDT :dichlorodiphenyltrichloroethane		
7.	Eutrophication.	C	Pond.
Expl.	The rich supply of nutrients from sewage collected in a pond is the cause behind Eutrophication.		
8.	Acid rain.	D	NO_2
Expl.	NO_2 produces Nitric and Nitrous acid during rain.NO2 formed due to the lightening and burning of petroleum product.		
9.	Bhopal.	F	MIC
Expl.	Methyl isocyanides are the poisonous gas which caused thousand death in Bhopal in 1984.		
10.	Ozone depletion.	G	CFCs
Expl.	CFCs break Ozone into Oxygen and cause Ozone layer depletion.		

Q: Type: [3] True or false. If false then rewrite the correct statement.

1) Oxygen present in air by volume is 21.856%.
2) Anthrax is a very common water-borne disease.
3) Pesticides mainly contain compounds of heavy metals.
4) Eutrophication could take place in a river.

5) MIC gas is a poisonous gas that caused the death of many people in Bhopal.
6) Air pollution is the main cause of cancer disease.
7) Progress in agriculture and industry is taken a general criterion of the development of any country.
8) Oil usually spread out rapidly across the water surface.
9) Non-biodegradable pollutants are domestic wastes that can be rapidly decomposed.

A: Type:[3] Answer:

1) [False] Oxygen present in air by volume is 20.94%.
2) [True]Anthrax is a very common water-borne disease
3) [True] Pesticides mainly contain compounds of heavy metals.
4) [False] Eutrophication could take place in Pond/lake.
5) [True] MIC gas is a poisonous gas that caused the death of many people in Bhopal.
6) [True] Air pollution is the main cause of cancer disease.
7) [True] Progress in agriculture and industry is taken a general criterion of development of any country.
8) [True]Oil usually spread out rapidly across the water surface.
9) [False] Biodegradable pollutants are domestic wastes that can be rapidly decomposed.

Q: Type: [4] Fill in the blanks:

1) Pollution is an ______________ change in the physical, chemical or biological characteristics of air, water and soil. Undesirable.
2) Typhoid is one kind of _________ borne disease. Water.
3) Manufacturers' should be encouraged to produce goods that are _________ friendly for Environment.
4) Wet scrubbers are used to control__________ pollution. Air
5) Interference is caused by _________ .noise.
6) Acid rain is caused due to pollutants released by__________. Vehicles.
7) Chernobyl disaster is related to __________ pollution. Radioactive.
8) Pollution is only caused by loss of resources by unnecessary _________ exploitation. wasteful
9) Excess potassium in soil decreases Vitamin ____ in vegetables and fruits. C
10) Pollution control involves funds, manpower, etc, for disposal of __________ and for developing control devices. Pollutants.
11) The ozone layer protects us from harmful ______ rays. UV
12) Biomagnifications is results of _________. Soil pollution.
13) One non degradable pollutant is __________.

A:Type:[4] Answer:

1.	Undesirable.	8.	Wasteful.
2.	Water.	9.	C
3.	Environment.	10.	Pollutants.
4.	Air.	11.	UV
5.	Noise.	12.	Soil pollution.
6.	Vehicle.	13.	DDT.
7.	Radioactive.		

Q:Type: [5] Write One effect of the following incidents:

SL No.	Components	On the following parameter.
01	Leaking refrigerator coil.	**Environment.**
02	Burning of solid waste unscientifically.	**Air pollution.**
03	Increase of water-borne vectors.	**Health.**
04	Nuclear power accident.	**Environment.**
05	Emission from vehicles.	**Rain.**
06	Incomplete burning of petrol.	**Environment.**
07	Use of chromium in pesticides.	**Skin.**
08	Sewages collecting in a pond.	**Nutrients of water.**

A:Type:[5] Answer:

1) **[Environment]**If the refrigerant is CFC it will create Ozone depletion.

2) **[Air pollution]** Due to incineration dioxin poisonous gas is released which is harmful an also burning produces CO_2 gas which is a greenhouse gas.

3) **[Health]**Water born vector such as mosquito-spread malaria, dengue etc.

4) **[Environment]**Continental air pollution due to radiation particulate spreading.

5) **[Rain]** Vehicle emission produces CO_2 and SO_2 gas which is a cause behind Acid rain.

6) **[Environment]**Incomplete burning of petrol creates hydrocarbon and Carbon monoxide pollution in the air which leads to cancer and death due to suffocation respectively.

7) **[Skin]** Chromium being a heavy metal is a cause for dermatitis.

8) **[Nutrients of water]** Due to accumulation of nutrients i.e. Eutrophication observed.

Q:Type: [6] Choose the correct answer:

1.The pollution which affects aquatic life is

a) Air pollution. **b)** Water pollution.**c)** Noise pollution.**d)** Soil pollution.

2. CFC stands for

a) Chlorofluorocarbons.**b)**caboflurochlorine. **c)**Carboflurocologen.**d)** None of the above.

3.Plastics and sewage litter on a crop-field will cause the pollution of

a)Soil. **b)** Air. **c)** Water. **d)**Scenery.

4. Effects of air pollution do not includes

a)Cough.**b)** Malaria.**c)** Asthma**d)**Lung cancer.

5.Which of the following does not pollute water?

a) Oil spill. **b)**Acidrain.**c)**industrial discharge**d)**Vehicular emission.

6. Which has been reported severe brain damage?

a)Sodium**b)** potassium.   **c)** Lead.**d)**Acid rain.

7. Most serious pathological effect of noise pollution is

a) Auditoryfatigue.**b)** Interference. **c)** Deafness. **d)**Impatient behavior.

8. The Chernobyl disaster took place in

a) 1985**b)**1986**c)**1984**d)**1996

9. Which of the following gas is responsible for acid rain

a) CO_2**b)**SO_2**c)**NO_2.**d)**All of the above.

10. Bhopal gas incident took place in

a) 1985**b)**1986 **c)**1984**d)**1996

A:Type:[6] Answer:

1.	Water pollution.	**6.**	Lead.
2.	Chlorofluorocarbon.	**7.**	Deafness.
3.	Water.	**8.**	1986.
4.	Malaria.	**9.**	All of the above.
5.	Vehicular emission.	**10.**	1984.

SECTION-II

Question-1:

Define the following
1. Pollution.
2. Smog.
3. Thermal pollution.
4. Eutrophication.
5. Biomagnification.
6. Pollutants.

Answer:

1)**Pollution:** Any undesirable change in the physical, chemical or biological characteristics of air, water and soil or land that may or will harmfully affect human or other living organisms or create a potential hazard to any living organism is called Pollution.

2)**Smog:**Smog is a combination of smoke and fog.It is generally observed in the industrial area during the winterseason. It occurs as a result of intense local pollution trapped by a thermal inversion. It is very hazardous toliving organisms.

3)**Thermal pollution:**It is the pollution due to the sinking of a large amount of waste heat from coal or nuclear power plants which carried away as hot water into the water stream.Thermal pollution increases the rate of chemical reaction which leads to a higher solubility rate of salt,increase the effect of toxin materials etc.Thermal pollution exerts a disruptive effect on the aquatic ecosystem.

4)**Eutrophication:**It is a natural process that happens due to the accumulation of nutrients through natural succession.This could be realised with the presence of Coliform bacteria which are found in humans or other animals intestine. Generally, drainage of sewage into a pond or lake cause eutrophication due to contamination with faecal materials.

5)**Biomagnification:** It is the process of accumulation of heavy material in living organism tissues through the food chain. Heavy material presence in pesticides will be washed out from the agriculteral field and enter in water. Aquatic plants receive those materials. Fish tissues are receiving those metal through the food chain and then it comes to other animals including human.Top members of the food chain receive the maximum quantity of heavy metals. This biomagnification is highly hazardous to any living organism.

6)**Pollutants:**The undesirable components or materials presents in the environment are called pollutants.

Question-2:

State three ways by which the following components of the environment gets polluted.

1) Air
2) Water.
3) Soil

Answer:

1) **Air**: a. Automobile emission.
b.Excessive burning of fossil fuels e.g. thermal power plants.
         c. Deforestation.

2) **Water**: a. Oil tanker leak into the ocean.
b.Illegal dumping of crude oil into the ocean to save money
to break up the oil.
c. Discharge of industrial waste and agricultural waste.

3) **Soil:**:a.Excessive use of inorganic fertilizers.
         b. Household waste like detergents, oils and solid refuses are
         added to the soil.
     c. Deforestation is the cause of soil erosion.

Question-3:

State three harmful effects of the following types of pollution.
1) Air
2) Water.
3) Soil

Answer:

1) **Air**: a. Acid rain.
b. Lung diseases.
c. Greenhouse effect.

2) **Water**: a. Instability in a marine ecosystem.
         b. Eutrophication.
         c. Spreading of water born diseases e.g. Anthrax, Typhoid etc.

3) **Soil**: a.Biomagnification.
         b.lead[Pb] through food has been reported to cause severe brain
         damage.
         c.Arsenic cause severe skin damage.

Question-4:

1. Explain any three causes and three consequences of eutrophication.
2. Mention any two environmental impacts of an oil spill.
3. Pollution has become a matter of great concern.
Discuss any three sources that affect air pollution.

Answer:

1) **Three causes of Eutrophication**:
   a. Drainage of sewage in non-flowing water sources e.g pond, lake etc.
   b. Natural enrichment of ponds and lakes.
   c. Contamination with faecal matter.

   Three consequences of Eutrophication:
   a. B.O.D will reduce.
   b. Underwater marine animals will be affected due to a lack of sunlight.
   c. Growth of Coliform bacteria.

2) **Impact of an Oil spill**:
   a. Huge marine organisms will die.
   b. Instability in a marine ecosystem.

3) **Three sources of air pollution:** 1.Automobile emission.2.Excessive burning of fossil fuels. 3. Deforestation.

Question-5:

1. **Explain any three dangers associated with the use of synthetic or chemical pesticides.**
2. **Name the gas that caused the Bhopal gas tragedy. Which organisation was responsible for the leakage of the gas.**
3. **Some fish in a pond found dead.there was a massive amount of algae.can you conclude the reason for the death of the fish?**
4. **Write three methods to control air pollution.**

Answer:

1) **Three dangers**:
   a. Birth defects.
   b. Delayed pregnancies.
   c. Lead used in pesticides causes brain damage.

2) Gas leaked in Bhopal during the Bhopal gas tragedy is MIC i.e. Methyl isocyanide. The name of the company responsible for the tragedy was Union carbide.

3) Due to the eutrophication of the pond,the massive amount of algae will produce which will reduce the oxygen content in water i.e. B.O.D and this leads to the death of the fish.

4) **Three methods**:
   a. Use more CNG in transport vehicles.
   b. Use air scrubbers and ESP devices in thermal power plants.
   c. Undertake more and more tree plantation programme.

EFFECTS OF POLLUTION ON ENVIRONMENT.

SECTION-I

Q: Type: [1] Name the followings:

1. The burning of fossil fuels and vehicular emission both producing this pollutant.
2. Acid rain pH value should be less than this.
3. This greenhouse gas presence in the atmosphere is maximum.
4. The term "greenhouse effect" was first termed by him.
5. This organic acid is produced due to forest fire.
6. A chemical that caused Minamata disease in Japan.
7. Marble cancer is phenomena that arise due to this.
8. The ozone layer is formed due to the presence of this ray.
9. The natural process which helps heat the earth surface.
10. Other than CFCs this gas also depletes the Ozone layer.
11. Overall greenhouse effect due to CFCs is about this.
12. New borne turtle sex depends on it.

A: Type: [1] Answer:

1.	CO_2	7.	Oil refinery pollutants.
2.	5.6	8.	Ultra Violet ray.
3.	CO_2	9.	Greenhouse effect.
4.	J. Furrier.	10.	Nitrogen Monoxide [NO].
5.	Formic acid.	11.	25%
6.	Mercury.	12.	Water temperature.

Q: Type: [2] match the column:

Sl. No.	Column A	Sl. No	Column B
1	Acid rain	A	Greenhouse gas.
2	Tajmahal.	B	Ozone-depleting gas.
3	Water vapour.	C	Marble cancer.
4	NO	D	Montreal Protocol.
5	CFCs	E	Industrial belts.

A: Type: [2] Answer:

Sl. No	Column A	Sl. No	Column B
1.	Acid rain	E	Industrial belt.
Expl.	Due to industrial pollutants e.g. SO_2 and CO_2 acid rain occur.		
2.	Tajmahal.	C	Marble cancer.
Expl.	Polluted fumes coming from Mathura refinery contains acid-forming gases e.g. SO_2 and NO_2. This acidic emission is responsible for marble cancer.		
3.	Water vapour.	A	Greenhouse gas.
Expl.	Water vapour in the atmosphere increase in response to global warming.		
4.	NO.	B	Ozone-depleting gas.
Expl.	Ozone + NO $\longrightarrow$ Oxygen + NO_2		
5.	CFCs	D	Montreal protocol.
Expl.	A landmark international agreement to phase out CFCs.		

Q: Type [3] True or false. If false then rewrite the correct statement.

1) Water vapour is a greenhouse gas agent.
2) The Montreal Protocol has come into existence in 1980.
3) The sex ratio of hatchling turtle depends on sea temperature.
4) Kyoto protocol is related to control the use of CFCs.
5) Di-hydrogen monoxide is not the cause behind the acidity of acid rain.
6) Acid rain mainly affects wild animals.
7) Forest fire is the cause of producing formaldehyde.
8) Acid rain can be defined as rain with a pH of less than 5.6
9) Stinking sensation observed after forest fire and rain thereafter.
10) William Currie is the father of the term "greenhouse effect'.

A: Type [3] Answer:

1) **[True]** Water vapour is a greenhouse gas agent.
2) **[False]** The Montreal Protocol has come into existence in 1987
3) **[True]** Sex ratio of hatchling turtle depends on sea temperature
4) **[False]** Kyoto protocol is related to control the use of greenhouse gas.
5) **[True]** Di-hydrogen monoxide [H_2O] is not the cause behind the acidity of acid rain.
6) **[False]** Acid rain affects all animals.
7) **[True]** Forest fire is the cause of producing formaldehyde.
8) **[True]** Acid rain can be defined as rain with a pH of less than 5.6
9) **[True]** Sticking sensation observed after forest fire and rain thereafter due to formic acid.
10) **[False]** J. Furrier is the father of the term "greenhouse effect'.

Q:Type [4] Fill in the blanks.

1) Most common Nitrogenous air pollutant is ____________.
2) Green house effect fist coined by____________.
3) CO_2 absorbs __________ rays.
4) The contribution of CO_2 alone towards the greenhouse effect is estimated to be about ____%
5) The capacity of methane to absorb heat is about ______ times more than CO2.
6) Acid rain can be defined as rain with a pH value less than ________.
7) Our immune system is damaged by ________ rays.
8) Ozone day is celebrated on ____________ September.
9) Kyoto protocol is related to control of ________ __________ gases. Green house.
10) CFCs break zone is found in ____________.

A: Type [4] Answer:

1.	NO_2	6.	5.6
2.	J. Furrier.	7.	Ultraviolet.
3.	Infrared.	8.	16.
4.	57%	9.	Greenhouse
5.	25%	10.	Stratosphere.

Q:Type [5] Choose the correct answer[MCQ]:

1. Ozone hole is a

b) Hole in the atmosphere. **b)** Hole in Antarctica. **c)** A thin layer of ozone over a particular area. **d)** Thin layer of ozone clouds.

2. Marble cancer is

b) The corrosive action of industrial effluents. **b)** Breaking of marble due to ageing. **c)** Change of marble colour due to algae formation. **d)** All of the above.

3. Water vapour is not considered as a significant greenhouse gas because

a) Concentration is globally in equilibrium) Concentration is very very less. **c)** Does not absorb infrared rays. **d)** Water vapour has very high specific heat.

4. Which of the following gas have the most impact as a greenhouse gas

a) Nitrogen oxide. **b)** Carbon di-oxide. **c)** Ozone. **d)** Methane

5. Climate change can be lead to the

b) Evolution of new organism. **b)** Extinction of many animals. **c)**Activation of non-functioning organs. **d)**All of the above.

6. Ozone hole was first observed in

a)1985**b)** 1980. **c)** 1987. **d)**1994

7. Due to the greenhouse effect, the average temperature of the earth is

a)Remaining constant **b)** Decreasing. **c)**Increasing. **d)** None of the above.

8. Phase-out of ozone-depleting substances was agreed upon in

a) Kyoto protocol. **b)** Montreal protocol **c)**Copenhagen protocol **d)**None of the above.

9. Greenhouse gas absorbed this

a) Infrared rays. **b)** Ultraviolet rays. **c)**X-rays. **d)**all of the above.

10. Which of the following is not responsible for depletion of the ozone layer

a) CO_2.   **b)**CFCs.   **c)** NO   **d)**Halon.

A:Type [5] Answer:

1.	c. thin layer of ozone over a particular area.	**6.**	b. 1980.
2.	c. Corrosive action of industrial effluents.	**7.**	c. Increasing.
3.	a. concentration is globally in equilibrium.	**8.**	b. Montreal protocol.
4.	c. Ozone.	**9.**	a. Infrared rays.
5.	b. Extinction of many animals.	**10.**	a. CO_2

SECTION-II

Question-1.

Define the following
1. A greenhouse gas
2. The main source of carbon-di-oxide.
3. A source of methane.
4. Acid rain.
5. Ozone hole.

Answer:
1) A greenhouse gas: The gases which prevent solar energy to escape from the earth and keeping the earth warm is called Greenhouse gas.

2) **The main source of carbon-di-oxide**: Automobiles.
3) **A source of Methane:** Gobar gas/forest biomass.
4) **Acid rain:** The rain with a pH value is less than 5.6 due to the presence of organic (Formic) or inorganic(Sulphuric acid, Carbonic acid] acids is called Acid rain.
5) Ozone hole: It is the location of the depleted ozone layerinthe stratosphere.

Question-2.

1. **Explain any four ways of preventing acid rain.**
2. **Discuss three effects of climate change on global warming.**
3. **Suggest two ways of reducing global warming.**

Answer:

1) a. Control air pollution as maximum as possible.
b. Use emission-reducing equipment like scrubbers, ESP [Electro Static Precipitators] to reduce air pollution.
c. Make a practice of adding a neutralising agent to the acidified water to increase the pH.
d. Formulate and implement laws to regulate emission and also improve public awareness through advertisement, event etc.

2) a. Due to global warming there is an increase in storms, damaging the breeding colonies of sea birds and sea animals.
b. Warmer seas could lead to some turtle species becoming entirely female, as water temperature strongly affects the sex-ratio of the hatching.
c. Global warming has led to negative glacier mean balance, causing glacier retreat around the world.
d.Global warming can slow down the circulation which can trigger changes in the ocean current.

3) a. Reduce energy use or conserve more and more energy as conservation of energy is equivalent to producing energy.
b.Shift carbon-based fossil fuels to alternative energy resources and nuclear energy.

Question-3.

1. **Mention any two economic effects of global warming.**
2. **Mention any two effects of Ozone depletion.**
3. **Discuss any three human activities that are responsible for climate change in recent years.**

4. How do CFCs break down Ozone in the stratosphere.

Answer:

1) a. Global warming increasing arrival frequency of natural disasters [forest fire, storm, flood etc] which leads to a loss in economic development.
b. Global warming increasing health issues and this leads to the erossion of personal economic stability.

2. a. Ozone depletion increase skin cancer, eye damage and damage to the immune system.
b. Ultraviolet rays also kill the minute aquatic plant life,the phytoplankton.

3. Three human activities are :
1. Use of methane gas for power production.
2. More and more use of plastics.
3. Huge expansion in the automobile sector.

4. Step-1: Ultraviolet rays release chlorine from CFC. This free cl reacts with Ozone gas. $Cl + O_3 = ClO + O_2$

Step-2: Due to instability ClO breaks down and produce O.
$ClO = Cl + O$

Step-3: ClO reacts with O and produces cl again.
$ClO + O = Cl + O_2$

Step-4: O_3 react with O and produce O_2.

$O_3 + O = 2O_2$

Question-4.

1. List down the sources of CFCs.
2. Name any two chemical that causes the depletion of the Ozone layer.
3. Name the two gases responsible for the formation of acid rain.

Answer:

1. **Source of CFCs**:
a. Refrigerator.
b. Aerosol can.
c. Plastic foam.
d. Fire extinguishers.
2. Chlorofluorocarbons(CFCs),Nitrogen monoxide (NO).
3. Sulpher Dioxide & Nitrogen Dioxide.